The Duration and Nature

OF

Future Punishment

Henry Constable

BIBLIOGRAPHIC INFORMATION

This reprint of *The Nature and Duration of Future Punishment*, 5th edition, was previously published in 1875 by KELLAWAY & COMPANY in London. Spelling, language, grammar, and punctuation have been gently updated.

an Ichthus Publications *edition*

ISBN 13: 978-0692408599

ISBN 10: 0692408592

www.ichthuspublications.com

CONTENTS

Preface

to the Fifth Edition

ABOUT EIGHT YEARS AGO we brought out the first edition of our work on the *Duration and Nature of Future Punishment;* and within that period the views advocated on our side have made very considerable progress. In Australia and India and America, as well as in Great Britain and on the Continent of Europe, numbers of persons of deep religious knowledge and undoubted piety have heartily adopted the great Scriptural doctrine of "Life in Christ." Very many of them have given proof of the sincerity of their opinion by suffering for the truth's sake.

When this view was prominently laid before the religious world of our day it was called a novelty, which would die out as soon as curiosity was satisfied. It has not, however, died out, but is steadily progressing year after year. It has stood its ground against misrepresentation, denunciation, and argument. It challenges the closest inquiry. Its appeal is to the Word of the living and true God.

For ourselves, we can truly say that the part we have taken in this question is one on which we look back with almost perfect satisfaction. If we have done anything which may deserve remembrance when we have passed away from this present scene it is what we have done in this great question. We adopted it from our study of God's Word. We advocated it because we felt it to be our duty to do so. Through the successive editions of our work, while we have introduced new matter into the later editions, and enlarged upon the arguments of our earlier ones, we have never seen occasion to modify even a single statement or argument which we put forward when we first came before the Christian public.

Henry Constable

London, 20th July, 1875

Preface

to the Fourth Edition

IT IS NOW SOME YEARS since I first brought the question here discussed before Christian men. I have carefully, and solemnly, and in the spirit of prayer, weighed all the objections which are brought against my view, and have only seen how futile and worthless they are: while, ever, as I study God's Word and meditate on God's character, the doctrine of life in Christ comes before me in clearer light as indeed the Gospel, the good news which the Son of Man came into our world to proclaim. I am deeply thankful that God has put it into my mind to vindicate His truth with whatever power I possess.

The doctrine of *life in Christ* is the key to the interpretation of Scripture. Read in its light, the Bible is a new book. The perplexities, the doubts, the surmisings of God that would force their way, the dark gloomy future, are all dispersed. This doctrine has made the Bible ten thousand times more precious to me than it was before: has made Christ more honored, and the Great Father more loved.

I no longer wonder that there should be fierce and inveterate opposition to the propagation of this grand doctrine. It was the very first truth which Satan sought to obscure and obliterate by the introduction into the Christian church of a specious and false philosophy borrowed from Greece and Egypt, and first taught by himself to Eve in Eden. He will not so easily part with a philosophy which has enabled him to do his work so well. Views that cover God with the aspect of injustice, or alienate men's minds from Him, or lead tens of thousands to infidelity, or enable men to get rid altogether of the idea that sin is a fatal and destructive thing, will not be easily given up. The doctrine that the soul is the true man, and that the soul is gifted with an inalienable immortality, brought in a mutilated shape into theology from the philosophy of Plato, has led to all this. It has led to Augustine's exhibition of God as a being of revolting cruelty, and to the future of much of his world as displaying only the most intense and harrowing misery: it has led to Origen's excision of vengeance from among the divine attributes, thereby opening the way to unbridled sin: it has led to the Roman purgatory, with all its attendant errors, as a refuge from what was felt to be too great a punishment to be inflicted by God upon ordinary offenders: it has raised against Scripture and the God of the Bible the derisive taunt and outcry of infidelity; it has caused the hearts of believers to mourn over a conduct on the part of God which they could not justify.

Altogether, no dogma whatever can be named which has been productive of one half the evil consequences that the dogma of man's inalienable immortality has produced. This is what we have gained by introducing into our theology under another name and under a specious disguise the old Manichaean heresy of the eternity of evil. I have no hesitation in saying that the eternity of evil as taught by the school of Augustine is a far fouler slander upon the character of God than this same error as it was propounded by the Persian Manes. Manes supposed evil to be an eternal and essential part of the constitution of the universe: the school of Augustine represents God as the perpetuator of evil by bestowing immortality upon the evil-doer. We cannot wonder that all the craft of the arch-deceiver should be put forth to maintain such a doctrine as this. Nor are men at all ready to part with long-established opinions. The triumph of the doctrine of life in Christ will produce a revolution in theology.

The standard works alike of the reformed and Roman churches are in great measure based upon the idea of the inalienable immortality of man. The interpretation of Scripture takes it as its starting point. When this comes to be acknowledged as a mere human conceit, many admired commentaries, treatises, sermons, confessions of faith, will be seen to have been based in great measure upon a foundation of sand.

But the truth will shine out the clearer for all this. To the truth we are ready to sacrifice a whole hecatomb* of human writings; and the truth is spreading far and wide. In Great Britain it is spreading, slowly but surely against prejudice and authority. In the United States it is spreading much more rapidly. From the Atlantic to the Pacific sea-board of the Great Republic, men of acute mind, who will not submit to the bidding of others no better able to judge than themselves, are examining the great question.

I have little doubt of the result. I look forward at no distant day to see the Christian mind shake of the false theology founded on a mutilated philosophy, and wonder that it could ever have submitted to it for a year or a day.

In the second edition of my work I called upon those who were opposed to my view to answer my arguments. That challenge has not yet been taken up. For whatever reason, men of leading position ignore the subject. It is not that it is unimportant. It is not that it has escaped their notice. I believe it to be because they begin to feel that the old arguments for what are called orthodox opinions do not possess the force they were once thought to have, and they have no others to supply their place.

I now repeat my invitation to the scholars and theologians of England and America. Let them answer me calmly, fairly, and fully, if they can. I now tell the teachers and preachers of the Gospel in these countries, the instructors of their young men for the office of the ministry, that their time-honored system is brought to the bar of public judgment. We who reject it are no longer to be classed among obscure heretics or scoffing infidels. We believe in God, and in God's Son, and in God's Word, and must be answered if we are to be put down. Misrepresentation, and lofty declamation borrowed from heathen sources, will not be enough.

---

* The 1828 edition of Noah Webster's *American Dictionary of the English Language* defines *hecatomb* thusly: "In antiquity, a sacrifice of a hundred oxen or beasts of the same kind, and it is said, at a hundred altars, and by a hundred priests."

In the present edition of my work I have carefully rewritten every chapter of the earlier editions, and added materially to many of them. I have also introduced several new chapters. My references to the opinions of the early Fathers are also much fuller, and will, I think, be found not uninteresting or unimportant. I have also given very many references to ancient and modem books, which will be of use.

I would here draw the attention of my readers to another work of mine, recently published, on *Hades, or The Intermediate State of Man*. The great question of the nature of man, which lies at the foundation of this whole matter, will be there found to be fully discussed. The proper understanding of this, as related to us by our Maker, will bc found of the greatest use for the more immediate object of the present work.

Henry Constable

1

Future Punishment Is Eternal

FUTURE PUNISHMENT FOR THE sins of the present life is universally allowed to be taught in Scripture: but with respect to its *nature and duration*, very different opinions have been and are entertained as being each of them the doctrine of God's word. We speak only of punishment to be inflicted subsequent to the General Resurrection and the Day of Judgment. Into the condition of the soul in the intermediate state in Hades we do not enter here.

There are three main opinions relative to this punishment. One of these makes it to be essentially of a *purgative nature*, to be *temporary* in its duration, and to have as its end the restoration of all to God's favor and eternal happiness. This was the theory of Origen. The second opinion makes punishment to be *eternal* in its duration; and to consist in *an eternal life of misery and evil.* This was the theory of Augustine. According to the third opinion, punishment is *eternal,* but it consists in *eternal death—i. e.*, the loss of eternal life or existence. This death is *attended and produced by such various degrees of pain* as God in his justice and wisdom thinks fit to inflict. The attendant pain with its issue in death are not two distinct punishments; but are one punishment, varying in degree of suffering according to the guilt of the object. This is the opinion which we here maintain. Its establishment sets the other two aside. Its eternal duration overthrows that of Origen; its involving a state of death overthrows alike that of Origen and Augustine. We rest the proof of it on the express, oft-repeated, and harmonious testimony of Scripture.

With respect to the eternity of future punishment we will here be brief. To us, as to the great majority of Christians of every age, it has always appeared that, as clearly as Scripture teaches that there will be punishment, with the very same clearness and distinctness it teaches that punishment to be absolutely eternal and without end. We will here give some of the chief grounds on which we rest our opinion.

In the first place its duration is described in the very same terms as the life of the redeemed: "These," saith Christ, speaking of the reprobate, "shall go away into everlasting punishment; but the righteous into life eternal" (Matt. 25:46). Here the same Greek word (*aionios*) is used for the *duration* of these opposite states. If, then, we suppose the life of the righteous to be everlasting, we must allow the punishment of the wicked to be everlasting also.

Again: Our Lord has repeatedly declared that there are persons who, at no time and under no change of dispensation, shall have forgiveness: "Whosoever speaketh against the Holy Ghost, it shall not be forgiven him, neither in this world (or age), neither in the world to come" (Matt. 12:31; Luke 12:10). This is wholly inconsistent with the idea that such persons should, after any period of punishment, enter into the peace of God.

What Christ has here said of one class of sinners he has elsewhere said in equally strong language of *all* who reject Him: "He that believeth not the Son shall not see life; but the wrath of God abideth on him" (John 3:36). If, after a certain purgation, such men passed from a state of punishment into one of bliss, these words of Christ—we say it with reverence—would not and could not be true; for such men would see life, on such men the wrath of God would not abide.

Again: There are persons of whom our Lord affirms that it would have been better for them if they had not been born (Matt. 26:24; Mark 14:21). Such an affirmation is incompatible with the idea that they should, after a punishment of any conceivable length, enter upon the life of bliss. The first moment of release would make amends for all past suffering; throughout eternity they would praise God that they had been born.

For these and other reasons which will appear in the course of our inquiry, we are persuaded that punishment will be of eternal duration. *The judgment once passed, God holds out no hope beyond.* Man now makes his choice of one or other of two conditions, each of which will be alike eternal. Here we fully agree with Augustine. As every grand error must needs have some truth mixed up with it to give it countenance and strength, so the eternity of future punishment is the great element of truth in the system of Augustine. It is that which gives its apparent strength to the fearful error with which he has mixed it up.

2

Eternal Death

IN WHAT WILL THE ETERNAL state of the lost consist?" This is now our question. We hold that it will not consist in an eternal life spent in pain of body or remorse of mind, but that *a state of utter death and destruction* is that state which will abide forever. The length of time which this process of dissolution may take, and the degrees of bodily or mental pain which may produce it, are questions which we must leave to that providence of God which will rule in hell as in heaven. Scope is here provided for that great variety of punishment which the reprobate will suffer hereafter, from that which in its justice is terrible to the sufferer, to that which, with equal justice, is by him scarcely felt at all.

We need not stop to argue that between this view of punishment and that which maintains an eternal existence in pain there is no comparison. The present life shows us this. When hope has ceased to cheer the future, men willingly lay it aside for death; when pain has made it a weary burden, the friends of the sufferer thank God for its termination. "Better not to be than to live in misery," was the judgment of Sophocles; and we ever find the wretched, when suffering has become excessive, calling upon death as upon a friend.[*] So the close of each agonized life in hell would be longed for there; would send a thrill of relief throughout the habitations of the blessed.

It will be well here to say a few words on the reason which has from a very ancient period led a majority of Christians, as from a period still more ancient it led a large part of the Jewish Church,[†] to hold the doctrine of an eternal life of pain; as it will be requisite to show that this reason is without foundation, before we proceed to the establishment of our own view. It will be seen that this same reason led another class of minds, with a like irresistible force and with an equal propriety, to the other great error here controverted, namely, Universal Restoration.

Before the preaching of the Gospel, the highest order of heathen philosophy had framed for its satisfaction a theory of the immortality of the soul. While the great mass of mankind had absolutely no hope of any future life[‡] and while far the greater number of philosophers taught that death was for all an eternal sleep;[§] there were "high spirits of old" that strained their eyes to see beyond the clouds of time the dawning of immortality. Unable, as we are able, to connect it with God as its source, and with his promise as their assurance, they framed the idea of an immortality self-existing in the human soul. Egypt, the prolific mother of religious error, appears, from the best authorities in our hands, to have

---

[*] Job 3:21; Jeremiah 8:3; Revelation 9:6; Witsius, *Covenants*, i., iv. xiv.; Baxter, *Saint's Rest*, c. v., 12; Cicero, *Tusc. Disp.*, i. 46.

[†] Jahn, *Archae. Bib.* s. 317; Bartlett, *Life and Death Eternal*, p. 384; Gibbon, *Decline and Fall*, c. xv.; Whitmore, *Doctrine of Immortality*, p. 21; Denniston, *Perishing Soul*, Letter xiii.

[‡] Ephesians 2:12; 1 Thessalonians 4:13; Justin Martyr, *First Apology*, c. lvii.; Tertullian, *On the Resurrection*, c. i.; Calvin, on 1 Thessalonians 4:13; Chambers, *Information for the People*, ii. 437; Plato, *Phædo*, para. 29.

[§] Athenagoras, *Plea for Christians*, c. xii.; Tatian, *Address to the Greeks*, c. xxv; Tertullian, *De. Anima*, c. iii.; *Ibid., De. Spectaculis*, s. 30; Cicero, *Tusc. Disp.*, i. 31; Gibbon, *Decline and Fall*, c. xv. 11; Landis, *Immortality*, c. iii. s. 25.

been the source of this idea.[*] But it was extracted from the tombs and the hieroglyphics of Egyptian priests by the brilliant and restless curiosity of Greece. Socrates, and his great pupil, Plato, presented it to the human mind where ever the Grecian intellect penetrated, and the tongue of Greece was known. Cicero recommended the theory of the Academy to his contemporaries in his "Tusculan Questions." They did not indeed teach it at all consistently, nor do they appear themselves to have relied with any firmness on its reality.[†] It was with them a great hope fitfully entertained, rather than a sober conviction. "I have perused Plato," Cicero sadly complains, "with the greatest diligence and exactness, over and over again; but know not how it is, whilst I read him I am convinced; when I lay the book aside and begin to consider by myself of the soul's immortality, *all the conviction instantly ceases.*" It is indeed doubtful whether any of the great minds of antiquity in their esoteric or inner faith held more than the tenet of Buddhism, which teaches that the soul, originally derived from Deity, is at length to be re-absorbed and lost in Deity again:

> "That each, who seems a separate whole,
> Should move his rounds, and fusing all
> The skirts of self again, should fall,
> Remerging in the general Soul."—TENNYSON

However this may be, those of whom we speak presented to the common mind an idea not so vague as this. The conception of it kindled their imagination, and the discussion of it afforded a theme for their logical powers. According to it, the soul was possessed of an inherent immortality. It had no beginning and could have no end. What was true of one soul was

---

[*] Perowne, J. J. S., *Immortality*, p. 37; Herodotus, b. ii., s. 123; Bunsen, *Egypt's Place in Universal History*, iv. 639; Whitmore, *Immortality*, c. i.

[†] Perowne, J. J. S., *Immortality*, preface vii., p. 45.

equally true of all souls, good or bad. They must live somewhere, be it in Tartarus, or Cocytus, in Pyriphlegethon, or the happy abodes of the purified. This idea, sublime for a heathen, passed readily and early into the theology of the Christian Church. Philosophers, converted to Christianity, brought with them into their new service too much of their ancient learning. Heedless of Paul's warning voice against philosophy in general (Col. 2:8; 1 Cor. 1:22; 3:19; 1 Tim. 6:28), they considered that a considerable portion at least of Plato's philosophy must be exempted from the apostolic condemnation. We find accordingly the Platonic philosophy of the soul's immortality running through and blending with the theological reasoning of Athenagoras and Tertullian, of Origen and Augustine.[*] Teachers who should have consulted only the oracles of God, leaving behind them their heathen lore as Moses left behind him the learning of Egypt, supplemented those living oracles with theories drawn from a brilliant Greek philosophy, which was in its turn suggested by the priest-craft taught in Egyptian temples. Their theory was that the life of the wicked must be as eternal as the life of those here redeemed and brought to Christ, because every soul of man was immortal.

A moment's reflection will show us that a dogma of this kind could not remain idle. It *must* influence irresistibly in one direction or another this whole question of future punishment.[†] It *must* mould the entire doctrine of the Church upon the subject. According as men connected it with one truth of Scripture or another, it *must* give rise to two opposite schools of thought. Connect the immortality of the soul with the scriptural doctrine of the eternity of punishment, and you inevitably create the dogma of eternal life in misery, *i.e., of Augustine's hell.* Connect it with

---

[*] Athenagoras, p. 31, A, 53 D., Edition Paris, 1615; Tertullian, *De Anima*; Origen, vol. i. 486 B; vol. ii. 108, C. E. Rothomagi, 1668; Augustine, *De. Civ. Dei.* xxi. 3.

[†] Hooker, *Eccl. Pol.*, v. 2.

another great truth of Scripture, the final extinction of evil and restitution of all things, and you as inevitably create *Origen's Universal Restoration.* For each of these opposing theories there is exactly the same amount of proof, that is—Plato's dogma and a dogma of the Bible; and if Plato's dogma could be proved to be a scriptural doctrine, then, by every law of logic, Scripture would be found supporting *two contradictory theories,* or, in other words, would itself destroy all its claims to authority.

Accordingly, this philosophical idea of Plato is found influencing most powerfully and most unfairly *the interpretation of Scripture from the second century down to our own time.* An example of this will probably snow this more forcibly than any words of ours. Tertullian is commenting upon our Lord's teaching in Luke 19:10, "The Son of Man is come to seek and to save *that which is lost*" (Vulgate, *quod perierat*). No one knew better than Tertullian the primary and proper meaning of the Latin verb *pereo,* and that it meant "to vanish," "to die," "to perish," "to be annihilated." Why would he not attach this meaning to it when he was commenting upon the text of the Latin version? Here is his own account:

> "We, however, so understand the soul's immortality as to believe it lost, *not in the sense of destruction, but of punishment,* that is, in hell. And if this is the case, then *it is not the soul which salvation will affect, since it is 'safe' already in its own nature by reason of its immortality;* but rather the flesh, which, as all readily allow, is subject to destruction."*

Such was the influence upon the interpretation of Scripture which his theory of the soul forced upon Tertullian. It led him to deny to the terms of God's word what he knew to be their primary and proper meaning, and to affirm that the salvation of our Lord had no relation to the human soul,

---

* Tertullian, *On the Resurrection,* c. xxxiv.

but only to the bodies of men! A similar influence this theory has had upon theologians down to the present day.

It is true, indeed, that while the Fathers as a general rule considered the question of future punishment under the impression that every soul of man was immortal, they did not attach to the soul the idea of an *essential immortality and an existence from all eternity* as Plato did. Their more just notions of the Deity prevented their going to this length; and they generally acknowledged the soul as the creation of God, having a beginning in time, and allowed that He who had given it existence, could take that existence away. But in supposing that God gave to the soul an *inalienable existence, i.e.*, an immortality not affected by any conduct upon man's part, of which no creature could deprive it, and of which God would not deprive it, they in effect laid down a dogma which had the very same influence upon their views of future punishment as if they had adopted the dogma of Plato to its fullest extent. An immortality that *never would* be taken from the soul, and an immortality that *never could* be taken from it, would have precisely the same bearing upon the future of man. In either case he must live on forever, whether in misery or in happiness. In a subsequent chapter we will show the actual influence of this dogma upon the doctrine of the Church, leading first to Augustine's fearful theory of everlasting misery, and then, in the revulsion of human thought from this, to Origen's theory of universal restoration.

Now the immortality of the soul, whether as held by Plato, or by the Fathers in general, was a mere fancy of the human mind. As to any *essential* immortality which belonged to it of its own proper nature there is no Christian writer or thinker of any weight who now dares to maintain it. It was, as Pliny justly called it a figment; and even Socrates, with all his noble language, evidently feared that his favorite notion was no sounder than the figment which the Epicurean Pliny contemptuously called it.* Scripture denies it altogether. An essential immortality it does not allow to be the attribute of any creature, however exalted. To one Being only—to God—does it allow to have "life in Himself;" of one Being only—God—does it allow such an immortality to be an attribute (John 5:26; 1 Tim. 6:16). Here, as in everything else, Scripture is the book of the highest reason. That which has had a beginning may have an end. That on which God has bestowed life He may and can inflict death. The highest intelligences as much as the lowest must depend on Him for the continuance of their life. Let Him withdraw his sustaining power and the mighty archangel becomes a thing of nought, as completely as the insect which dances in the sunbeams for an hour and then passes away forever. Says Calvin, "Immortality does not belong in the propriety of speech to the nature either of souls or of angels; but is derived from another source, the secret inbreathing of God."†

The idea that God has bestowed upon men, or upon any part of human nature, an inalienable immortality finds just as little sanction in the Scriptures. The expression "immortality of the soul," so common in theology, is not once found in the Bible from beginning to end.‡ In vain do men, bent on sustaining a human figment, ransack Scripture for some expressions which may be tortured into giving it an apparent support. The phrase, "living soul," applied to man at his creation (Gen. 2:7), has been by many Christian writers, utterly ignorant of Hebrew, supposed to imply such an immortality. *The very same phrase, however, in the original language of Scripture, had been applied to the lower creation before it was*

---

* Pliny, *Natural History*, b. vii. c. 56; *Apology of Socrates*, c. 32 and 33; Calvin on 2 Corinthians 5:1.

† Calvin on 1 Timothy 6:16.

‡ Mr. Maude's paper on Immortality, *Rainbow*, March, 1869; Rev. W. Ker's *Popular Ideas on Immortality*, p. 31.

applied to man (Gen. 1:20-21). The threefold description of man, as having body, soul, and spirit, has been by others supposed significant of his inalienable immortality. Whatever be meant by this distinction, it cannot in any measure support the inference based upon it; as the lover creatures are allowed in Scripture to be possessed not merely of body and soul but of spirit likewise (Gen. 7:15-22; Ps. 104:29; Eccl. 3:19-21).

But an *inalienable* immortality is expressly asserted in Scripture *not* to have been bestowed upon man at his creation (Gen. 2:17). We do not deny that man was made in God's image; and that a very important part of this resemblance consisted in man's not being subject to death as the lower creatures were. Immortality *was* given to man at his creation.[*] This priceless gift was one of the gifts which a bountiful Creator bestowed upon a favored creature. *But it was alienable.* It might be parted with; it might be thrown away; it might be lost. So He, the Lawgiver, said, when, in giving immortality, He also added the warning, "In the day thou eatest, thou shalt die." What is more: *this immortality was alienated: this priceless gift was thrown away and lost.* Man sinned, and lost his immortality. As Irenaeus expresses it, "Man, disobedient to God, was cast off from immortality."[†] And so God said Himself, when to fallen Adam He declared: "Dust thou art; and unto dust shalt thou return" (Gen. 3:19). *Sinful* man is not by nature immortal but mortal. He has lowered himself to the level of the beasts that perish. If immortality is to be his again, it must be as *a gift restored, and not inherited.* It must become his by virtue of some new provision of grace which reinstates him in the place he lost. *This was the Gospel of Christ.* It was to give back the eternal life which man had

[*] Wisdom, ii. 27; Denniston, *Perishing Soul*, pp. 127-131; Plato, *Phædo*, para. 55.

[†] Irenaeus, *Against Heresies*, b. iii., s. ii.; Landis, *Immortality of the Soul*, p. i., c. iii., s. 26.

forfeited, that he came into the world: "God was manifested in human form for the renewal of eternal life."*

> "If then, as annihilated by sin, the soul was ever forfeit.
> Godhead paid the mighty price, the pledge hath been redeemed;
> He from the waters of oblivion, raised the drowning race.
> Lifting them even to Himself, the baseless Rock of Ages."

Subsequent examination will, however, show us that Christ has not, as some suppose,† bestowed this priceless gift on all; but on some only of the fallen race. It is the believer only who can say with David, "He redeemeth my life from destruction" (see Ps. 100:3-4; 102:28; John 5:20, 40).

Before we proceed to establish our view of future punishment by the direct testimony of Scripture, it will be necessary to remove an objection very commonly made to it, and which has great force with very many minds. The objection is this—that what is no longer *felt to be punishment by the party who is punished is no punishment* at all: that it ceases to be a punishment the moment it ceases to be sensibly felt. This was one of Tertullian's chief reasons for his view of eternal misery.‡ He reasoned precisely as those heathen reasoned, who, in trying to reconcile man to his inevitable fate, tried to reason him into the belief that *death was no evil.*§ Yet, when even such men looked on into the limitless future, into that endless life which man can conceive of and longs to make his own, because in truth it was his birthright once, they corrected their idle reasoning, and without the Christian's promise of eternal life in Christ, called *endless*

---

* Ignatius, *To the Ephesians*, c. xix.; Landis, *Immortality*, p. i., c. 3. s. 21.

† Denniston, *Perishing Soul*, p. 131.

‡ *On the Resurrection*, c. xxxv.

§ Cicero, *Tusc. Disp.*, i. 36-37; Lucretius, b. iii.

death an endless injury,[*] Such it is even to him who has ceased to feel the loss of life, and, since the life restored to man through Christ is an eternal life, it follows that its loss, inflicted as a punishment, is a punishment of an everlasting nature.

And here the first death affords a perfect analogy to the second. From the earliest records of our race *capital* punishment has been reckoned as not only the greatest but also the most lasting of all punishments; and it is only reckoned the greatest because it is the most lasting. A flogging, inflicted on a petty thief, inflicts more actual pain than decapitation or hanging inflicts upon a murderer. Why then is it greater and more lasting? Because it has deprived the sufferer of every hour of that life which but for it he would have had. *Its duration is supposed co-existent with the period of his natural life.* "The laws," says Augustine, "do not estimate the punishment of a criminal by the brief period during which he is being put to death; but by their removing him forever from the company of living men."[†]

The conclusion drawn from this is sometimes sought to be got rid of by representing the real punishment of death to consist in its exposing the party put to death to those sufferings which are supposed by many to follow during the intermediate state from death to resurrection.[‡] Whatever may be believed of the reality of such sufferings, it is, however, certain that human governments in their apportionment of punishments never took anything of this kind into their thoughts at all. Death, as a legal punishment, is reckoned the very same punishment, *whatever be the character of the person thus punished,* whether he has been an upright or a wicked man, one likely to suffer punishment or reward. The idea of death

---

[*] Cicero, *Tusc. Disp.*, i. 47.

[†] *City of God*, xxi. 2; Abp. Tillotson, *Eternity of Hell Torments*, p. 412.

[‡] Bartlett, *Life and Death*, 289.

as the most lasting of all has not been confined to Christian nations; or to believers in a future life of rewards and punishments; but was accepted before the time of the Gospel, and by individuals and nations who did not believe in a future life at all. The Sadducee, the Epicurean, and the Atheist, held it just as well as the Platonic philosopher, the Christian father, or the Egyptian priest. Justin Martyr expresses the idea well, when, speaking of heathen persecutors who, as he expressly states, "believed that there was nothing after death," says: "They kill us with no intention of delivering us; but cut us off that we may be deprived of life and pleasure."[*]

Now all this is readily applied to the future life and to future punishment. The loss of every year of the life which the sinner might have had is a punishment, and because the life is eternal the punishment is eternal also. There is here no straining of argument to make out a case. The argument is one which man's judgment has in every age approved as just, whether it agreed or not with his view of future retribution. "Good things," says the Christian father, Irenaeus, who held our view, "good things are eternal, and without end with God, and, therefore, the loss of these is also eternal and never-ending." "May it not," says the great Dutch divine, Hermann Witsius, who himself held the Augustinian view of punishment, "may it not, in its measure, be reckoned an infinite punishment, should God please to doom man, who is by nature a candidate for immortality, to total annihilation, from whence he should never be suffered to return to life?"

And President Edwards, of America, who also held the Augustinian view, yet distinctly agrees with us. "*Endless annihilation,*" he says,

> "*is an endless or an infinite punishment.* It is an endless loss of, not only all the good a man at present enjoys, but of all that good which he would have enjoyed throughout eternity in the state of bliss to which he would have

[*] *First Apology*, c. lvii.

> been admitted, if he had never sinned. This, in an endless duration, would have amounted to an infinite quantity of good. Annihilation, therefore, is an infinite punishment, both as it is *endless*, and as the quantity of good lost is infinite. . . . Final annihilation then is an infinite evil, as it is inflicted in disapprobation of sin."[*]

In arguing thus we have argued at the greatest disadvantage to ourselves, for we have confined our attention to the parties actually punished, while we have left out of sight the grand object of all-wise punishment, namely, the lesson taught by it to those who have not offended. Viewed in this light, eternal death inflicted, on sinners *is eternally felt,* and has an eternal influence on the parties whom it was intended principally to affect. The actual sinner suffered as he deserved—if not less, certainly not more. His death then intervenes to afford its eternal lesson to all future times. Those who rejoice in immortality are forever warned by the aspect of its loss. Milton draws the fallen angels as shuddering at the thought of the loss even of their life lowered, shattered, with no aim or object but evil:

> "To be no more: sad cure; for who would lose,
> Though full of pain, this intellectual being,
> These thoughts that wander through eternity?"

And the genius of Pascal rebukes the thought that makes light of the loss of existence: "Is it a thing to speak of flippantly? Is it not a thing, on the contrary, to speak sadly of, as of all sad things the saddest?"[†]

---

[*] Irenaeus, *Against Heresies*, iv., v. 27; xi. 4; Witsius, *Covenants*, i., v., xlii.; Blain, *Death Not Life*, 12th ed., p. 80; Denniston, *Perishing Soul*, p. 80; *Pensées* De Pascal, S. P., art. 11; Wesley's Sermons, "Of Hell," sermon lxxviii.

[†] *Pensées* De Pascal, second part, art. 11; Young, *Night Thoughts.*

A vast amount of misconception, and consequently of needless controversy, has arisen from the mistaken idea that eternal death is not properly eternal punishment. One class of reasoners, holding eternal punishment, think it necessary to argue against eternal death as not being its equivalent; while another class, holding more or less the doctrine of eternal death, feel bound to argue against the eternity of future punishment, from not perceiving that the eternal death which they hold is in truth its full equivalent. One class, again, imagines that in proving eternal punishment they prove eternal life in torment; and the other that, in overthrowing the notion of the latter, they have overthrown the former also.[*]

We will here merely add that the terms "everlasting destruction," "eternal death," etc., taken by us as properly descriptive of our theory of the future non-existence of the wicked, are the very terms used by the best writers of the periods before and after the birth of Christ, when they would describe the eternal loss of life and existence by beings who had once possessed life. The Grecian writer calls such a condition "a death that never dies;" the Roman Cicero calls it "everlasting death;" Lucretius calls it "immortal death," "eternal death;" even Tertullian, though his theory constantly compelled him to confound life with death, when he would describe a state from which there was no resurrection to existence, can find no stronger, truer description of it than "eternal death," "everlasting destruction."[†]

---

[*] *Eternity of Future Punishment*, G. Salmon, D. D.; *Eternal Punishment*, J. W. Barlow, M.A.; *Religious Tendencies of the Times*, J. Grant, i. 268.

[†] θάνατος ἀθάνατος Amphis Gynæcocr, i.; mors. simpiternum malum; Cicero, *Tusc. Disp.*, i. 42; mors immortalis, mors æterna; Lucretius, Lib. Tert; mors æterna Æternus Interitus; Tertullian, *On the Resurrection*, c. ix.

3

Testimony of the Old Testament

HAVING IN OUR LAST CHAPTER removed all obstacles arising from an erroneous notion of the nature of the soul, we proceed to consider the direct proofs of our view. We will first advert to the testimony of the Old Testament. This is indeed by no means so clear either as to the future of the redeemed or the lost as the New Testament; but there are undoubtedly in it many places, not only in its later but in its earlier portions, which speak of both (Acts 3:22-25).

Death was the penalty which God originally pronounced against human sin. All that God purposed to inflict upon Adam and his posterity in case of transgression is included in that word "death." "In the day that thou eatest, thou shalt die" (Gen. 2:17). It is of the utmost consequence then that we should understand what God meant by death; nor is there the smallest difficulty in doing so if we will only attend to what reason and justice require, and what Scripture expressly declares. Its meaning, then, we contend to be, when it is thus attached to sin as its penalty, *the loss of life or existence.*

One of the first principles of justice requires that parties threatened with a penalty for transgression should have the fullest opportunity of understanding *what the penalty is.* God, accordingly, speaks to Adam of death as a thing whose nature Adam knew. Now Adam knew very well what death was in one sense, and *in one sense only.* He knew it to be the law of the lower creatures, and to *consist in the loss of their being and existence.* He knew nothing of any other senses of death, such as "death in sin" or "death to sin;" for, in his innocence, he did not know what sin was at all. Still less did he understand by death an eternal existence in agony. He had one clear, well-understood sense for death—the loss of life and being. When God, therefore, threatened death to Adam as the penalty of disobedience, Adam could only know that penalty to mean that he would become like the beasts that perish; and therefore, in agreement with a fundamental principle of justice, such an end was that which God threatened to inflict for sin.

So fully persuaded indeed are the advocates of the Augustinian theory, that Adam could not possibly have understood death in their fearful sense, that they are compelled to deny a fundamental principle of law—that parties living under it should have the means of knowing to what they expose themselves if they violate it. "It is not essential," writes Professor Bartlett, the ablest advocate of the Augustinian theory that either this country or America has produced, "it is not essential to enquire whether the first pair understood all that was involved in the penalty, 'Ye shalt surely die!'" And he then goes on to lay down the astounding proposition that "neither the judicial dealings of God nor man" require that "the extent" of penalty should be "unfolded" before the minds of those who may expose themselves to it if they offend![*] If this Professor of Theology had consulted a Professor of human Jurisprudence, he would have been informed that when a man is incapable of knowing the nature of a penalty, he cannot be subjected to it. He must at least have a fair opportunity of knowing it, or human law will not make him liable. If the

[*] Bartlett, *Life and Death*, 48.

Professor had consulted that divine law which he has undertaken to teach, he should have known that justice is one of the qualities that the divine Lawgiver claims as the foundation of his throne. The old morality of the land of Uz was higher than that breathed in the Theological Seminary of Chicago: it spurned the idea that a mortal man could be more just than God (Job 4:17).

The only meaning which Adam could attach to death as the threatened penalty for transgression is that which God himself expressly attached to it. As soon as Adam transgressed, God came to him and repeated to him in other words the penalty he had just incurred. It was, "Dust thou art; and unto dust shalt thou return" (Gen. 3:19). God's definition of the death inflicted for the first transgression is frequently repeated in the later Scriptures. Paul tells us that it is the death which all men actually undergo, whether they are among the saved or the lost; and therefore an eternal existence in pain can be no part of its meaning (Rom. 5:12, 14, 17; 1 Cor. 15:22). Such too was the death which Christ endured for human sin—the very same penalty to its full extent to which man was exposed; and therefore spiritual death, or an eternal life in misery, can form no part whatsoever of its meaning (Phil. 2:8; Acts 2:24; Rom. 5:7-8).

We have thus, if we are satisfied to accept God's teaching, the clearly-expressed sense of death. It was not spiritual death: that was the sinner's guilty act, but not the penalty for his sin. It was not an eternal existence in pain. It was simply the withdrawal of a life whose true aim and object had been lost. God said nothing in the first instance of transgression as to whether this death would be temporal or eternal; but what the death was He fully explained both by word and by example. He gave life to the race of man, and He would withdraw that life if man sinned. Such was the simple scriptural meaning of that word "death," about which Christian theologians have written whole libraries of confused jargon and hopeless nonsense, ever since the introduction of the Platonic dogma of the inalienable immortality of man compelled them to hold that all men must live forever. If our readers would wish to judge for themselves of the effect which the dogma has had upon scriptural exegesis, let them compare the lucid comments of the Christian father Irenaeus, who was unacquainted with it, with the flounderings of Moses Stuart, when both are discussing the same grand subject—death, the penalty of sin.[*]

This old sense, first stamped on it by God Himself, in the opening period of human history, has also been the universal idea formed of it wherever man has lived and died. It is always the primary, and in the case of the great majority of mankind the only meaning of the word, in every language and every tribe of the earth. "The world," says Athenagoras, "regard death as a deep sleep and forgetfulness."[†] So strongly impressed indeed was this primary sense of the word upon the human mind, from the perpetual recurrence of the thing itself among all the creatures, that while numberless words in the progress of time have assumed senses wholly alien or contrary to their original meaning, this word "death," has remained true to its original in its various applications. Thus we have in Scripture the expressions "dead to sin," "dead to the law;" in our Catechism we have the phrase, "a death unto sin;" in ordinary life we speak of persons being "dead" to certain passions or affections. All such expressions are derived from physical death, and are true to its original sense. They imply the departure, and consequent *non-existence,* of relations and feelings which were once living and strong—*their death.* Sin has ceased to be dear to the renewed mind: the old relation of the law has ceased to be for the believer: the former friend no longer loves. In every case, something has disappeared from existence. To the sense thus imposed on death in all times and by all nations, in its primary and its

[*] Irenaeus, *Heresies*, v. xxiii; M. Stuart, on Romans 5:12.

[†] Athenagoras, *Plea*, c. xii.

secondary significations, there is *one exception—that given to it in the theology of a portion of Christendom.* Compelled by a false dogma and a terrific creed of punishment arising from it, *death* is made to mean its direct opposite, *life*—some "condition of being or existence."*

But this late meaning attached by many Christians to the term death, in one of its applications, namely, to future punishment, has not the smallest force as regards its use in the Old Testament. There the word must be taken in the sense God has stamped upon it, and left unchanged. It is there over and over again described as the end, in the future age, of obstinate transgressors. For such God declares He has "provided the *instruments of death:*" of such as hate divine Wisdom that Wisdom says, "they that hate me *love death:*" to the wicked God saith, "thou shalt surely *die,*" "the soul that sinneth it shall *die*" (Ps. 7:13; Prov. 8:36; 11:4; Ezek. 3:18; 18:4; 33:8). While, as plainly as words can express, it distinguishes between the sinful acts and state of the sinner, *i.e.*, his moral death, and that death which God will at a future period inflict upon him as its punishment (Ezek. 18:11, 16). Two things, perpetually confounded by the Augustinian theorist, are as perpetually kept distinct in the Scriptures, that is, man's moral degradation, and God's penalty.

No one, we suppose, will apply the death pronounced in the above passages upon unrepented and unpardoned sin to that death which all men alike, whether saved or lost, undergo as the children of Adam. They can only apply it to future punishment. Death, then, is, according to the Old Testament, to be after judgment the result of sin, as life is the result of righteousness. Can we suppose a God of truth, of justice, and of mercy, to mean by this well-understood phrase something unknown to his hearers, of a character the very opposite to what they had from his own teaching conceived, and conveying a doom unutterably greater? The very idea is an

---

* *Rainbow*, for 1869, p. 254; Grant, J., *Religious Tendencies*, ii. 141.

insult to God. But hence it follows, as a matter of course, that loss of life is the doom pronounced against sinners in the Old Testament.

But the loss of life is not merely implied, it is distinctly stated to be the punishment for sin (Ezek. 3:18; 13:22). We have only to enquire what is meant in the Old Testament by "life." Life in common language means "existence." A man is said to be yet alive, though his moral condition may be of the most degraded character, though his happiness is utterly gone. This sense however would not suit the Augustinian. He has recourse to some secondary sense; and, because life is frequently associated with its proper action and with happiness, he assumes these to be its sense when spoken of in Scripture.

"Life," says Professor Bartlett, "signifies true functional action, welfare, prosperity, happiness, and the like."* Now while we are perfectly satisfied that life, *as given by God and unaltered from the state in which he gave it, is always* associated with true functional action and happiness, and so in such a state may from invariable association come to be synonymous with them, we yet see that they are really two distinct and different things, from the fact that they may be and are frequently disassociated. If life were identical with true functional action and happiness, then, where these had ceased to exist, there life too would cease to exist. But this is not in conformity with the language of the Old Testament. There the utterly wicked are said to be possessed of life, which they value, and would fain perpetuate forever; and the wretched to be possessed of life so unutterably wretched that they long for its departure (Ezek. 3:18; 13:22; Job 3:20). Life, then, and life's happiness, are distinct things. While the creature keeps the condition in which he was created they are, from the Creator's loving nature, inseparable; when he abandons it, they are seen to be distinct. The life which the wicked man has, and which false teachers promise him that

* Bartlett, *Life and Death*, p. 41; Grant, *Religious Tendencies*, ii. 141.

he will continue to have in the future age, that life God tells him he will be deprived of in that solemn time when He will "bring every work into judgment, with every secret thing, whether it be good, or whether it be evil" (Eccl. 12:14).

But it is not only through the terms "life" and "death," that the Old Testament describes the punishment of the ungodly. By every expression in the Hebrew language significant of loss of life, loss of existence, the resolution of organized substance into its original parts, its reduction to that condition in which it is as though it had never been called into being—by every such expression does the Old Testament describe the end of the ungodly. "The *destruction* of the transgressors and of sinners shall be together;" "prepare them for the day of *slaughter;*" "the *slain* of the Lord shall be many;" "they shall go forth and look upon the *carcasses* of the men that have sinned;" "God shall *destroy* them;" "they shall be *consumed;*" "they shall be *cut off;*" "they shall be *rooted out of the land of the living;*" "blotted out of the Book of Life;" "they *are not*" (Is. 1:28; 66:16, 24; Jer. 12:3; Ps. 28:5; 37:20; 73:27; 38:38; 52:5; 69:28; Job 27:19). The Hebrew scholar will see from the above passages that there is no phrase of the Hebrew language significant of all destruction, short of that philosophical annihilation of elements which we never teach, that is not used to denote the end of the ungodly. The English reader need only turn to his English dictionary to see that the *primary sense of all the above terms* is *significant of the loss of existence.* At a subsequent page we will show that the primary sense of words is the *only* sense that is allowable where a lawgiver is laying down for the guidance of men his penalty for transgression.

For the sake of greater plainness we will present instances of the meaning of some of these phrases in things that relate to this present life. We are thus enabled to see clearly their exact force. There are several Hebrew words applied to future punishment translated by the word "perish." *Abad* is one of the most common of these. When Heshbon was utterly cut off by the sword of Israel: when a sentence of extermination was pronounced against the house of Ahab: when the memory of the wicked has departed from the earth: when Esther apprehends her death at the hands of Ahasuerus: it is this word which is used: they have, or will, or may perish (Num. 21:30; 2 Kgs. 9:8; Job 18:17; Esth. 4:16). *Haras* is another term in frequent use for future punishment. What is its meaning in common life? When the altar of Baal was thrown down, stone after stone: when the strongholds of Zion were levelled to the ground: when a wall is broken down so that its foundations are discovered: this is the term used (Judg. 6:25; Lam. 2:2; Ezek. 12:14). Again: God will "destroy" the ungodly. One Hebrew word for this is *Tsamath.* It is used in the sense of utterly cutting off and destroying from a place (Ps. 69:4; 101:5, 8). Another Hebrew word is *Shamad.* It is significant of utter extinction. When the women of the tribe of Benjamin had been slain: when the nations of Canaan disappeared before the sword of Israel: when Moab ceased to be a nation: this is the word used for their destruction (Judg. 21:16; Deut. 12:30; Jer. 48:42). Again: the wicked will be "cutoff." The Hebrew is *Karath* in Nifal. What is its use in common life? When truth has become extinct from a sin-loving people: when weapons of war are broken in pieces: when life at the period of the flood perished from off the earth: when the life of an offender against the law of Moses was taken: this is the word used: "they are cut off" (Jer. 7:28; Zech. 9:10; Gen. 9:11; Exod. 30:33). By another word, *Nathats,* God threatens future destruction. In matters of this life, it indicates destruction of an utter kind. When the infected house of the leper was cast down and dismantled: when the images of Baal were broken in pieces: when the stones of the altar of the Sun were ground into powder: this is the word used for the process of destruction (Lev. 14:45; 2 Kgs. 11:18; 33:12).

We need go no farther at present in order to ascertain the clear, distinct, oft-repeated testimony of the Old Testament. By every unambiguous term, it has pointed out the punishment of the wicked as consisting, not in life, but in the loss of life; not in their continuance in that organized form which constitutes man, but in its dissolution; its resolution into its original parts, its becoming as though it had never been called into existence. While the redeemed are to know a life which knows no end, the lost are to be reduced to a death which knows of no awaking: for ever and ever. Such is the testimony of God in the Old Testament. If Christian divines refuse to accept it because Plato, and before him Egyptian priests, taught a doctrine of the soul's essential immortality, let them see to it. We prefer the word of God to the logic of Plato and of Egypt.

Our readers may perhaps have remarked that we have avoided hitherto the use of a very well-known term in this question, that is, "annihilation;" and have, in our only reference to it, disclaimed it in one of its senses. If they have any acquaintance with the controversy as conducted by our opponents, both of the schools of Origen and Augustine, they will also have known that this is the term by which our theory is almost invariably described by them. They are never tired of repeating this long Latin word. It is never out of their mouths. If we may judge by their pertinacious use of it, it seems absolutely essential to their cause; and, indeed, their ablest men have confessed that its use by them *is* absolutely essential.* If they were to cease for a moment calling our theory one of "annihilation," and describing us as "annihilationists," they seem to feel that it would be all over with them and with their cause. The terms are long ones; Latin ones, and therefore not so grateful to the Saxon ear; somewhat obscure, and therefore distasteful to those who would prefer clearness of expression; but still, use them they must, and use them they do, until at any rate the sound of the terms, if not their sense, is very well known. We must then say a few words about this term "annihilation," before we hand

* Bartlett, *Life and Death*, Preface.

it back to our opponents, and return to the good old words of our Saxon version of the Bible.

We have not the smallest objection to the word "annihilate," *if* it is used in *one of its senses.* The greatest authority in the English language, Webster, tells us in his Dictionary that, "to annihilate" means "to destroy," and "to destroy" means "to annihilate." Our theory is therefore one of "annihilation," because it is one of destruction. But the word has also a *philosophical sense,* and in this sense means *reducing those parts of which organized bodies are composed to nothing.* In this sense philosophy concurs with the saying of Bacon—"*It is impossible for anybody to be utterly annihilated.*" And now we may see why and wherefore our opponents persist in calling our theory one of "annihilation;" and why we prefer calling it by the scriptural phrase of "destruction." Paraded before the unenquiring mind as a theory of "annihilation," while that mind is at the same time carefully taught that all philosophy denies that there can possibly be such a thing as "annihilation," we are represented as maintaining a system at variance with the maxims of human knowledge. Whether such a mode of conducting a great controversy is ingenuous, or candid, or commonly honest, we must leave our readers to decide. For our part, we do not think it is. For we do not hold, any more than our opponents, that annihilation of parts which philosophy denies. We challenge them to produce one word of ours, or of any advocate on our side, which affirms it. We now take our leave of this matter with one parting remark. When our opponents charge us with holding a theory of annihilation in that sense of the word which philosophy denies, they bring against us a false accusation. When they charge us with holding a theory of annihilation in its well-established sense of destruction, they only charge us with holding a theory which Scripture from beginning to end maintains. For *the destruction of the wicked is the testimony of the Word of God.*

4

Testimony of the New Testament

WE NOW TURN TO THE New Testament. We shall find in it perfect agreement with the Old. Before, however, bringing forward its statements, we will make a few observations on a new feature here introduced, viz., the change of language adopted in the publication of the Gospel revelation.

We remark, then, that the writers of the New Testament must not only be supposed to follow the sense already fixed on the terms expressive of future punishment in the Hebrew Scriptures, but they also give us another guarantee as to their meaning by their usage of the Greek tongue. The Gospel, revealed and recorded chiefly by Jews, is recorded, not in a provincial dialect, but in the language of the Roman world. We have here a guarantee as to their meaning; whose overpowering force upon the present question we will show a little farther on. Paul and Luke, and John and Peter, used a language which they had no hand in forming or moulding, but which was already provided for them to be the vehicle of their thoughts. They made no claim to alter the world's tongue, but to alter the faith of the world through the medium of that tongue which the world used and understood when they were children, learning the meaning of its words from their elders,[*] The ordinary Greek lexicon—not lexicons of the New Testament, frequently colored and tainted by theological opinion—is the true guide to the Greek of the New Testament. It is only where an opinion new to the human mind is brought before it that we have a right to look for a new or modified phrase, whose sense is to be stamped upon it by the teachers of the novel truth. Neither a future life, however, nor judgment and punishment to come, were ideas novel to man. Heathen poetry and prose perpetually discussed them before the preaching of the Gospel. Nor have we throughout the whole of the New Testament Scriptures, addressed as the several portions of these were to men of different races and religions over the broad surface of the Roman world, the smallest hint or indication that the language used differed in any way or degree from that in established use. Had we but one text from John or Paul, affirming that they wrote in a Grecian tongue different from that of Hesiod and Homer, of Plato, Aristotle, and Epicurus, we should then no longer possess in the New Testament an intelligible language, but an unknown, an unintelligible, and a useless tongue. We should have to lay it aside as of no service until God should again raise up within the Church the spiritual gift of interpretation of tongues.

We will first draw attention to the fact that the punishment of the wicked is as frequently described as *their death* in the New Testament as in the Old, without the smallest effort to show that its terms "death" or "to die" have any new sense placed on them.[†] These words, as all other words on this subject, are used without any explanation, as words whose sense was long established and generally known. Thus our Lord, speaking of Himself, says, "This is the bread which came down from heaven, that a man may eat thereof, and *not die.*" And again He says, "Whosoever liveth

[*] Discussions on the Gospels, Rev. A. Roberts, M. A., pp. 35-42.

[†] θάνατος, *thanatos;* ἀποθνήσκω, *apothnesko.*

and believeth in Me shall *never die*" (John 6:50; 11:26). In these passages he implies that they who do not believe in Him *shall die.* What our Lord implies of the ungodly Paul affirms of them: "If ye live after the flesh, ye *shall die*" (Rom. 8:13). Very frequent are the passages in which the expression "death" is used for future punishment. Thus our Lord says, "If a man keep my sayings, he shall never see death." Paul affirms of wicked works that their end is death—"that the wages of sin is death:" of those who perish, he says, that to such "we are the savor of death unto death." James declares that "sin, when finished, bringeth forth death," and that "he which converteth the sinner from the error of his way shall save a soul from death." John declares that the ungodly shall suffer "the second death" (John 8:51; Rom. 6:21-23; 2 Cor. 2:16; Jas. 1:15; 5:20; Rev. 20:14). We have thus, in repeated places, death described as the lot of the wicked in the coming age, nor is there in a single passage the least attempt made to show that death had any other than its usual sense—the loss of existence.

We now proceed to examine another very frequent description of future punishment, namely, as consisting in the loss of life.* The uniform testimony of the New Testament is that "eternal life" hereafter will be the exclusive possession of the just, and that the wicked will certainly not obtain it: "He that believeth on the Son hath everlasting life; and he that believeth not the Son shall not see life" (John 3:36). We are here tolerably agreed as to the sense of "everlasting:" our simple enquiry is, what is the proper and natural sense of that Greek word, *zoe,* here and elsewhere translated "life."

If we were only to ask what was its *primary* sense, we should have no difficulty. All allow *existence* to be its primary signification. We will hereafter show that the primary sense of this term is the only one admissible; but here we will not further insist on it. We will here only ask

* Ζωή, *zoe.*

if there was *one universal sense* attached to this term; so that while there might be to a greater or lesser extent *a variety* of senses attached to it in one place or other, still, as accepted by all mankind speaking the Grecian tongue, it had one sense which was everywhere accepted as a true sense, and by some accepted as the only sense. Here too we are able to come to a certain conclusion. That sense of "existence" which is undoubtedly the primary sense is as undoubtedly a sense accepted by every Grecian speaker as a true sense, and by very many Grecian speakers accepted as its only sense. Our opponents themselves cannot and do not attempt to deny this. "The unenlightened heathen," says Mattison, "understood the terms life and death as implying *simple existence or non-existence.*"*

A fact of this kind would seem sufficient to decide the question as to the meaning of "life" in the New Testament. "The unenlightened heathen" may appear to some minds a very unimportant portion of mankind; but they, in effect, formed the vastly-preponderating number of persons to whom the Gospel was preached. If Christ's own words were almost exclusively addressed to the Jewish cars, they were recorded for a world-wide circle of readers. If the founder of Christianity spoke mainly to the lost sheep of the house of Israel, his apostles addressed and wrote to the heathen as well, and these heathen hearers, outside of Palestine, outnumbered their Jewish hearers as a thousand to one. No one will pretend that "life" as spoken by Paul to a heathen meant something different from "life" as spoken by Christ to a Jew. The word throughout must have the same sense, and as that word was addressed to hearers, the majority of whom only understood it in its sense of "existence" then we can but suppose that it was really intended to have this sense throughout the New Testament.

* *The Immortality of the Soul*, Philadelphia, 3rd ed., p. 127.

If "life," spoken of to the heathen, had a sense different from what the heathen addressed put upon it, then it would have required to have been explained to them. We know how our opponents, both of the schools of Origen and Augustine, labor hard to explain the term in this sense. Page after page, chapter after chapter, are devoted by them to persuade their readers that "life" means "well-being," "true functional action," "prosperity," "harmonious moral development, and fulfilment of the great moral aims of human existence," "the happiness or the glory of heaven," and so on.* But there is not throughout the New Testament one attempt at explaining the word in such a sense. For unenlightened heathen, or converts lately rescued from heathenism, there would have been an absolute necessity for such explanation of the word were it used in this sense so new to them. But of such explanation we do not find a trace. Where we do find an inspired writer defining the meaning of "life," he defines it exactly as a heathen would do: "What is your life?" saith the apostle James: "It is even," he replies, "a vapor, that appeareth for a little time, and then vanisheth away" (Jas. 4:14). Life, with St. James, himself a Jew, meant but what it meant with a heathen, *existence.*

But we have abundant proof from the New Testament that it does not use this important term "life," in that figurative sense which the Augustinian theorists put upon it. This we will now proceed to show. The importance of the point will be our full justification for dwelling upon it. The life which Christ bestows upon his redeemed is, according to our opponents, a true functional action, imparted to the believer by the renewing work of the Holy Spirit upon his heart and mind; and may be said to comprehend that great work of grace, commencing with repentance and faith, which issues more and more in the restoration of the human mind in its love for God and holiness, to a life of obedience; all this

* Bartlett, *Life and Death*, c. iii; Grant, *Religious Tendencies*, ii. 141.

producing that peace of mind, that well-being and happiness, which may be attained even in this present state. Such is a fair explanation of what they suppose to be meant by the eternal life which Christ bestows upon His people. It is identical with their repentance, their faith, their sanctification, their present peace and joy in believing.

Now we will find that what is thus supposed to be identical with "life eternal," is in the New Testament *distinguished* from it. Paul has done so, plainly and explicitly. "Eternal life," with him, is not the present obedience, or the present faith, or holiness of the believer; it is not the new hopes, desires, aspirations, joys, planted within him by divine grace: *it is that which is hereafter to crown and to reward,* through the goodness of our Father, *such a work as He has Himself here effected in the hearts and lives of his people:* "to them who by patient continuance in well doing seek for glory and honor and immortality," he tells us, *"God will render eternal life"* (Rom. 2:6-7). That eternal life which so many confound with God's present work of grace upon the heart, is by the apostle distinguished from it, and taught to be its result, its consequence, its reward, its crown, in the coming age ushered in by the resurrection of life. The same distinction is observable in other Scriptures (Acts 11:19; Rom. 6:22; 8:13; Matt. 7:13). Life is ever the end to be obtained, not the way that leads thereto. Man is first prepared by a divine work of grace, wrought now, for the true enjoyment and use of life, and then the eternal life is bestowed upon him in which to glorify God and to be blessed.

In exact conformity with this, Scripture represents eternal life as a gift, *not yet enjoyed* by the children of God. If it were identical, as many suppose with that "true functional action," produced in man by God's work, in that case eternal life would be here *begun.* In this present world, before death came to take him from it, before resurrection restored him to existence, the believer hi Christ would already have had his eternal life, as truly, though it may be not as fully, as at the resurrection. But this is not the case.

While there are no doubt many Scriptures (John 3:36; 5:24), which describe the believer as *now having* everlasting life, we are expressly told elsewhere that this consists in his having God's pledge and promise of that everlasting life; but not its actual possession and enjoyment. It is common in Scripture to speak of that which God intends to do as already done. It is significant of God as invariable in his purposes: "As I have thought, so shall it come to pass; and as I have purposed, so shall it stand" (Isa. 14:24-27). This is accordingly the way in which eternal life is spoken of. It is sometimes spoken of as already given, because it is pledged and promised; but it is far more frequently spoken of as a future thing, because it is not yet actually bestowed and enjoyed. Thus St. Paul, in a passage already referred to, tells us that "eternal life" is a thing which God *will hereafter render* to his people at the same time that he will render to the wicked their tribulation and wrath. Our Lord tells us that it is at this same coming time that the righteous will go into life eternal. Hence, Peter describes believers as "heirs of the grace of life;" Paul describes them as living "in hope of eternal life, which God hath promised;" while the Epistle to the Hebrews describes their exact position and standing here, namely, as "*called to receive the promise of eternal inheritance.*" Eternal life, then, is a great gift promised by God, but not yet bestowed: the possession of his people in His unalterable purpose, but not yet placed within their hands. It is not yet theirs to use and to enjoy. It will not become theirs in the intermediate state when the spirit has left the body. God's heirs of life will enter upon its enjoyment when their Redeemer comes again to call them to the resurrection of everlasting life.

Having thus established the scriptural force of the word "life," as signifying "existence," we will see at once its bearing upon our present question. As the wicked are not to have an eternal life hereafter, it means that they are not to have an eternal existence then. Their existence, then, after their resurrection to judgment will but resemble their existence now; it will be temporary, and will pass away.

There is another Greek word constantly translated "life," in the New Testament,* With respect to this word, one thing is certain, specifically, that it never bears in classical dictionaries, nor even in dictionaries of the New Testament, so far as we know, that sense of "happiness," "well-being," or "true functional action," which is so often, attributed to the term *zoe.* Another thing is equally certain, namely, that in passages where this word can only mean "animal life," such as we share with the lower creation, this life, it is expressly declared, shall be lost hereafter by the ungodly. Let us consider one such passage. In Matthew 10:39, our Lord declares, "He that findeth his life shall lose it; and he that loseth his life for my sake shall find it." What is this life which the fearful and the unbelieving prolonged by their denial of Christ, and which martyrs lost by their confession of Christ? It is, and can be, *nothing but animal existence. It is the life which the good and the bad have in common.* It is that which both alike value and would prolong, but which one are content to lose, and do lose, for Christ, and which the other will not lose for His sake. That which these latter have here prolonged for a little while, the Lord of Life tells them they shall lose in the future retribution, *i.e., they shall cease to exist.* Christ's words here can have no second meaning. If we want to have His great apostle's commentary on what is meant by the loss of a soul or life, we will find it in Acts 27:22. And our conclusion is only in agreement with all Scripture. Immortality is nowhere spoken of as the possession of fallen man; but it is described as a blessing to be *sought* by him, as much as the "glory and honor" of the future state (Rom 2:7; 6:23).

And here we will refer for a moment to a passage in the history of Moses which strongly confirms our view. Moses intercedes with God that

---

* ψυχή, *psyche*; Matt. 2:20; 10:39; John 10:11; Rom. 11:3.

Israel may be forgiven, and asks that, if his prayer be not granted, he may be blotted out of the book which God had written (Exod. 32:32-33). This book can be no other than that "book of life" frequently referred to in Scripture, and in which the names of the redeemed are written (Ps. 69:28; Luke 10:20; Rev. 20:15). What then did Moses mean by his receiving the doom of sinners, and being blotted out of the book of life? We cannot suppose that he could even for a moment have wished throughout eternity for a life of pain and moral corruption. He could only have wished for the utter cessation of a life which he then felt would be intolerable if his prayer was refused. Since this must be his meaning, it follows that what he asked for himself shall be the condition of the ungodly; for God declared that what Moses sought for himself He will inflict on them—"Whosoever hath sinned against Me, him will I blot out of My book."

We now proceed to consider other expressions significant of future punishment. Of these none is more common than the Greek noun, *apoleia,* translated by the term "destruction."* "Broad is the way that leadeth to destruction," saith Christ; and Paul speaks of the ungodly as "vessels of wrath fitted for destruction" (Matt. 7:13; Rom. 9:22). *There is not in the Greek language a word more strongly significant of the utter loss of existence.* Its *proper* meaning, says Schleusner in his Lexicon, is "*the destruction of anything so that it ceases to exist.*" Schleusner, who gives this as its proper sense, himself held the Augustinian theory of punishment. We will show from some passages in the New Testament that it uses the word in this its proper sense. In Acts 8, we read of the intercourse of Simon Peter with Simon Magus at Samaria. The latter offers money to the apostles, in order that he may have bestowed upon him a power equal to theirs. He is met by the indignant rebuke from Peter: "Thy money perish with thee," literally "thy money go with thyself to *destruction.*" Here we see

* Απώλεια, *Apoleia.*

Peter's sense of destruction. It had the same meaning when applied to a man as it had when applied to metal: disorganization and wasting away until it should disappear, was the idea which Peter attached to it in both cases alike. The notion of the perpetual existence of anything which met with destruction was absent from his mind. From another example of the word in this book of Acts we find that such was the sense attached to it in the common usage, and accepted by the inspired writer, Luke (Acts 25:16). Festus here tells Agrippa that it was not the "manner of the Romans to deliver any man *to death*" (literally, "to destruction"), before the accused had an opportunity of defending himself. Festus here calls the "destruction" of a man his "death;" and as Festus doubtless, with almost every man of his station at that time, ridiculed the very idea of any future life after this, he could only have intended by the "destruction" of a man, the putting him out of all existence. Luke, by using, accepts the term in the sense of Festus, and we have thus in the usage of two of the inspired writers of the New Testament, Peter and Luke, the sense of "destruction" established as the putting out of existence. Such, we are told, will be the end of the wicked.

Besides the Greek noun which we have just spoken of, its verb, *apollumi,* is constantly employed to signify the punishment which God will inflict in hell upon wicked men and wicked spirits.* This is a most important word, and deserves special attention. We will now take the verb in its *active voice.* In this voice, it is used either in *an active* or a neuter sense. In this latter sense, it signifies "to lose utterly:" in *its active sense, when applied to persons,* it means "to destroy utterly, kill, slay." In this its active sense it is applied to God's treatment of wicked men and devils in hell. A close search into classical writings may perhaps discover a very few instances, and these even doubtful and disputed, where the term has a

* Απολλυμι, *apollumi*; Matt. 10:28; Luke 4:34.

lower sense, but, beyond any doubt, its true, well-established, general, if not absolutely-invariable sense is, "to kill" or "slay."

That such is its meaning in classical Greek, we assert on the authority of Greek classical dictionaries (see *Liddell and Scott's Dictionary*). If our opponents can disprove our assertion let them do so, and we will withdraw it. Till they do so, we take it as an established fact that *apollumi* in its active sense, and as applied to persons, never has any other established sense in classical Greek writers than to deprive those persons of existence. This fact *ought* to be sufficient to decide the sense of this term so used *in the New Testament.* For we maintain that the Greek of the New Testament differs in no imaginable respect from the ordinary Greek of its own place and period. We challenge our opponents to show that it does. Let them remember that, if they succeed, they also succeed in converting the Greek of our New Testament into an unknown tongue.

But we will not rest satisfied with asserting on the authority of classical dictionaries that the above sense is that of the word, we will show that such is its invariable sense in the New Testament itself. We will for this purpose refer to its use, in two of our Gospels, that written by the Jewish Matthew and that written by the Gentile Luke. We will refer to every place in these two Gospels where the word is *thus* used. We are thus referring to books which use the term more frequently than any other of the New Testament Scriptures, and which also show its sense as well with Jewish as Gentile writers. The whole of the New Testament is open to our readers to confirm or to controvert our statement.

The verb *apollumi,* to destroy, is used in its active sense and as applied to persons, *five* times in the Gospel of Matthew. Herod's attempt to take the life of the infant Jesus: the Pharisees' plot to deprive of life that same Jesus when he was grown to manhood: the Lord of the vineyard decreeing death to the unfaithful husbandmen: the King punishing with death the slayers of his servants: these are four of the places where the word is thus used in Matthew: the fifth passage is that solemn one wherein Christ declares that God can "destroy both body and soul in hell" (Matt. 2:13; 12:14; 10:28; 22:7). This same verb is used as above *seven* times in the Gospel of Luke. To take away life from man: the universal death produced by Noah's flood: the plots of the enemies of Christ against his life: the decree of death to the unfaithful husbandmen: these occupy six of the places where the word thus occurs in the Gospel of Luke: the seventh place is where wicked spirits, meeting with Christ, are filled with terror, lest He should have come, before they expected, to destroy them (Luke 4:34; 6:9; 9:56: 17:27, 29; 19:47; 20:16).

We have thus seen the usage of this word in the New Testament, and have seen that it agrees exactly with its usage in other Greek writings. In ten of these passages it speaks of the loss of existence here: in the other two it speaks of the loss of existence hereafter. For this second loss of life, the second and eternal death, hell has been provided. The bodies and souls of wicked men will there suffer eternal destruction. There devils, whose well-being and happiness and moral order have long since departed, will suffer the loss of that existence to which, with all its present drawbacks, they fondly and desperately cling. Annihilation is a fearful thought to the mind of angels, fallen though they be: annihilation they know to be their doom.

We will not here enter any further into the sense of this verb *apollumi,* when, in its *middle voice,* applied to future punishment. We will merely say that we could here too show it, as used in the New Testament, to signify the loss of existence by the wicked. We wish to avoid tedious, because needless, verbal discussion. To the verb, as used in its active voice and sense, we invite the attention of our opponents. We challenge their contradiction of what we have written. We assert that they do, not willfully but really and grossly, put false senses upon the plainest words of Scripture. We reaffirm the indignant protest of one of the best Greek scholars of the day against their perversion of language, when we record a portion of a letter from R. F. Weymouth, Head Master of Mill-Hill School, addressed to the Rev. Edward White, in which he says,

> "My mind fails to conceive a grosser misinterpretation of language than when the five or six strongest words which the Greek tongue possesses, signifying 'destroy,' or 'destruction,' are explained to mean maintaining an everlasting but wretched existence. *To translate black as white is nothing to this.*"

Even the leading modern advocate of the Augustinian view, who all but closed his literary labors in the defense of this wretched cause, looking in blank dismay at these words of doom, can only say of them that they "do not *invariably* mean annihilation."* We, on the contrary, assert that such is in the New Testament, as used of the wicked, their invariable sense: they are there ever connected with death (Matt. 7:13-14; 10:28; 2 Cor. 2:15-16).

We now proceed to consider some of the other terms in the New Testament relative to future punishment. Thus Paul, in his solemn warning to his Jewish hearers at Antioch, in Pisidia, adopts the teaching of the Old Testament as truly descriptive of future punishment, and sums it up in these words, "Behold, ye despisers! and wonder, and *perish*."† The Greek word here translated "perish," when, as here, used in the passive voice, means properly "to become unseen, to disappear, and to be heard of no more." We have a striking instance of its sense in the active voice in an address of Titus to his soldiers. He is speaking of the immortality which bravery in war would secure for the brave in a future life, while the sluggish and the cowardly would in death be reduced to annihilation. He thus describes the latter process: "A subterranean night *dissolves them to*

* Religious Tendencies, J. Grant, i. 34.

† Αψανιζω, *aphanizo*, Acts 13:41.

nothing."[*] We have in Josephus' account of the doctrines of the Jewish sects a yet stronger instance of the recognized force of this word. He is describing the views of the Sadducees who taught there was no future life at all either for wicked or good men. He describes their view in these few words: "The doctrine of the Sadducees is this, that *souls perish with their bodies.*"[†] Josephus, a contemporary of the apostles, and whose Greek corresponds perhaps more closely to that of the New Testament than that of any other writer, here shows that there is no ambiguity about the phrase. It means with him, plainly and without a doubt, when applied to human life, its vanishing utterly and entirely away. And exactly so we find it used by the apostle James when speaking of the transitory nature of this present life (Jas. 4:14). Such is the word which Paul uses to describe the consummation of retribution. That which the Sadducees taught would happen to all men at the first death the apostle tells us will be to unbelievers the sad result of the second death: they will rise from their graves and see what they have rejected, will marvel at their folly, and will vanish out of existence.

Another Greek verb, translated "destroy," "corrupt," "defile," and used to express future punishment, has, when applied to man, two main senses.[‡] One is to deprave and corrupt: the other to destroy by depriving of existence. As it would be impious to suppose that God will ever do Satan's work of corrupting, we can only take the word in the second sense (1 Cor. 3:17; 2 Pet. 2:12). A good example of these different senses is found in 1 Corinthians 3:17, "If any man *defile* the temple of God him shall God *destroy.*" It is the same Greek verb which first here signifies "defile," and

---

[*] Josephus, *Jewish Wars*, vi., i., v., namely: ὑποφειοζ ἀψανίζει.

[†] *Antiquities*, xviii., i., iv.

[‡] Φθειρω, *ftheiro.*

afterwards "destroy." The first is the sinner's guilty act; the second is God's punishment hereafter by destruction.

This verb in its composite form has also the same two senses, while it intensifies their force.[*] It signifies to "destroy utterly," to "kill," as well as "to lead astray," and "corrupt." In that book of Revelation, which is so frequently and so vainly supposed to teach the Augustinian error, it is used to describe future punishment, where John tells us that God will "*destroy* them that destroy the earth" (Rev. 11:18). The verb occurs twice in this passage, and is in both cases translated "destroy." There can be no doubt that our translators here should have made the same distinction which they made in translating the simple verb in 1 Corinthians 3:17. The Vulgate has carried out the true sense which is translated in the Rheimish Testament, "shouldest *destroy* them who have *corrupted* the earth."[†] The sense of the word, as signifying wasting away to utter destruction, is constantly found in the New Testament (see Luke 12:33; 2 Cor. 4:16).

The Greek noun of this verb has in the same way the two senses of "moral corruption" and "destruction by death," and is frequently applied to future punishment.[‡] When spoken of as what God will inflict in punishment, it can only bear the latter sense. We would direct attention to the passage in 2 Peter 2:12, as affording indubitable proof that it is thus used in Scripture with direct reference to future punishment. Speaking of the ungodly, Peter says, "These, *as natural brute beasts, made to be taken and destroyed,* shall utterly *perish in their own corruption.*" Here *the same Greek word is used* of the end of beasts *and* the end of the ungodly. We know what is the end of beasts taken and destroyed: even such, Peter

---

[*] Διαψθείρω, *diaftheiro.*

[†] "Tempus exterminandi eos qui corruperunt terram" (Vulgate).

[‡] Φθυρα, *fthora,* Galatian 6:8; 2 Peter 2:12.

declares, will be the end of the ungodly in the future life: *they shall perish there as beasts perish here.*

Another Greek verb and noun, translated "destroy," "destruction," is properly and primarily significant of utter extermination by death.[*] It is applied in the New Testament to the punishment of sinners hereafter: "Every soul which will not hear that prophet shall be *destroyed* from among the people;" "the wicked shall be punished with everlasting *destruction* from the presence of the Lord" (1 Thess. 5:3; 2 Thess. 1:9; 1 Tim. 6:9).

We will now call attention to but one other phrase of the New Testament significant of future punishment.[†] It occurs in Paul's wish that he "were *accursed* from Christ for his brethren"—a passage affording an exact parallel to the prayer of Moses already referred to.[‡] There can be no doubt that whatever Paul here means by being "accursed from Christ," it is that condition in which the ungodly will hereafter be (1 Cor. 16:22). What then *could* Paul here wish for himself? Less of him than of almost any man that ever lived, are we to suppose that he could for a moment wish for himself an eternal life of blasphemy and moral corruption, which, according to the Augustinian theory, is the condition of the reprobate throughout eternity? We can only suppose him to mean that he could suffer an eternal death, a blotting out of his own name from the book of the living, if, by so doing, he could gain for his kinsmen the life he had surrendered for himself.[§] This sense is in exact agreement with the use of the term "accursed" among the Greeks, by whom it was applied to any animal devoted to death and removed out of the sight of man, in order to avert calamity. We will also find abundant confirmation of our view in the

---

[*] Εξολοθρεύω, *exolothreuo*; Ολεθρος, *olethros*.

[†] Αναθεμα, *anathema.*

[‡] Romans 9:3, see Alford.

[§] Bengel in Romans 9:3.

usage of the corresponding Hebrew term, *cherem,* in the Old Testament, when applied to things devoted to cursing (Deut. 7:26; 13:16; Josh. 6:17-21; 7:13-25). Utter death where there was life, utter destruction where no life existed, was the end of persons and things devoted to a curse.

We have thus gone through the various phrases of the New Testament which describe the end of the ungodly after the judgment. We have seen the proper and primary sense of each of these terms. We have seen that such a sense carries out precisely the theory which we here maintain—the destruction or annihilation of the wicked. In subsequent chapters we will proceed to show that the sense thus put upon them is in harmony with the sense of the words in the Grecian language—that the primary sense is the *only* sense that we are warranted in putting upon them—and, that even when taken in any of the secondary senses which the Greek tongue bears, they do not admit of that view of future punishment which the theories either of Augustine or Origen teach.

5

The Greek of the New Testament

WE HAVE IN OUR LAST chapter brought forward a variety of phrases from the New Testament descriptive of future punishment. All must see that on the true sense to be given to these terms our views of the doctrine of the New Testament must very mainly rest. Other considerations indeed, and these also drawn from Scripture, will occur, bearing with vast power upon the momentous question before us, but still the proper and true sense of the terms just discussed must ever occupy a leading place in the mighty argument. We must therefore, even at the risk of appearing tedious, dwell somewhat further upon them.

The New Testament was, in the wise purpose of God, written in the Grecian language. Well may we thank God for this selection; for in no other language of the old world could His mind have been conveyed to man with equal perspicuity and clearness. In this Greek tongue all the phrases we have been speaking of are found in constant and perpetual use. Before the Gospel was preached, their meaning was fully established in the cultivated and the common mind of the human race. What is more, they were all in common use, and applied to, and their sense established, *with reference to this very point now under discussion.* Immortality was not a question for Jewish and Christian thought alone: it was the question of questions for the universal human mind. Made originally for immortality, the thought of it, even when man is fallen from it, still lingers in his breast. It comes up to him like a dream of the olden time, or some bright vision or horrible phantom of a time to come. According to the circumstances of his life and the tone of his mind, it is regarded as a boon most devoutly to be longed for, or an evil most earnestly to be shunned, or a weary burden at which the spirit of man faints, and longs, rather than endure it forever, for annihilation, or reabsorption into the Great Spirit of the universe.

The question of the immortality of the soul, accordingly, was the question of questions in the various schools of Grecian philosophy. The resurrection of the body to eternal life, which was the grand hope of primitive times (Job 19:26), and which is the grand article of faith brought to light by the Christian revelation, took no place in heathen speculation. It may seem from researches into Egyptian tombs and hieroglyphics that some traces of the primitive tradition of a resurrection lingered in the old land of the Pharaohs. But when Grecian sages brought the lore of fertile Egypt to the rocky promontory of Attica, they brought with them certainly no idea of Egypt's faith in a resurrection, if such were really there ever entertained. Such an idea, if presented to the Greek by the priest of Zoan or of Memphis, was to the Grecian intellect but as foolishness. They saw the body return to the dust, and there they left it forever, and even thought that its complete destruction was a gain. Their whole thoughts, and speculations, and hopes, and fears, and reasonings, and raillery, were directed to the soul or life of man. When man's immortality was discussed in the schools and by the philosophers of Greece—by some gravely maintained, by others as gravely refuted, and by the majority treated as a jest—the entire grand question of man's immortality turned upon *the immortality of his soul.* If we look to the reasonings of our *Christian* teachers from Tertullian to Bishop Butler, to the theses of our *Christian* schools from Alexandria to Oxford and Paris, we will find that they have followed with docile spirit the impulse given by Epicurus, Aristotle, and Plato.

One of the noblest specimens of human reasoning that has ever charmed, exalted, or, for our part we must add, bewildered the human intellect, is found in the dying discourse of Socrates to his friends, handed down to a deathless fame in the *Phædo* of Plato. Its object was to prove the immortality of the soul—that it could never cease to be—that through whatever changes it might pass, whatever pollutions it might suffer, whatever fearful torments it might endure, there was that deathless principle of the human soul which asserted an eternal life and utterly refused to die. It could never be, according to Plato, a thing of yesterday, an existence of the past but not of the present, a figure once jotted down in the book of life and then blotted out of it forever.

In what terms is the denial of its mortality conveyed? In the very terms in which the punishment of the wicked is asserted in the New Testament! When the latter says the soul shall die, Plato says it shall not die; when the latter says it shall be destroyed, Plato says it shall not be destroyed; when the latter says it shall perish and suffer corruption, Plato says it shall not perish and is incorruptible.[*] The phrases are the very same, only that what Plato denies of all souls alike the New Testament asserts of some of the souls of men. But the discussion of this question was not confined to the school of Plato, or to his times. Every school of philosophy took it up, whether to confirm Plato's view, or to deny it, or heap ridicule upon it. All the phrases we have been discussing from the New Testament had been explained, turned over and over, handled with all the powers of the perfect masters of a perfect language, presented in every phase, so that of their sense there could be no doubt, nor could there be any one ignorant of their sense, before Jesus spoke, or an evangelist or apostle wrote. The subject

[*] Plato, *Phædo*, pars. 38, 14, 29, 23, 8, 55, 37, 41, 44, 17, ed. Bekker.

had not died out before the days of Christ. It never could and never will die out. In every city of the Roman world were schools of Grecian thought in the days of the apostles. In every school the question before us was discussed in the phrases and language of the New Testament. In Jerusalem and Rome, at Athens and Corinth, in Ephesus and Antioch—wherever a Christian preacher opened his mouth to speak to man of his future destiny—were Platonists, or Epicureans, or Stoics, or Alexandrians, to whom the question of immortality was a question of solemn thought, with whom the phrases in which the preacher addressed them as to their solemn future were familiar household words.

And what did the Christian preacher declare, and the Christian writer write, to that world-wide community, which was ruled and bound together, not merely by the power of Roman will, but by the scepter of the Grecian tongue? In sermon and disputation, in Gospel and history, in epistle and revelation, the propagators of the new religion asserted of the persons of the wicked—*i.e.*, of souls and bodies reunited at the resurrection—that which Plato had denied could happen to any soul. The cultivated intellect of the world, as well as the popular mind, read in the words of Christ, of Paul, of John, of Peter, of James, that what one of its schools of philosophy taught could happen to no soul, and what another taught should happen to all souls, the rising school of the Nazarene taught would happen to those whom its phraseology described as "unjust," "wicked," "unbelievers." Plato's noble conception, itself, in an imperfect shape, but the utterance of the longing of the human heart for its original inheritance, was taken up by the New Testament, only that it had here given to it its true direction, and had the eternal life after which it yearned connected with the God of life manifested in his Son. In Jesus Christ was that "life" which Plato fancied might exist in the soul itself. This "life" He would bestow upon His people, realizing for them more than the conception of Plato. But, away from Him, there was no life. On those who would not come to Him there would come, finally—after stripes, few or many—the end pictured for all by Epicurus. The Gospel brought together the fragments of truth scattered through all human systems, and in them all poisoned with error. Those who would soar, the Gospel raises to God; those who would revel in the sty of sensuality, or live without God in the world, it sinks to the level of the beasts that perish.

We will apply these general observations somewhat more particularly. In its descriptions of future punishment, the New Testament uses the terms we have been discussing in the following way: "If ye live after flesh, ye shall *die:*" "the wages of sin is *death:*" God will "*destroy* them that corrupt the earth:" "as many as have sinned without law shall *perish* without law:" the disobedient "shall be punished with everlasting *destruction*:" "he that soweth to the flesh shall of the flesh reap *corruption*." These texts comprise most of the Greek terms under consideration.

Now according to the schools both of Origen and Augustine, all these terms, applied to the condition of the wicked after the judgment, are in perfect harmony with the idea of their immortality. According to the school of Origen, these terms—"death," "corruption," "destruction," and others—describe the salutary process through which the wicked will be in the coming age brought to the blessed life of the just. According to the school of Augustine, these terms are most properly descriptive of the endless misery of the lost. We think it is the late Professor Stuart of Andover who has said that the copious Greek language affords no other terms so properly descriptive of a life of misery. We will put this claim to the test.

Plato was a Greek, and one of the greatest masters of the Grecian language. Plato also held precisely the Augustinian view of future punishment. Indeed it is from him that our Christian divines have derived it. Rome follows him more implicitly than our great Protestant theologians; for she has accepted his purgatory, which these latter have rejected: but in the doctrine of an endless life of misery for some, hereafter, Plato is at perfect accord with the majority of Christian teachers. We should expect then that since Plato held the Augustinian view he would use these *appropriate* terms in describing it! This master of the Greek tongue would lay hold of the very best words in his language to set forth his views! Or, at least, if by some unaccountable oversight he never once used them, we should certainly expect and demand that *he would not explicitly reject them as unfit and unsuitable words* to describe this view of his. But this is the very thing which Plato has done. He has told us, over and over again, by every variety of expression, that these phrases, one and all of them, are utterly unfit and improper to describe such a life as the Augustinian inflicts on the sinner, or indeed to describe a life of any kind at all. He lays down that these terms cannot, and ought not to be applied to any immortal being: that they are wholly inconsistent with the very notion of existence. When therefore we find that the New Testament constantly uses these terms to describe the future condition of the ungodly, we must either admit that in so doing the New Testament denies their immortality, or we must assert that the Greek of Plato and the Greek of the New Testament are two distinct and different languages. But this latter is a theory which no Greek scholar will maintain. If it were established, we might close our New Testament as a useless book. If it cannot be established, then we must admit that the New Testament, in thus describing the future of the wicked, denies the immortality of their existence, and thus overthrow the fallacies alike of Augustine and Origen.

We will apply this test to another writer. Josephus was a contemporary of the apostles, and his Greek is universally allowed to correspond to that of the New Testament. He has not written much as to his own views of future punishment; for it is seldom maintained now, that the discourse on Hades, attributed to him in an uncritical age, is from his pen. When he does come to speak upon the subject it is where he describes for his Gentile readers the theological views of the chief Jewish sects. He would have smiled at the idea that in addressing Greeks he did not speak the language of their great writers, and would have asked for what purpose he wrote to Greeks if he did not write in their tongue. But in giving his account to the Greeks of the religious views of the sect of the Essenes he expressly states that the views of these latter were identical with those taught to the Greeks, evidently referring especially to that doctrine of the immortality of the soul which was taught and vindicated by Plato.*

Josephus thus adopts the ordinary terms among the Greeks, and in especial the terms of Plato, as having the same meaning with him as they had with them. If there could be any doubt upon this point, of which we cannot see the possibility, Josephus would remove it himself; for he has, in describing the various opinions of the Pharisees, Sadducees, and Essenes, used several of the most important terms in use in the New Testament and in Plato in the very same sense that Plato has used them.† We have then to say of Josephus what we have said already of Plato, that in his idea of the meaning of the Grecian language the terms which the New Testament has most constantly used to describe future punishment are altogether inconsistent with the idea of the immortality of the wicked. This is altogether a different question from what were Josephus' own opinions of the nature of future punishment. We only here lay down the indisputable position that, if Josephus himself held the Augustinian view, he would have described it in different terms from those which we have seen the New Testament most commonly to use, and would have said that the use of those terms was totally opposed to a theory which maintained for the wicked an eternal life of misery, or indeed any existence at all. He would

* *Jewish War*, ii., viii., xi.

† *Antiquities*, xviii., i., pars. 3-5; *Jewish War*, i., vi., 5; ii., viii., 11; ii., viii., 14.

have described these terms as only expressive of a theory which taught annihilation.

We will apply another test. Plato held the Augustinian view that some would be punished by an everlasting life of misery. What are the terms in which he describes this everlasting condition? It will not be denied that Plato knew or used the best and most appropriate language in which to set forth his views. He tells us then that the soul of the reprobate will not be "destroyed," will not suffer "destruction," will not "perish," because it possesses "immortality," and is "indestructible," and "immortal."[*] Such, according to Plato, are the proper terms by which to describe an eternal condition. *Not one of these are ever used in the New Testament to describe the future condition of the lost.* Let our opponents, whether they follow Augustine or Origen, show us but one such term applied to the wicked, and we will allow that we are wrong. Surely God, in setting forth the future of the wicked, would use the language that would best express it.

We will show from the language of Professor Bartlett, of Chicago, the exceeding importance which our opponents attach to the use of such terms as we have above referred to in the present controversy. He is showing from the apocryphal book of Enoch that the Augustinian view of future punishment was held by some in the Jewish Church at a period considerably before the birth of Christ. He quotes for this purpose the following words: "They shall go with the wicked, and like them, but their souls *shall not be put to death* in the day of judgment, nor shall they come out from hence." Professor Bartlett's comment on these words is: "*There is no ambiguity here.*"[†] He tells us, and he is perfectly right in telling us, that one such expression as stating that the wicked will "not be put to death" in the future retribution puts it beyond any dispute that the use of such

[*] *Phædo*, pars. 14, 18, 37, 38, 41, 44.

[†] *Life and Death Eternal*, 386.

language held the eternal misery of the lost. Why then does Scripture *never* use these unambiguous words in describing the punishment of the wicked? There can be but one answer given, specifically, because Scripture never teaches the immortality of the wicked. Its teaching is unambiguous, but in the opposite direction: its teaching is that "the soul that sinneth, it shall die."

We will apply another test. There were at and before the time of Christ very many who taught the doctrine of annihilation. They held that there was no future life of any kind for any man, but that when men died they completely perished, and that soul as well as body were alike and forever destroyed. Such was the Epicurean school of philosophy among the Gentiles, and the Sadducean school of theology among the Jews. Now in what terms and by what language did such men set forth their views? *Simply and entirely by their application to all men alike of the very terms which the New Testament applies to the future punishment of the wicked.* Every scholar knows this to be the case. The friends with whom Socrates conversed on the day of his death, as related in the *Phædo* of Plato, were Epicureans, whom he sought to reason into the adoption of his own grander views. The writings of Epicurus are lost, but we know from some fragments of his preserved by other writers what his terms on this question were. We know how the Sadducees spoke, from Josephus and other authors. The composition in the Latin tongue by the Epicurean philosopher Lucretius shows us what were the corresponding terms in Latin used by those of his school. Now from these and other sources we learn that the Epicurean philosophy described its miserable theory of the final annihilation of all at death by exactly the same terms in which the New Testament sets forth that which will happen to the wicked in hell. If the New Testament by the use of these terms is supposed to teach an eternal life of misery for the wicked, then the Sadducees and Epicureans of that same period must also be supposed to have taught such a life for all mankind. We could with just as much truth and reasonableness establish an eternal life of misery for mankind from the writings of Epicurus and Lucretius as we can from the writings of Scripture; for if "to die," and "perish," and "be destroyed," mean "to exist in misery," these are the very terms in which Epicurus and Lucretius spoke of the end of all men. Will our opponents tell us that the apostles of Christ taught *the doctrine of Plato in the language of Epicurus?* They really hold this strange view; but which of them will venture to defend it? If it could be maintained it would give a fatal wound to the authority and value of Holy Scripture as speaking an intelligible language.

Even at the risk of wearying our readers, we will apply yet one more test of the true meaning of the terms of the New Testament applied to future punishment. There are, scattered throughout heathen writings, at and before the time of Christ, various descriptions of such an eternal misery of being as the Augustinian theory maintains. Whether such descriptions were really believed by those who gave them is another question; but, both in poetry and prose, we have such descriptions given. Now we call upon the holders of eternal misery to select from all these descriptions a single one of those phrases which the New Testament has constantly applied to future retribution. According to them, these terms are the very best, the strongest, and the most suitable to express its exceeding misery. If they are, let them bring forward but one example from the writings contemporaneous with the New Testament to show that they were so considered. If they cannot do this, let them honestly confess that the terms of the New Testament are unsuitable to express their view, and therefore do not express it.

Such a confession has virtually been made. In the second, third, and succeeding centuries of Christ, Christian teachers taught the theory of Plato. We say they *introduced* it into the Christian Church: our opponents say that they only taught what had been *handed down* from apostolic days:

but both we and they allow that Athenagoras and Tatian, Tertullian, Athanasius and Augustine, taught beyond a question the eternal misery of the wicked. Now we cannot and do not mean to deny that these writers, at least most of them, used the terms of the New Testament which we have been discussing, and applied them to future punishment. As they were Christian teachers, they could not possibly avoid doing so; for these terms were so applied in the Scriptures of which they were the defenders and the expounders. *But they were not satisfied with these terms. They have shown their dissatisfaction by the adoption and perpetual use of other terms never once applied in the New Testament as they apply them.* The old nomenclature of Plato is revived by the Fathers of the Christian Church.

We hear in Christian writings the voice that never speaks from the New Testament. We hear from Athenagoras what we do not hear from Paul, that the wicked are incorruptible: we hear from Tertullian what we do not hear from John, that the souls of the wicked are immortal: we hear from Augustine what we do not hear from Christ, that the existence of the lost is as indestructible as that of God himself. These are their favorite expressions when they explain and vindicate their theory of punishment. The terms of the New Testament, considered in our previous chapter, are more rarely used; or are painfully explained away; or are sometimes positively contradicted: while the terms derived from Plato overlay and supersede them. Of what is this the confession? It is the confession that the above terms of the New Testament are *insufficient* to express the Augustinian theory, *and therefore do not express it.*

The Primary Sense of Terms Indicated

If the various words descriptive of future punishment, which we have discussed in the last two chapters, had in human usage *one sense only,* there could be no room for doubt but that the view wo advocate was that of Scripture: for it is not questioned that all those words have the sense which we have put upon them. Nor is it even attempted to be denied that this sense is their *original* and primary sense. Every dictionary in every language of the earth is our witness for this. Our opponents, both of the schools of Origen and Augustine, would deny this if they could; for these words, when taken in their primary sense, *overturn both of their systems alike.* If the wicked cease to exist in hell, there is no room either for Origen's restoration or Augustine's endless life of anguish.

But most words in common use, and especially in an advanced stage of knowledge and civilization, have several senses. Most of the terms in question have such. They are words too important, and too much in constant use, not to have gathered to them in course of time several senses derived from, and more or less different from their primary sense. These are called their *secondary senses,* and in certain circumstances are frequently used, and in some circumstances even more frequently used than the primary sense from which they are derived. It is in this fact that our opponents take refuge. They assert that the words of Scripture applied to future punishment are not to be taken in that primary sense *which in the beginning of language was their only sense;* but in one of those secondary senses, which, in the course of time, men came to attach to them. The schools of Origen and Augustine here agree. They differ indeed when they come to settle *what* secondary sense is to be taken, but they unite in saying that *some* secondary sense it certainly is. To this important question we will now attend. We will endeavor to arrive at the true principle of interpretation of these words. Our enquiry is this: are they to be understood in their primary sense, or are they to be understood in one or other of their secondary senses?

This is a most important question. Here are words which bear with awful power upon myriads of myriads of beings throughout eternity. Understood in their primary sense, they consign the wicked to eternal oblivion: understood in one secondary sense, they consign him to eternal evil and misery: while understood in another, they promise him restoration to holiness and to happiness. Are the advocates of these several schools to be forever arraying the various senses of these words against each other without any *principles of interpretation,* which are, with fair and candid minds, to set the matter at rest by showing that one, and only one of them, is that which God means us to accept. They are not. We have full means of knowing that in the great question before us *the primary sense can alone be taken* and that the secondary senses are here one and all alike to be laid aside.

We will not here enter into the question of the origin of human language. For our part we believe it to have been directly from God, *i.e.,* that Adam did not invent language by any process more or less rapid; but that he found himself immediately on his creation endowed with a power of language fully suited to and sufficient for all the requirements of the condition in which he was created by God. Be this, however, as it may, there is no doubt that before the fall of man, the penalty attached to sin, namely, death, *had but one sense, and that sense the primary.* It was the introduction of sin which led gradually to those various secondary senses derived from the primary one of loss of physical existence. As this was the *only* sense which death had when it was first spoken of to Adam, we are compelled to take it in its primary sense when the word was first used in the sense of a penalty. Surely this one fact ought to be sufficient to guide us through all the later Scriptures which speak of death as the penalty of sin. God Himself stamped this as its original sense, and we may not dare to alter it without authority from Him. The penalty was first promulgated in the primary sense: it must be understood ever since so, unless God tells us He has altered its sense. The primary sense attached to *one* of the terms descriptive of future punishment determines that it is to be attached to *all the terms.* "Destruction" is to be understood in the same sense as "death."

But there is besides this a well-known and universally-accepted principle of interpretation among mankind which decides this question. The principle of interpretation is this, that *all language relative to law and jurisprudence,* all language descriptive of the sanctions of government, all language setting forth the penalties of crime and disobedience, *is to be accepted in its primary sense and in no other.* Examine the terms of any human law, ask the men whose life-study relates to law whether as legislators or administrators, all will reply that in all documents relating directly or indirectly to law and jurisprudence, no sense but the primary is for a moment allowable. Thus, when death is announced as a penalty for crime, no controversy would for an instant be admitted as to its meaning. No lawyer, for or against the criminal, would search for dramatic or poetic secondary senses. If the criminal himself were gravely to plead that his physical existence was not to be taken from him because he had understood the legal penalty of death in a secondary sense, it is quite possible that he might be saved from the scaffold and the hangman; but it would only be by his being sent to a lunatic asylum as an incurable madman.

Here, then, is a great principle of interpretation in use among all mankind: it is that all documents and terms relating to human conduct, as affected by law, are only to be interpreted in then primary sense. A secondary sense may be more usual and more proper *elsewhere, but not here.* Poetry and the drama, the literature of passion, imagination, and feeling, may use these terms differently; but their use is not to affect in the smallest degree *the interpretation of a law.* Here we take our stand. Here we are on sure and steady ground. The terms we have been discussing are the terms of the *Divine Law:* the jurisprudence we have been discussing is *Gods jurisprudence.* The Great Governor is laying before his subjects the penalties which attach to sin. He speaks to them in the only language they can understand—their own language. He puts no new rules of interpretation upon it, when He addresses them. He accepts, adopts, and uses the language of those to whom He speaks. We can then only interpret the divine penalty for sin in the sense which man has put upon all such penalties—in the primary sense. It is only claiming that God's penalty for crime against His law should be interpreted in analogy with all law. It is only saying that God speaks to men in their own tongue. It would be an outrage upon human law to interpret its sanction in some figurative and secondary sense; but that God's jurisprudence should be interpreted in this way, his awful penalty for sin explained by the tropes of poetry and the hyperbole of grief, is an outrage of a graver kind, because mixed up with a higher destiny and the Great Judge of the universe. On this principle, then, we set aside *every secondary* sense from the terms relative to future punishment: *on this principle we accept their primary as their only possible sense:* and on this principle the theories of Augustine and Origen fall together—the theory that inflicts eternal misery on man, and the theory that brings him back, through a death to sin, to holiness and happiness.

If any justification of this principle were required it is readily found. The primary sense is *one unchanging sense,* universally understood by every reasonable being of every stage of civilization, and *every* variety of religious belief. The secondary sense is various, changing, differently regarded by different minds. Thus death in its primary sense is always one and the same. Down from its first example and enunciation to the present day, it has preserved this sense unbroken and unchanged, and is understood alike by the savage and the civilized, by the ignorant and the learned, by the degraded and the sensitive mind.* But when we come to the secondary sense all this is changed. There are several secondary senses! These secondary senses are ever varying with the opinions and circumstances of men! Some of these secondary senses are absolutely unintelligible to multitudes of minds, as those of children, persons of blunted moral feeling, and savages, who were yet all intended to be affected by the terms used.

In order to show the uncertainty which arises the moment we leave the primary sense of these terms and try to fix upon them a proper secondary sense, we will just show how one of the most important of these terms, death, is regarded by two opposing schools who both insist on the propriety of taking it in a secondary sense. *The Augustinian* fixes upon a sense, and interprets the word as signifying "death to all holy feeling," "death to all happiness"—*i.e.*, misery, and moral corruption. But this is not its only secondary sense. The *Universalist* claims it in another! With him it is "death to sin," a process resulting in happiness! Who is to decide which of these is right? Scripture simply calls it "death." If the Augustinian tells us that it is a punishment, and is therefore to be taken in an evil sense; the Universalist will reply that punishment is at least as often inflicted for the correction of the criminal as in vengeance; and that it is therefore at least

* Bickersteth, *On the Prophecies*, 5th ed., p. 69.

as probable that it is here to be taken in a good sense. If the Augustinian will remind us that pain accompanies the death mentioned in Scripture, and that it is therefore evil, the Universalist will reply that pain and tears and anguish accompany the process of repentance and recovery, and that his view is therefore probable. If the Augustinian will urge that sin is of an infinite demerit, and should consequently receive infinite punishment, and that too forever felt by the sufferer, the Universalist will set in opposition that love of God which is much more certainly infinite, that compassion of His which is boundless, that yearning which the Creator feels for the work of His own hands; and will argue hence, with an infinitely greater force, that He who brought back blood-stained David, and Saul the persecutor, and the woman who was a sinner, will, in the vast *aionial* period, bring back Balaam, and Judas, and Demas, and even the Archangel, now dark, but once a son of the morning. In a contest such as this, it were indeed difficult to decide. The adoption of the primary sense puts an end to all such contests. It removes dispute by removing ambiguity. It is essential to all law, most of all to the law of God. The graver the penalty for disobedience, the greater the necessity for certainty.

As it is in all legal documents absolutely, so it is to nearly the same extent in *historical composition.* A secondary sense is all but banished from its terms. When we read of Lord William Russell losing his life through a prosecution instigated by the Court, we never dream of his becoming very "unhappy," or losing his "well-being," from the cessation of Court favor. Or, when we read of the loss of such a number of lives in such a battle, we never dream that twenty thousand men on one side became very unhappy at some national calamity, and that ten thousand men on the other side, "in generous sympathy," also became unhappy at sight of their foemen's tears. Such interpretations of men's writings are simply ridiculous. Yet such are the interpretations which learned theologians, and right reverend bishops, and long-robed preachers, put upon writings which, while we rejoice to know them to be divine, are also as purely human as the writings of Coke or Lyttleton, of Macauley or Hume.

For Scripture, while it gives us in its wonderful variety specimens of every variety of composition, from the sublimest poetry to the baldest prose, is preeminently the code of the Divine law, the history of God's dealings with man. To insist that in writings of tins kind the primary sense of words is to be abandoned and the secondary figurative sense substituted, is just as absurd, as unreasonable, as inadmissible, as to interpret the language of Coke or Hume by the tropes of the highest poetry. When God gravely and solemnly tells us how He will deal with us in the future world for our conduct in this, we are not only justified, but we are imperatively compelled, to take his solemn words explanatory of our future condition *in their primary sense.* So interpreted, "life" is "animal existence," and "death" is the "loss of animal existence;" and, so interpreted, away fly into the clouds all those secondary senses which writers, from Tertullian and Origen and Augustine, to their modern representatives, Messrs. Grant, and Jukes, and Angus, have been putting on them with such pertinacity and assurance that the Christian world has all but universally believed that the sense universally attached to these terms in the common language of mankind is never attached to them in the most awfully solemn documents that ever addressed their teaching to the human ear. But this we need not suppose, we cannot suppose, we dare not suppose. Addressed to human ears, to man's highest hopes and his profoundest fears, these terms have the sense commonly attached to them by those to whom they are addressed. God does not describe the awful penalties of violated law under the figures of poetry.

If the primary sense of the terms be established as the true sense, there is an end of this controversy. But we will submit the matter to another test. We will give a table of the various terms applied to future punishment: we will append to them *every meaning* attached to them in the ordinary Greek language: and we will then show that the force of these aggregate terms admits of our view, while it absolutely rejects the views of Augustine and Origen. We take our meanings of the terms from Liddell and Scott's Greek-English Lexicon, allowed to be an authority of the highest order. What their views were upon the question itself we do not know, and do not care to enquire. What we ask from them is all the senses put upon a certain set of terms in that Greek language in which the New Testament was written. We will first give the table of words and then draw the inference from it.

TABLE OF GREEK WORDS AND THEIR MEANINGS					
θάνατος, *thanatos*	Death, natural or violent	Death by judgment of court	Death, sister of sleep	A corpse	
αποθνήσκω, *apothnesko*	To be ready to die	To be put to death			
ἀπόλλυμι,[*] *apollumi*	Destroy utterly	Kill	Slay	(Spoken of things) To demolish	(Spoken of things) To lay waste
ἀπόλλυμαι,[†] *apollumai*	To perish	To die	To be undone	To be lost	To slip away
απώλεια, *apoleia*	Destruction	Loss			
ἀφανιζω,[‡] *aphanizo*	To make unseen	To hide from sight	To suppress	To do away with	To make away with
	To drink off	To keep out of public			
φθείρω,[§] *ftheiro*	To corrupt	To spoil	To ruin	To waste	To destroy
φθείρομαι, *ftheiromai*	To go to ruin	To perish	To be deranged	To put to death	To be slain

[*] Additional definition includes: "to lose utterly."

[†] Also, "to banish."

[‡] Also, "to kill and bury secretly," "to drive away," "to destroy utterly," "to obliterate," "to steal," and "to tarnish good repute."

[§] Also, "to put to death," "to kill," "to debauch," and "to mix together colors."

φθορά,[*] *fthora*	Corruption	Decay	Destruction	Loss	Ruin
ἐξολοθρεύω, *exolothreuo*	To destroy utterly				
ὀλεθρος,[†] *olethros*	Ruin	Destruction	Death	Plague	Loss
Ζωή, *zoe*	A living or property	Life opposed to death			
Ζάω, *zao*	To live (spoken of animal life)	To be full life and strength			
ψυχή,[‡] *psyche*	Breath	Life	Spirit	The soul or immortal part of man	The seat of the will

We will thank our readers to look carefully at the foregoing table. It contains the words by which the New Testament describes future punishment, either in the way of infliction or deprivation, as that the wicked will suffer death (*thanatos*), and will be deprived of life (*zoe*). It contains *all the meanings* which the speakers of the Grecian language applied to the above terms. We here take these terms simply and by themselves as they are used in the New Testament on this question, as in the text "the wages of sin is *death,*" or, "if ye live after the flesh ye shall *die.*" Let each theory of future punishment *give a plain definition of what it means.* Let this definition be applied to the above table. It is quite plain that in order to be the theory revealed in the New Testament it must suit *one or other of the meanings of every one of the above words.* It will not be enough that it occurs among the meanings of some, or of many, of these terms: *it must be found in every one of them.* Now tried by this plain test

[*] Also, "Perdition," "death," "debauching," and "mixing of colors."

[†] Also, (to others) "a plague," "a curse," and "a ruin."

[‡] Also, "reason," "anima mundi," "a moth," and "psyche."

we must reject the theories of Augustine and Origen, and can only accept that here maintained.

A single glance will show that what we understand as the terrible punishment of the wicked, that is, their "loss of existence," is found under every one of the above terms. But when we come to the definitions given by the Augustinian and Universalist we find that neither meets the requirements of the case. Thus the Augustinian means by future punishment "an existence in misery and moral pollution." He thinks, and perhaps justly, that this view of punishment agrees with some of the senses of some of the above terms; as, for example, that it may very well agree with a sense of *apollumai* " to be undone;" or of *phthora* and *olethros* as significant of "loss." We need not dispute this with him; but this concession leaves him still at a far distance from his object. He must show that his view of punishment consorts with a meaning of every one of the terms. One of the meanings of *phthora* is "mixing of colors;" but we never suppose that this sense describes the punishment of the wicked. Why? Because though it is a meaning of one of the terms it is not any meaning of the rest. And so we say of the Augustinian view. It is not enough for him to say that his view suits several, or most of the above terms. This is what he is always doing. He *selects* some of them and keeps his hearers occupied solely with these. But Scripture has used a great many terms—a great many more in the Greek than we find in the corresponding terms in English, in order that on this vital point there may be no ambiguity. Now if the Augustinian could show that his view *agreed with every one of the above terms with but a single exception, that single exception would exclude his view as effectually as if his view were not found under one of them.* But our readers will see that the Augustinian view is not among the senses of several of the above words, as, for example, of *thanatos, apothnesko, aphanizo, exolothreuo.*

It is yet more hopeless when we come to the Universalist. When we come to ask him what he means by that "death" and that "destruction" which God says that He will inflict upon sinners hereafter, he tells us that in his opinion these terms mean "the extinction *of sin*" the "destruction or obliteration *of pride* and self-will" in sinners, through which their restoration is to be effected. But when we come to compare his definition with the terms in question, *we do not find it the sense of a single one of them.* He will not find in the Greek language that *thanatos, taken by itself,* ever means "the extinction *of sin,*" or that *apoleia,* taken by itself, ever means "the obliteration of any evil quality." These words occur simply and by themselves in the New Testament, and we will allow no man to subjoin other words to them.

Tried then by this simple test the theories of our opponents fall to the ground. It is not simply that the meaning which they put upon the terms of Scripture is not their *primary* meaning, but that in very many instances it *is not their meaning at all.* If they want to show that their sense of the words is their true sense in the New Testament, they must first undertake the task of showing that the Greek of the New Testament is a *language in itself,* different from the Greek spoken and written by ordinary men in the apostolic days; a sacred language, peculiar to the writings of the evangelists and apostles; quite distinct from the Greek of Josephus and Philo, of Demosthenes and Plato. When they shall have succeeded in establishing the evidence of this *sacred language* they will have also succeeded in establishing an *unintelligible hieroglyphic, i.e.*, that the words about which we are speaking cannot be shown to have any sense at all. We however take our stand upon the intelligible principle that the Greek of the New Testament is part and parcel of the grand tongue of Greece, from which it cannot be dissevered, from which it would be its death to sever it; and, standing on this ground, we call upon our opponents to abandon theories, which, opposed to the established usage of the Grecian language, are contrary to God's holy Word.

Before we bring this chapter to a close we will show our readers how truly and really the terms of Scripture are opposed to the theories of Augustine and Origen, by showing them that their advocates, in explaining fully and completely the theories which they maintain, are compelled in doing so to contradict in plainest contradiction every one of the strongest declarations of Scripture relative to future punishment. Neither of these theories can be explained without contradicting Scripture. If the simple language of the New Testament is exclusively adhered to, it will not set forth, but will contradict their views. If they only speak of "death," and "destruction," and "loss of life," as the lot of the wicked, they know perfectly well that the ordinary sense of these terms is ruinous to their systems: if they say that the wicked will be "consumed," "burnt up," reduced to "ashes," they are but too keenly aware that these terms express the opposite to what they teach. When they want, then, to be *plain,* when they want, beyond any ambiguity of phrase, to set forth their horrible or delusive theories, they are compelled by dire necessity to introduce a language not merely not used by Scripture but flatly contradictory to what it does use. In order to show this we will draw out tables of some of the chief of those terms in which the Scripture speaks of future punishment. We will give these terms in the Greek, Latin, and English languages. Those who are unacquainted with the former can pass them over.

THE TABLE			
	AUGUSTINIAN THEORY	**SCRIPTURE**	**THEORY OF DESTRUCTION**
LIFE	"The fact of the never-ending life of Satan and lost sinners" (James Grant, *Religious Tendencies*). "Disbelief affirms what it denies. It unawares asserts immortal life" (Young's *Night Thoughts*).	"He that believeth not the Son shall not see life" (John 3:36).	"The wicked will not live forever" (Rev. S. Minton). "The loss of life is the essence of future punishment" (Rev. H. Constable).
LIVE	"The wicked live on forever" (Tatian). "How wilt thou endure to live on forever" (R. Baxter, *Saint's Rest*). "The sinner shall live on through eternity" (James Grant). "The wicked shall live forever" (J. Angus, *Future Punishment*). "In hell they must live" (Rev. J. C. Furniss).	"Lest he eat, and live forever" (Gen. 3:22). "If any man eat of this bread he shall live forever" (John 6:51).	"Only they who eat of the bread Christ gives will live forever" (S. Minton). "If you defile your flesh, you will not live" (Hermas).

DEATH	"Death cannot happen to the soul" (Athenagoras). "The souls of the wicked will not be put to death" (*Book of Enoch*). "No death will deliver them from punishment" (Hippolytus). "How will they call and cry: O death, wither art thou now gone?" (R. Baxter). "Does death come? No; he flies away from him" (Rev. J. C. Furniss).	"The wages of sin is death" (Rom. 5:23). "This is the second death" (Rev. 20:14).	"Envy leads to death" (Clemens Romanus). "The ungodly are condemned to death" (Barnabas). "They are debtors to death" (Irenaeus). "The doom of the wicked is death" (S. Minton). "Death is the essence of future punishment" (H. Constable).
TO DIE	"The soul of the wicked cannot die" (St. Augustine). "It does not die in hell" (Clementina). "The wicked shall never die" (James Grant). "And tried and wished to die; but could not die" (Pollok). "I cannot, must not die" (Bunyan).	"If ye live after the flesh ye shall die" (Rom. 8:13).	"The wicked will hereafter die" (H. Constable).

TO DIE ***(Cont.)***	"O, that I might once at last die" (Richard Baxter). "They shall burn eternally without dying" (Jeremy Taylor).		
DESTRUCTION	"The soul of the wicked is lost, but not in the sense of destruction" (Tertullian). "The eternal destruction of human life, at or after death, is among the theological errors of the day" (James Grant). "The soul cannot suffer destruction" (Tertullian).	"Broad is the way that leadeth to destruction" (Matt. 7:13). "Who shall be punished with everlasting destruction" (2 Thess. 1:9).	"The heathen considered death to be final destruction" (John Calvin). "The language of Scripture points, not to endless misery, but to destruction" (S. Minton). "The end of the wicked is destruction" (H. Constable).
DESTROY	"God meant, not to destroy, but root them (devils) out of heaven" (Milton). "The evil one will never be destroyed" (James Grant). "God will not destroy one single soul or body which He has created" (James Grant).	"Art thou come to destroy us?" (Mark 1:24). "God is able to destroy both body and soul in hell" (Matt. 10:28). "All the wicked will God destroy" (Ps. 145:20).	"God destroys both the serpent and those angels and men who are like him" (Justin Martyr). "He who chooses other (evil) things shall be destroyed" (Barnabas). "God will destroy the wicked in hell" (H. Constable).

DESTROY ***(Cont.)***	"Pained, yet coming out undestroyed" (C. H. Spurgeon). "Rebuilt in union indestructible" (Pollok).		
TO PERISH	"God has not made us that we should perish" (Athenagoras). "From such an idea my very soul turns away with abhorrence" (James Grant). "The soul's imperishable nature" (James Grant).	"Them that perish" (2 Cor. 2:15). "They shall utterly perish" (2 Pet. 2:12).	"To perish rather, swallowed up and lost" (Milton). "According to Epicurus, the entire man perishes" (Hippolytus). "The heathen think that whatever is taken away from the world has perished" (John Calvin). "The wicked must in due time perish" (S. Minton). "To perish is truly descriptive of future punishment" (H. Constable).
TO CONSUME	"The bodies of the wicked shall burn, and never be consumed" (Jonathan Edwards). "Burning continually, yet unconsumed" (Pollok).	"The wicked shall consume: into smoke shall they consume away" (Ps. 37:20). "God is a consuming fire" (Heb. 12:29).	"The wicked will consume away" (H. Constable).

TO CONSUME (*Cont.*)	"The fire of hell does not consume" (Bunyan). "The wicked shall never be consumed" (Richard Baxter). "Their bodies will never be consumed" (John Wesley). "They shall always suffer without consuming" (*Nelson's Festivals*).		
BEING—TO BE	"If our substance be indeed divine, and cannot cease to be" (Milton). "The being who has sinned cannot cease to be" (Robert Baxter). "The eternity of being in man" (*Ditto*).	"The wicked shall not be" (Ps. 37:10). "Let the wicked be no more" (Ps. 104:35). "He is not" (Job 27:19).	"The end of sinners is the blotting out of being" (Constable).
CORRUPTION	"The soul is superior to corruption" (Athenagoras). "The corruptible body of the wicked puts on incorruption" (*Ditto*).	"He that soweth to the flesh shall of the flesh reap corruption" (Gal. 6:8).	"God shall raise all from the dead, and appoint *some* incorruptible" (Justin Martyr). "Corruption represents death or destruction" (S. Minton).

CORRUPTION (*Cont.*)	"The bodies of the wicked shall be rendered incorruptible" (Thomas Scott). "The evil changed corruptible to incorrupt" (Pollok). "The bodies of the wicked shall be changed to fit them for eternal torment without corruption" (Jonathan Edwards). "Their bodies are incorruptible" (John Wesley).		"Corruption is the end of the ungodly" (H. Constable).

We are not at present able to present to our readers a table of Universalist terms such as that just given of the opposite school. We have just put down as below a few of such terms which occur to us at present. They will show, so far as they go, the same tendency to contradict the language of Scripture. Should our work extend to another edition, we propose to enlarge this table; and would feel obliged if any of our readers would furnish us with examples which they may meet with in their studies.

	UNIVERSALIST THEORY	SCRIPTURE
LIFE	"Not one life shall be destroyed" (Tennyson). "No life may fail beyond the grave" (Tennyson).	"He that believeth not the Son shall not see life" (John 3:36).

DESTROY	"Not one life shall be destroyed" (Tennyson). "The wicked shall not be destroyed" (*One of the Laity*).	"All the wicked will God destroy" (Ps. 145:20).
PERISH	"The soul is exempt from perishing" (Origen).	"Them that perish" (2 Cor. 2:15).

In order to show the extreme danger of such a principle of interpretation as that we have controverted in this chapter, we will show how readily it may be applied to overturn the cardinal doctrine of Christianity, for instance, the resurrection of Christ, and our resurrection as a result of His. It is simply effected by attributing to the terms descriptive of it their secondary or figurative sense instead of their primary and literal one. And for such an interpretation there is fully as much, in our opinion much more, ground, than for adopting it in the case of future punishment.

The noun "resurrection," and the verbs "to rise again," have in common use a primary and a secondary sense. According to those with whom we reason, the secondary figurative sense is in Scripture the most important, the highest, and the most common sense.* As being such, in their judgment, they have interpreted all the terms relative to future punishment in conformity with it. "Death" is, with them, "moral disorganization:" "life" is, with them, "well-being:" "destruction" is, with them, "the overthrow of happiness:" and so on through all the terms. Now upon what principle can they refuse to the terms "resurrection" and "rise again from the dead," a similar figurative sense. They are certainly so used in Scripture (Luke 2:34; Col. 3:1; Eph. 5:14; Col. 2:12). Why should not this

* S. C. Bartlett, *Life and Death Eternal*, c. ii.

be their use whenever there used? We ask our opponents for a single reason why these should not be thus used. In the application of such terms to bodily resurrection the New Testament introduced a use all but unknown to the Gentile mind, which was not at all the case with regard to the terms of punishment. Why then should they deny to the terms relating to resurrection some such figurative sense as they know so well how to apply to the terms of punishment? Why should not resurrection be "an awakening out of the sleep of ignorance and sin," a "resumption of vigor," or some such "high" sense, and not the "low" "material" sense of awaking dull matter from the dust? On some such principle the early heretics would appear to have gone, who denied the bodily resurrection of Christ, and denied that there would be any bodily resurrection for man (Luke 2:34; Col. 3:1; Eph. 5:14; Col. 2:12). They too could descant upon the superiority of the figurative sense. What could our Augustinian theorists reply to such men? Nothing that could not be overturned from their own practice in other cases. What could they reply to a modern sect who have in England assumed the name of "Shilohites," and who reject the ordinary doctrine of our Lord's resurrection and that of his people on the very identical ground on which they reject the final destruction or annihilation of the wicked, that is, their rejection of the *literal* sense of the terms of Scripture? When such airy reasoners say, "We believe that all mankind will be redeemed by the Spirit and power of God from all evil, and put into the possession and enjoyment of all good, so that pain and sorrow shall be no more: and we believe that this is the resurrection spoken of in the Scriptures" (1 Cor. 15:13; 2 Tim. 2:18), what can our Augustinians reply?

Nothing.

How can they rebuke them? They cannot rebuke them. They have been teaching for centuries the principle of interpretation on which the Shilohites act in a particular case. They cannot deny that it is just as applicable to the doctrine of the resurrection as it is to that of future punishment. And, indeed, by their common view of the believer's death as, according to them, introducing him at once into the glory and bliss of heaven, they remove the grand reason and object of the believer's resurrection.

7

The Illustrations of Scripture

THAT THE WICKED WILL come to an end and cease to exist in hell, we have seen to be the direct teaching of Scripture in what we have called its legal terms. We have submitted those terms to every possible test, and seen that they can fairly bear no other interpretation than that which we have put upon them. But these terms by no means exhaust our argument. We will find our conclusion supported in many other ways. We now proceed to support it by drawing our readers attention for a short time to the *illustrations of Scripture.*

The illustrations of Scripture on the subject of future punishment are very numerous, are presented in every variety of aspect, and are every one of them harmonious with the rest. We will compare them with the illustrations selected by men who hold every variety of opinion as to the future of man—from the Augustinian, who gives to the wicked an endless life of anguish, to the Epicurean, who holds that there is no future life for any man at all. We have no hesitation in saying that the illustrations of Scripture, so varied, so numerous, so harmonious, are *by themselves* sufficient to decide this great question in our favor. They overthrow alike the theory of eternal misery and of universal restoration. *It may be remarked that the advocates of these opposite errors are wonderfully guarded in their reference to this leading feature of Scripture.* We do not wonder that, holding their views, they almost pass it by in total silence. We will not however permit them to do so.

We find in the Old Testament the following illustrations of future punishment: the wicked shall he dashed in pieces like a potter's vessel (Ps. 2:9); they shall be like the beasts that perish (Ps. 49:12, 20); like the untimely fruit of a woman (Ps. 58:8); like a whirlwind that passes away (Prov. 10:25, see also Hos. 13:3); like a waterless garden scorched by an Eastern sun (Isa. 1:30); like garments consumed by the moth (Isa. 51:8): they shall be silent in darkness (1 Sam. 2:9); like a lamp put out (Job 18:5; Prov. 13:9); like a dream which flies away (Job 20:8). The wicked shall consume like the fat of lambs in the fire; consume like smoke (Ps. 37:20); melt like wax (Ps. 68:2); burn like tow (Isa. 1:31); consume like thorns (Isa. 34:12); vanish away like exhausted waters (Ps. 58:7).

The illustrations of the New Testament are of the same unmistakeable character. The end of the wicked is there compared to fish cast away to corruption (Matt. 13:47-48); to a house thrown down to its foundations (Luke 6:49); to the destruction of the old world by water (Luke 17:27), and that of the Sodomites by fire (Luke 17:29; 2 Pet. 2:5-6); to the death and destruction of natural brute beasts (2 Pet. 2:12). They shall be like wood cast into unquenchable flames; like chaff burnt up (Matt. 3:12); like tares consumed (Matt. 13:40); like a dry branch reduced to ashes (John 15:6).

Such are the illustrations of Scripture. These are the images which God has selected from the world that is open to our inspection, in order to let us know what shall happen to the ungodly hereafter. We have no hesitation in saying that they are, one and all, irreconcilable with both Augustine's and Origen's theories of hell. *If it was true,* as both these theories insist, *that the wicked never cease to exist, these illustrations would be every one of them, not merely unsuitable, but positively false.* The wicked will *not* be, according to either theory, like the beasts that perish, or a whirlwind that passes away, or garments consumed by the moth. They will *not,* according to them, consume like the fat of lambs in the fire, or consume into smoke, or melt like wax. They will *not* be like wood cast into quenchless flames, or like chaff burnt up, or like tares consumed, or like a dry branch reduced to ashes. All these lose their form, substance, and organization, and become as though they had never been, which the wicked never do according to the theory of their eternal misery or their ultimate restoration. The illustrations of Scripture are therefore *fatal to both views alike.* Every one of its images points, not to the preservation of being in any state, whether good or evil, but to the utter blotting out of existence and being and identity.

Let us now compare these illustrations of Scripture with those of ordinary writers, and see if the comparison does not fully bear out our view. We will first examine the images which writers who hold the theory of eternal misery select as suitable to illustrate their theory. We will take our examples from the writings of the Christian fathers Augustine and Tertullian, both of them men of great power of mind and force of language. Is it not most significant that these men, perfectly familiar with the illustrations of Scripture, turn away from them as unsuitable to their purpose, and select with much pains, from a survey of nature as it was understood by them, a series of illustrations not only absent from Scripture but of a *nature diametrically opposed to those of Scripture.* According to Tertullian, the wicked will be like *mountains which burn but are not consumed;* like a body struck by lightning whose *organization is uninjured* and itself *not reduced to ashes.* According to Augustine, the wicked will be like *worms that exist in hot springs*; like *salamanders which are not destroyed* in the fire; like *diamonds* which are *indestructible in scorching heat;* like *Vesuvius and Etna which burn but do not consume.* These are not the illustrations of Scripture. They contradict those of Scripture. According to Scripture the wicked will *not* be like the salamanders, or boiling-water worms, or burning mountains, of Tertullian and Augustine. They will, on the contrary, be destroyed, consume away, be reduced to ashes, as the fat of lambs, or the dry wood and thorns.

There is one illustration in Scripture which we have sometimes wondered has not been laid hold of by the Augustinian theorists as an illustration of their view. *It is an exact and complete illustration of it.* It represents substance as burning in fire but remaining perfectly unconsumed. We refer to the burning bush seen by Moses in the Wilderness of Horeb (Exod. 3:1-15). It exactly illustrates the Augustinian theory—that the wicked will burn in the fire of hell, but not be consumed by it.

Apposite as this illustration is, familiar as it is, we do not know that it has ever been used by any Augustinian writer. They have doubtless often thought of it with this view, and examined it very carefully; but, somehow, one and all of them pass it by.

Why?

It must be unsuitable after all or surely they would all have used it over and over again. But this illustration, so familiar to us all, which we have admired since first we heard in childhood the grand story of Moses, the man of God, is an illustration in its way subversive of Augustine's fearful hell. The burning bush was a *miraculous* sign. It tells us, therefore, that without the miraculous interposition of God no substance could burn with fire *without being consumed.* And it also by its significant language, "*burnt but teas not consumed*" points to the *opposite* language in which Scripture speaks of the end of the wicked in that fire which *does consume* and reduce them to ashes. The burning bush was emblematic of the children of God who passed through a fire which did *not* consume them: it is not emblematic of the lost who enter into a fire which kindles upon them and consumes them, because God does not put forth his almighty power to save them from its devouring flame.

We have seen what kind of illustrations the advocates of eternal life in pain select as suitable to their theory. We will now draw attention to the fact that the advocates of this view, when not sufficiently careful, and when desirous to express beyond any doubt their sentiments, by showing *what the wicked are not like, constantly contradict the very illustrations which Scripture has selected to show what they are like.* "God has *not* made us," says the Christian father, Athengoras, *"like beasts that perish;"* and Mr. James Grant repeats the old father's renunciation of a scriptural illustration in still more emphatic terms, by telling us that, from the idea that the wicked should become like beasts that perish, *his "very soul turns away with abhorrence."** The celebrated author of "The Night Thoughts," one of the great masters of the English tongue, rejects disdainfully another of the illustrations of Scripture:

> "To toil, and eat,
> Then make our bed in darkness,"

in his description for that state of non-existence of the wicked against which he directs a considerable amount of poetry but no logic. It is by one of the illustrations of Scripture that the greatest of French thinkers, Pascal, has expressed that idea of annihilation against which he strenuously reasons, asking whether it is cause of joy to be told that "our soul is nothing but a *puff of wind or smoke.*" We have thus the Augustinian theorists insisting that the illustrations which Scripture uses of the end of the ungodly are exactly and unmistakably illustrative of their destruction or annihilation.

Having seen how the advocates of eternal evil unconsciously contradict the illustrations of Scripture, we will now show how men who

* *Religious Tendencies*, i. 132.

held the Epicurean notion of the utter extinction of being at death, or who, though not holding it themselves, wished to describe this Epicurean idea, have used the very same illustrations which the Scripture uses for the destruction of the wicked after judgment. Thus an illustration of Scripture referred to in the last paragraph is that the wicked "shall consume *like smoke.*" This we are told by Plato was the usual illustration used by Epicurean theorists to express their idea that after death the entire being and existence of man came to an end. It vanished, according to them, "*like a breath of wind or smoke.*" Accordingly we find the Epicurean poet, Lucretius, using this very illustration:

> "As the smoke disperses into the air,
> So believe that the soul also is dissolved."

The ending of the wicked "in darkness" or "night" is another illustration in common use in Scripture. It is the illustration which Titus uses in his address to the Roman soldiers when he speaks of "souls that wear away in and with their distempered bodies, on which comes a *subterranean night to dissolve them to nothing.*" It is also the very illustration which the Epicurean poet, Catullus, uses when he exhorts his mistress to catch at each pleasure of life because there was no bright hope of any after existence:

> "Let us live, and love, my Lesbia,
> Suns can set and come again:
> For us, once our brief day has sunk,
> Is only the sleep of an *endless night.*"

This is also the very image which that consummate master of language, our own Tennyson, uses to express the same idea:

"T'were best at once to sink to peace
Like birds the charming serpent draws,
To drop head-foremost in the jaws
Of vacant darkness, and to cease."

And another of our great English writers, Thomson, uses the same illustration when he makes his heroine to prefer death to Roman bondage, even though persuaded that

"It were a long *dark night* without a morning."

The comparison of the destruction of the wicked to a dream or vision that flies away is also an illustration of Scripture. We find the very same illustration used by Homer in one of those moods of his when he abandoned the Platonic idea of the immortality of the soul for the Epicurean idea of its dissolution:

"Like fleeting vision passed the soul away."

Once more we find in one of the Apocryphal books that the most usual illustrations of Scripture to describe the end of the wicked were the very ones used by Epicurean theorists:

> "We are born of nothing," they said, "and after this we shall be as if we had not been; for *the breath in our nostrils is smoke,* and speech a spark to move our hearts, which, being put out, our body shall be as ashes, and our spirit shall be poured abroad us soft air, and our *life shall pass away as the trace of a cloud,* and shall be dispersed as a mist, which is driven away by the beams of the sun. *For our time is as the passing of a shadow.*"*

---

* Plato, *Phædo,* par. xiv.; Josephus, *Jewish War.* vi., i., v.; Tennyson, *In Memoriam,* xxxiv.; J. Thomson's Works, *Sophonisba;* Wisdom ii., 2-5.

We thus see that when Epicurean theorists would describe their theory of annihilation they can find no better or stronger illustrations to describe it by than those which the Bible uses for the final destruction of the wicked; and that when the great masters of our English tongue wish in the most appropriate and most striking language to describe the Epicurean theory, they are forced to borrow the very illustrations which Scripture from first to last uses when it speaks of the end of the wicked in hell.

A little industry could multiply examples of this kind a hundred-fold. They show us unquestionably, that the illustrations of Scripture are by themselves sufficient to overthrow the false systems both of Augustine and Origen. They all teach, as the universal law of language proves, that the end of the wicked, after they have been raised to judgment, and to stripes few or many according to desert, is to vanish into that nothingness which the Epicurean falsely taught would be the end of all men upon death. Every one of them point, not to the preservation of life in any condition, whether miserable or happy, but to the loss of all life, the utter blotting out of existence. Scripture does not use the illustrations of Epicurus to describe the theory of Plato. This our opponents of the Augustinian and Universalist schools say that it does. This monstrous satire upon Scripture they do not scruple to assert in favor of theories begot by human error mingled with divine truth.

How are our opponents to get over these illustrations of the Word of God which is to judge them at the last day? What can the Augustinian theorist say of them? He finds it said that the wicked shall be like the beasts that perish; that they shall consume like thorns; that they shall be burnt up like chaff; that they shall be reduced to ashes like a dry branch! What is his comment on these vivid emblems? He tells us that they are strong poetic figures! We see nothing to object to this, and merely ask him *of what* are they strong poetic figures? After an immensity of talk, we find him replying that they *are poetical figures representative of the very opposite to that which they teach.* The wicked perishing like beasts, means that they are never to perish, and are exceedingly unlike beasts: the wicked, consuming like thorns, means that they never will consume at all, and will never bear the remotest resemblance to thorns which have been consumed: the wicked beings burnt up like chaff, means that they are never to be burnt up, and that they will never be like chaff that has been burnt up: and their being reduced to ashes; like a dry branch, means that they cannot by any possibility be reduced to ashes, or bear the faintest likeness to a dry branch which has been thoroughly consumed! Whether such a handling of God's Word as this is deceitful or not, let our readers and our opponents judge.

And how do Universalists avoid the force of these illustrations? In a manner no way more creditable or more ingenuous than the Augustinian reasoners. They apply those illustrations which Scripture directs against the *persons* of the wicked *to their sin.* They do not deny that "perishing" and "being destroyed" indicate certainly that *something will cease to exist.* That something is, however, *not the sinner himself, but his sin.* It is thus that one of the latest of the advocates of this view, the author of *Future Retributive Punishment*, puts his case:

> "As the result of awful chastisement, the second death, all the myriads of the ungodly, *their former defiant aspirations* to be as gods, unaccountable, independent, *being* utterly *'destroyed;' their expectations* indulged in this life *'perished,' 'broken to shivers,' 'burnt up as chaff,'* shall themselves be brought to bow and submit to Christ."*

Our readers will not fail to mark here the striking and wholly unwarranted departure from the language of Scripture. The Scripture says that it is the *ungodly themselves* who shall be destroyed and perish like

* *The Rainbow,* 1871, p. 91.

chaff burnt up in the fire: the Universalist says it is the *"aspirations and expectations"* of *the ungodly* which shall thus perish, *while they themselves are preserved.* We deny him the right thus flagrantly to tamper with Scripture. If man may be allowed thus to alter it, he may make it speak anything he pleases. We characterize such a treatment as simply a barefaced and impudent alteration of the Word of God by man.

If anything further were required to expose this view it would be found in the language of Scripture as it addresses itself to those who are here brought to God through Jesus Christ. The chastening and the trials of this life are to them precisely what, according to the Universalist, the sorer chastisement of the second death will be to the ungodly. These are the "fires" and the "waters" through which they pass in their subjugation of the "expectations" and "aspirations" which possessed them likewise. But is such a process ever described in Scripture as their "destruction," or their "perishing," or their being "burnt like chaff"?!

Never.

We ask the Universalist to produce one such comparison. We read of their becoming "dead *to sin,*" of *"the body of sin being destroyed,"* of their "crucifying *the old man,*" and similar phrases indicative of the *destruction of evil within them* while they themselves were undestroyed, but we never once read of such terms applied to them as are invariably applied to the punishment of the ungodly hereafter. Nay, *the very contrary language is applied to them*: "We went through fire and through water," the people of God say, but they add *"Thou broughtest us out into a wealthy place;"* for He whom they serve has pledged His word to every one of them, "When thou passeth through the waters, I will be with thee; and through the rivers, they shall not overflow thee; when thou walkest *through the fire thou shalt not be burned; neither shall the flame kindle upon thee*" (Ps. 66:12; Isa. 63:2).

There is no speech about their being destroyed or consumed like chaff in that "fiery trial" which purifies them for the kingdom of their Father. The "bush which burned with fire and was not consumed" is the emblem of God's people in their chastisement: the "withered branch" which is consumed and burned up is the emblem of the ungodly in their future punishment. Surely these opposing emblems do not illustrate processes identical in their nature. Surely they point to results as different as light from darkness, or as life from death.

8

The Resurrection of the Wicked

WE NOW PROCEED TO A very important question in connection with our subject, the resurrection of the wicked. As yet this point has not been very much discussed. It is however one of prime consequence, and must be thoroughly sifted. We will endeavor to lay it before our readers as we find it revealed in God's word. We are aware of its difficulty; but that must not deter us from its examination. We invite close and candid scrutiny into what we say, and are ready to make any alterations that criticism, whether hostile or friendly, shall show us to be called for. We fully believe that this question of resurrection, fairly and honestly discussed, will form one link in that vast accumulative line of evidence which binds us irresistibly to the belief in the final destruction of the wicked as the doctrine of God's word.

With Paul, we believe that there shall be "a resurrection of the dead, both of the just and of the unjust" (Acts 24:15). We believe that all men shall rise in their bodies to give an account of their deeds. While we know that the passages in Scripture which speak of a resurrection of the wicked are few in comparison of those which speak of the resurrection of the just; while we know that in passage after passage of Scripture which speaks of resurrection, that of the wicked is not spoken of, alluded to, or *included*;

we also know that there are passages which teach their resurrection in the body with the same clearness and distinctness that that of the just is elsewhere spoken of. We have no sympathy with those who deny the resurrection of the wicked. We know that there are writers who hold our view of the destruction of the ungodly, who also, from a variety of alleged reasons, hold that they will never rise to judgment. We know that such writers are numerous in America, though, we are scarcely aware of their existence in England. But now, once for all, we disavow any connection or sympathy with them on this point. We think their view false, and mischievous in the extreme. We hold it calculated to throw discredit upon our grand cause; and therefore to be one of the devices of Satan to hinder the progress of our truth. For ourselves, we have no doubt that the resurrection of the wicked is taught as plainly as that of the just, and that if we give up the one we may just as well give up the other.

But while this is our faith, we also just as firmly hold a fundamental and essential difference between the resurrection of the wicked and that of the just. We hold it to be not only that the one is raised to shame and to pain, and the other to glory and to joy; but that the one is raised to die a second time, and the other never to die any more. In other words, we believe that the bodies of the just are *changed* at their resurrection, then putting on incorruption and immortality, and thus becoming "spiritual bodies;" while those of the wicked are raised *unchanged,* not putting on at resurrection either incorruption or immortality, but still natural bodies as they were sown, resuming with their old life their old mortality, as such subject to pain, and as such sure to yield to that of which all pain is the symptom and precursor, physical death and dissolution.

It will be seen that we rest our conclusion of the resurrection of the wicked to mortality mainly on the supposition that *no change passes on them at their resurrection.* If no change passes on them then, if they are raised to punishment in the same mortal corruptible bodies which here they had, it cannot but be allowed that those bodies will and must die in hell a second time. The presence of pain is not only a token of mortality, but a producer of death. Such we know from experience. Pain, by God's ordinance, produces death here. The frame may battle long and sorely against death—the longer and the sorer in exact proportion to its physical vigor; but sooner or later pain brings the iron frame of the strongest to the release of death. So it would be, so it must be, in the scene of future woe, if the bodies of the wicked were raised *unchanged.* If no change passes upon them they must needs yield to the bitter pains which accompany the second death.

It is not merely we, or reasoners on our side, who say this. The thing is so plain to reason that our opponents insist upon it as much as we do ourselves. They are not silly enough to suppose that a "*mortal body*" *could live forever under any circumstances,* far less *under those awful circumstances* of pain and anguish and remorse which belong to the lost in hell. All that is mortal must yield to death even though there be no pain, as we see from the example of the lower creation: but pain, whether of body or mind, and especially when both are united, is a wonderful hastener of the solemn issue. It is so in the merciful dealing of God.

Accordingly our opponents insist upon *a change* passing upon the bodies of the lost at their resurrection. They acknowledge it freely and unreservedly as essential to their system. As the wicked are, according to them, to endure pain forever *in the body,* they are just as much compelled to insist upon their having an *immortal body* as on their having *an immortal soul.* Their Christian faith has superadded to their system a difficulty which Plato did not meet. The great ardent mind of Socrates failed him when he regarded the subtle train of reasoning on which his grand theme of the soul's immortality rested: but surely he would have thought of it with blank dismay, and utterly have refused to face it, had he been compelled to assert for the human body that immortality which he asserted for the soul.

This, however, is the very thing which our Augustinian opponents have to do. They have to prove the immortality of the body as much as of the soul. Scripture teaches the resurrection of the wicked: it teaches us that their future punishment, of whatever nature it be, is endured in the body: if then its punishment be, as no doubt it is, eternal, and if it consists in an eternal life of pain, then their bodies, thus eternally suffering, must be endowed with an immortality of being. For this purpose they must be *changed* at the resurrection; for in this life they are but poor frail mortal bodies, unable to resist the ceaseless sappings of time, far less able to resist the gnawing inroads of perpetual pain.

Accordingly, on a change of an essential kind the Augustinian theorists insist. We find them irresistibly compelled to it from the moment they began to broach their doctrine, and we find them compelled to uphold it down to our own time. "*This corruptible must put on incorruption,*" says ono of the earliest upholders of everlasting misery, Athenagoras, quoting Paul's grand words in 1 Corinthians 15, "*in order that* those who were dead, having been made alive by the resurrection, each one may, in accordance with justice, receive what he has done by the body, *whether it be good or bad.*"[*] Augustine too, though he feels sadly perplexed by what fit term to describe it, insists that a change of *some kind* is absolutely essential to fit the body for the endurance of endless pain. He solves his difficulty by the desperate subterfuge that there are *two kinds of* "*incorruption,*" one an incorruption which is incapable of pain, that of the just, and another *an incorruption which may endure the corruption of pain,* that of the unjust! He too uses the language of Paul of the "corruptible putting on incorruption," though he felt compelled to explain the very

---

[*] Athenagoras, *Resurrection*, c. xvi., xviii.

extraordinary sense in which he used "incorruption" as applied to the ungodly. But the change to "incorruption" which he insisted on, while he held it to be a blessed change for the righteous, he held it to be "*a change for the worse*" for the wicked. What we thus see in the earlier advocates of a monstrous caricature of Divine justice we find also in its modern upholders. "The bodies of the wicked shall lie *so changed,*" says Jonathan Edwards, "as to fit them for eternal torment *without corruption.*" Thomas Scott says: "The bodies of the wicked will be *rendered incorruptible.*" Pollok says:

> "The good and *evil,* in a moment, all
> *Were changed, corruptible to incorrupt,*
> *And mortal to immortal*
> Her loud, uncircumcised, tempestuous crew,
> How ill-prepared to meet their God! *were changed.*"

We thus see that not only does the reason of the thing necessitate, but the advocates of the Augustinian theory admit and insist upon the necessity of *a change* passing upon the bodies of the lost at resurrection, in order to enable them to endure eternal torment. And not only do they insist upon *a change*; but they also, one and all, describe *the particular change required* for their horrid purpose. It is the change which St. Paul in 1 Corinthians 15 describes as passing upon the bodies of the redeemed at their resurrection! If our readers will turn to this grand chapter they will find the apostle giving in different parts of it descriptions of the same resurrection varying somewhat in language. The first is contained in verses 42-44:

> "So also is the resurrection of the dead. It is sown in corruption; it is raised in incorruption: it is sown in dishonor; *it is raised in glory:* it is sown in

> weakness; it is raised in power: it is sown a natural body; it is raised a spiritual body."

The second description is given us in verse 53: "This corruptible must put on incorruption; and this mortal must put on immortality."

Any candid mind, unblinded by a cherished theory which must be maintained at all hazards, would see that these two descriptions, varying in language, *are identical in sense.* There is, however, *one expression* in the description which no Augustinian theorist, so far as we know, has ever dared to apply to the resurrection of the wicked—that which describes the body as being "raised *in glory.*" They remember Daniel's description of the wicked being raised "to *shame and to contempt*" and therefore *dare not* appropriate this description to the resurrection of the wicked. They do, however, what is just as bad and impudent. The description in verse 53 is most certainly only a more condensed form of the description in verses 42-44: in some of its most important expressions it is identical. While then they dare not because of one phrase in the former—"raised *in glory*"—attribute it to the resurrection of the wicked, they do dare to apply to that resurrection a description which the apostle Paul has given us as identical: they affirm of the wicked, as of the just, that their "corruptible must put on incorruption; and their mortal must put on immortality." *This is the change required to fit them to endure eternal agony.*

We have no doubt that they use this language *unwillingly.* We have no doubt that they wince and shrink as they apply the language of 1 Corinthians 15 to the resurrection of the wicked. They would not do so if they could help it. But it is a sad necessity of their position. They have adopted a theory which demands it. They cannot uphold their theory in any other way. With inexorable claim it calls upon them to do so. To uphold a theory which perpetuates evil and pain in the world of a merciful, powerful, and just God, they must needs describe the resurrection of the wicked in the very same language in which Paul describes the resurrection of the just! We will take the liberty to examine by what right and upon what grounds they do so.

And, first, they all tell us that *a change* will pass upon the wicked at their resurrection! We ask for proof. They cannot say that there cannot be a resurrection without a change; for, unfortunately for them, there have been resurrections where no change has taken place. All the resurrections before that of Christ were such. He was the "first fruits from the dead," *because* in the case of others raised before him *no change from mortality* took place. They cannot say that there cannot be a resurrection followed by death; for, again, the cases of Jairus' daughter, and the widow's son, and Lazarus, would confront and confound them; for all these, after they were raised, died again. We ask them for proof that the bodies of the wicked will undergo *any change* at their resurrection. *We ask for proof in vain.*

There is but one passage in Scripture which directly states that *a change* will take place in the body at the resurrection (see 1 Cor. 15:51-52). It is where Paul says "the trumpet shall sound, and the dead shall be raised incorruptible, *and we shall be changed.*" Do our opponents say that Paul here *includes the wicked?* They must do so if they would bring forward from Scripture any direct assertion that they will be *changed.* Which of them will come forward and maintain that Paul speaks in this chapter of any resurrection but that of the just? We challenge proof. A few words we will here say why we hold that in this chapter Paul speaks *only* of the resurrection of the just, and does not include or hint hi the remotest degree at that of the wicked.

That Paul might speak of the resurrection without including in his mention of it any idea whatever of the wicked is quite plain from the fact that such mention is very usual in Scripture. Our Lord Himself has given the example (Luke 14:14; 20:33-34). In fact, as we have already stated, when resurrection is spoken of in Scripture, it is *only* the resurrection of the just that is spoken of, *except in such places as expressly mention that of the wicked.* It we had not such exceptional passages, we would never suppose from the Bible that there would be any resurrection of the wicked, and it is on this fact that the deniers of the resurrection of the unjust must mainly depend for their erroneous opinion. But most certainly the passages of Scripture, which, speaking of resurrection, include that of the wicked, *are the exception, not the rule.* We believe it will be found that where ever the resurrection is *simply* spoken of, and invariably where, when thus spoken of, the Greek article is prefixed, it will be found that *the resurrection of the just is the only idea present to the mind of the inspired writers.*

A sufficient reason for this is found in what we have no doubt to be the truth of Scripture, meaning, that the *only resurrection which is a fruit of redemption is the resurrection of the just.* This is a most important question in the present controversy and we will therefore attend to it for a short time.

To raise the dead to life is not *in itself* any more the fruit of Christ's redemption than any other miracle. This we know from the fact that the resurrection of our Lord Himself was the "*first fruits*" *from the dead,* produced by His redeeming work (1 Cor. 15:20, 23). Such resurrections therefore as that of Lazarus, or Jairus' daughter, were no more the fruits of *redemption* than was the dividing of the Red Sea by Moses, the raising of the Shunamite's child by Elijah, or the cure of the paralytic by Christ Himself. They were works of power attending a messenger from God, if you will, *figuring* redemption, but certainly not a fruit of redemption. If they were, it would not be true that Christ's resurrection was *the first fruits* of them that slept. If then there was resurrection *before Christ rose* which *was not* a fruit of His redemption, it is quite plain that there may be resurrection *after He has risen* which will not be any more than the former the fruit of His redemption.

But we have from our Lord's own lips the positive declaration of the connection between *Himself as Redeemer and the work of resurrection* (John 11:24-26). Martha expresses her belief in the resurrection of all alike, good and bad, at the last day. Such was the opinion of most of her people, derived from the prophecy of Daniel and other parts of the Old Testament; and such belief she probably gave expression to here. Christ had just told her that her brother would rise again. In her reply she evidently takes it as a mere matter of course that it would take place at the last day. When all would alike rise, of course her brother would rise with the rest. She does not seem to have thought that Christ, as Redeemer, had anything in especial to do with resurrection. But Christ proceeds to teach her the close relation in which He, as Redeemer, stood to resurrection: He was its cause, its source, its very self: without Him, there would not be resurrection: in Him, by Him, through Him, from Him, and Him alone, the resurrection was to spring—"I am the resurrection."

He tells Martha to look upon Him, the Redeemer, the Christ, as the *fount of resurrection.* Such a thing as she spoke of was not to be hoped for away from Him. Put Him away; suppose Him not come; imagine His work unaccomplished; and the dark shadow of death would never be lifted from the face of the sleeping dead. But of *what resurrection* did He thus proclaim Himself the source? *The resurrection of life.*

"*I am the resurrection and the life*" (John 11:25). Here is that of which, *as Redeemer,* He is source. The resurrection procured by Him is *to life,* and not to death. Resurrection, as a fruit of redemption, is one with, identical with, inseparable from, *life.* Christ does not here connect Himself as Redeemer (for it is in His capacity of Redeemer He is speaking) with any resurrection except a resurrection of life, and that life *an eternal one* (v. 26). In fact, if we connect the resurrection of the wicked with redemption as its source, we will find it extremely difficult, if not absolutely impossible, to deny Origen's theory of universal restoration, or at least that modified view which Mr. Birks has presented in his *History of Divine Goodness.*[*] But the Savior, who has connected the resurrection to life with Himself as His work of redemption, has elsewhere expressly guarded us against such an idea by telling us that it is only *some,* and not all, who shall partake of the "resurrection of life" (John 5:29).

What our Lord in the place just referred to teaches that it is not the resurrection of *all men,* but only the resurrection of His people, which is a fruit of redemption, is also apparent from other Scriptures. There can be no doubt that "the resurrection of the dead," or rather "from among the dead," spoken of by Paul to the Philippian church (Phil. 3:2), was that resurrection of which Christ as Redeemer was the source. If Christ as our Redeemer procured the resurrection of *all men alike,* whether they were good or evil, there could be no doubt but that Paul, like all others, would obtain it. There could be no question as to his obtaining it. Whether it were desired or dreaded, it would as a matter of course be bestowed. But this is not at all the light in which Paul regarded it, or teaches us to regard it. He tells us it is a thing *which may, or may not, be obtained*: which man must strive for if he would obtain. The resurrection, then, procured by Christ as Redeemer, is *not the resurrection of all men,* it is only that of His people.

We are taught the same truth elsewhere. "The quickening of the mortal body," spoken of by Paul to the Romans (Rom. 8:11), was the resurrection procured by Christ's work of redemption. According to all our opponents, whether of the Augustinian or the Universalist schools, *every mortal body,* whether it be the body of a good man or a wicked man, *will be quickened* by God. But it is a remarkable fact that, throughout the New Testament, the word "quicken"[†] is never applied to the wicked in any way: it is exclusively confined to the just. And in the passage immediately

---

[*] See pp. 183-188.

[†] Ζωοποιεω, *zoopoieo.*

before us Paul expressly thus confines it to them. He says: "*If* the Spirit of Him that raised up Jesus from the dead dwell in you, He that raised up Christ from the dead *shall also quicken your mortal bodies* by His Spirit that dwelleth in you" (Rom. 8:11). Here we see that the quickening of the mortal body, which is the fruit of redemption, is *not bestowed upon all:* it is only bestowed upon those who are renewed in the spirit of their minds. In other words, the resurrection of the wicked is not in any way, form, or degree, a fruit of the redemption of Christ.

The same inference is clearly drawn from Luke's description of apostolic teaching (Acts 4:2). We will take the liberty to translate the description referred to more literally than it is done in our authorized version. The original Greek exactly carries out that essential distinction between the resurrection of the wicked and the just which is insisted on all through Scripture, and also teaches us how much of resurrection is to be ascribed to redemption. We read then that the Sadducees were "grieved that they (the apostles) taught the people, and preached *through Jesus the resurrection; that, namely, from among the dead?*" Here Luke tells us that the apostles made a marked distinction in their description of resurrection: that they spoke of *two* different resurrections, those of the just and of the unjust: that they described the resurrection of the just as a resurrection from among the dead; while they would describe the resurrection of the wicked by these expressions which, we find used in Scripture, as a resurrection to "shame," "damnation," and so on. Our point here, however, is that "the resurrection from the dead," of which Luke speaks, is the resurrection of *the just.* The way in which it is spoken of in the passage itself plainly distinguishes it from another resurrection, which can be only that of the unjust; while its correspondence *in character* with the other descriptions given in Scripture of the resurrection of the just identifies it with them. The "resurrection *from among the dead*" is plainly the same as the "resurrection *of life,*" the resurrection of those who "*can die no more,*" the resurrection of those whose "*mortal bodies are quickened,*" etc. (John 5:29; Luke 20:36; Rom. 8:11). All these descriptions are plainly descriptions of one and the same resurrection—*that of the just.*

And now for our further step. *What resurrection,* according to the teaching of the apostles, is "*through Jesus,*" *i.e.*, through His work of redemption? *The resurrection of the just*: this is the apostles' teaching. The resurrection of the just is the fruit of redemption: the resurrection of the unjust has nothing to say to it. And is not this alone worthy of the work of Christ? It supposes Him to bestow blessing, and *only blessing,* through His resurrection. He came to give no *fatal gift* which should force everlasting existence upon myriads who asked not for it, and would shun it with all their heart. He did not come to give what he called a blessing but which millions would find a curse. True it would be, in the case of those at least who had heard His Gospel, solely and entirely their own fault. But how does this mend the matter? Still we should have myriads actually *receiving a fruit of redemption, and find it an unmitigated curse.* Surely such a view as this is most derogatory to Christ. Surely the only worthy view of His work, from first to last, in each particular and in all its parts, is that *it is a blessing*: that he who receives any part of it receives only blessing! To call the resurrection of the wicked a *work of judgment and damnation,* which it is, and at the same time to call it *a fruit of redemption,* seems to us more absurd than to say that "black *is* white" or "sweet *is* bitter."

No; the lost do not partake of redemption *in whole or in part.* If they were to partake of any *iota* of it, it would indeed be difficult, to our mind impossible, to reject the dream of Origen that *all* would follow in the ages to come. But they do *not* partake of *redemption.* They do not partake of any part or parcel of it. They do not lose one part of it, and gain, even to their utter loss, another. It is all gained, or all lost. It is like the garment of Christ, a work without seam. It is a grand whole which cannot be broken into parts. We have it all in the realms of life and of bliss. We have no shivered fractured part in the realms of the lost. It may not be that in the gloomy prison house of hell is a something which the lost can in bitter derision and utter despair call the fruit of redemption procured by Christ for them. But from all this it follows, that the resurrection of the wicked, being a resurrection to shame, being a work of judgment, and being felt to be a curse and a curse only, is *no part of,* no fruit of, redemption.

Having seen that the resurrection of the damned is no part of redemption, but is simply an act of power and of judgment, we can readily see why Paul not merely *may not* speak of resurrection without including that of the wicked, but that he *could not in 1 Corinthians 15, include it at all.* For he is speaking to the Corinthian Christians on *the idea that they would really obtain that salvation which Christ came to give.* "Brethren," he says, "I declare unto you the Gospel which I preached unto you; which also ye have received, and wherein ye stand; *by which also ye are saved, if ye keep in memory what I have preached unto you*" (1 Cor. 15:1-2). He is here therefore speaking to them on the supposition that they were and would continue to be genuine and true professors of the Gospel of the Redeemer. *On this idea* he proceeds to unfold to them the blessing which would result to them as believers, and in especial to give to them *a view of resurrection.* If, as we have seen, the resurrection of the wicked is no part or result of redemption, it is quite plain that the apostle *could not include it* in his description. Speaking only of the blessed fruit of redemption he could not introduce a thing which was not a fruit of redemption. He *must* leave out the resurrection of the wicked as an idea foreign to his present subject. He might as well include the despair of the fallen angels, the weeping and wailing of the wicked, as the resurrection of the latter. If it was no fruit of redemption it could not be included in a chapter which professed to describe only what was the fruit of redemption. "Scripture," says Bengel, "*everywhere concerns itself with the faithful,* and treats especially of their resurrection: *with regard to the resurrection of the wicked it only treats of it in a casual incidental way.*"*

But it is said, and very frequently said, that Paul here tells us that he speaks of the resurrection of all men, whether they be just or unjust. The passage invariably, and we believe almost exclusively, claimed for this purpose, is verse 22: "As in Adam all die, even so in Christ shall all be made alive." The "all" in the second clause is supposed to be identical with the "all" in the first clause, and as the "all" in the first clause undoubtedly includes every one sprung from Adam, whether just or unjust, it is argued that the second "all" comprehends the same parties, and therefore must include the resurrection of the unjust.

Now we do not deny that there is considerable plausibility in this argument. We do not deny that if this text stood alone, it would bear this interpretation fully as well as any other. We do not deny that the second "all" must be in some true and proper way *equally comprehensive* with the first. Both terms are plainly *universals*, and must be interpreted as such. We only hold that while both are equally universal, *they are not the same universals*. As to the term "all," it has every variety of comprehension, and no stress can be laid on it. "All men" may mean the inhabitants of a province, of an empire, or of the earth. The only force of the argument is that "all" being in two clauses of the same verse contrasted cannot in that verse apply except exactly to the same parties. There is here much apparent, but no real force. We are faulted as though we would paraphrase the verse thus: "As in Adam *all* mankind die, whether just or unjust; so in Christ shall *some* of these be made alive, specifically, the just who believe in Christ."

We freely admit that *so represented* we appear to trifle with the text. We seem to handle it in a disingenuous way, and not with that simplicity

---

* Bengel on 1 Corinthians 15:22.

of interpretation that alone is becoming learners from God's word. But we do not think it fair to represent us thus, and will proceed to give our view which, we maintain, will be found consistent with sound honest interpretation, while it will have the incalculable and decisive advantage of being in harmony with the general reasoning of the apostle, and with his own express words elsewhere. Of two interpretations of a particular text, both equally probable as regarded the text itself, or even where one was less obvious than the other, that one must be selected which is in harmony with other Scriptures, and especially with other sayings of the same writer.

"All," then, in both clauses, is a universal term, and in both equally comprehensive, and yet the terms are applied in the two clauses to different parties. Universals are meant in both, but *different universals.* We thus paraphrase the passage: "As in Adam all related to him, as their head, die; so in Christ all who are related to him, the second Adam, as their head, shall be made alive." Here we see at once that we make "all" to be in both clauses a universal term, and an equally universal one. In both clauses it embraces every individual referred to. And is not this a natural interpretation of the passage. Why does the first "all" *include all mankind, and exclude all except mankind?* Because it refers to those, and to those alone, *who owe their physical existence to their* connection with the first man. Interpreted in strict analogy with this, the second "all" refers to all those, and those alone, who owe their spiritual existence to their connection with Christ the second man. Both terms are equally universal in their proper and evident application. The first "all" includes *all men,* and excludes all who are not men, because it applies to natural generation and descent. The second "all" includes *all who are believers,* and excludes all who are not believers, because it applies to spiritual generation and descent, and has nothing whatever to say to anything else. If you are *"in Adam,"* you are included in the first "all;" if you are *"in Christ"* you are included in the second "all." Both are equally universal terms, and both are equally comprehensive of the *all* to whom they refer. Nothing beyond this is required by the text, though we fully admit that the text would fairly admit of another interpretation if it was considered solely by itself. When we know that such a critic as Bengel adopted this view we may well admit that it can fairly bear it; for, of all theorists, they cling to the other interpretation, who hold, as Bengel did, *the Universalist theory.* We may well imagine an Augustinian theorist to pause before he accepts the interpretation that the words, "so in Christ shall all be made alive," refers at all to the resurrection of the wicked. We may well imagine him to tremble as he does so, knowing well, if he has any clearness of vision, *the use* that will be made of such an admission by a school to which he is almost as much opposed as he is to ours. But the Universalist on this interpretation finds indeed a powerful argument for his theory. He connects the wicked with Christ in one blessed fruit of redemption: he knows the force of the word "quicken" in the other writings of the apostle Paul: it will indeed be difficult to prevent him from following out this to universal restoration as its inevitable result. When Bengel then, a Universalist, admits that this text bears the interpretation which we have put upon it, we may conclude that such an interpretation is no forced or unnatural one.

This once conceded, there remains no difficulty. Our interpretation is in harmony with the entire argument of this chapter, which, as we have seen, addresses itself only to genuine believers in Christ. Besides this we must allow Paul to be *his own interpreter.* He here tells us that "in Christ all shall be *made alive.*" Our opponents say that he here teaches that *the wicked* will be "made alive." We say that he does not say that the wicked will be "made alive," and that he here speaks only of the just. Let us hear Paul on his own language. The words "made alive" is the Greek Ζωοποιεω, *zoopoieo.* Does Paul allow or forbid the idea that *he* thinks this term applicable to the resurrection of the wicked? He forbids it. He elsewhere expressly *confines it to the resurrection of the just.* With him it *only* refers to what his Master called the "resurrection of life," and what Daniel called the resurrection "to everlasting life." Here are his words: "If the Spirit of Him that raised up Jesus from the dead dwell in you, He that raised up Christ from the dead *shall also quicken your* mortal bodies" (Rom. 8:11). It is the same Greek word which is translated "quicken" in Romans 8:2, and "made alive" in 1 Corinthians 15:22. Paul, in the former, tells us that he does not allow the word to be properly applicable to any resurrection except that of those in whom the Spirit of God dwells. We may not then accept that interpretation of 1 Corinthians 15:22, which attributes to Paul a use of language which he has expressly disclaimed.

And we may readily see a good and sufficient reason why Paul, with his knowledge of the life which man had at creation and would regain through redemption, would refuse to describe the resurrection of the unjust as their being "quickened" or "made alive." *Life for man is eternal life.* Man's condition, as he came from his Maker's hands, and as he is restored by his Redeemer's work, is *a condition of immortality.* A brief fading life is not man's *true life.* Such a life was given to the brutes; such a life became man's as fallen, and by his fall. But it is not man's life, either as created or as redeemed. Man's condition as fallen is called a state of *death.* In the midst of the life we inherit from our fallen parent, we are in death. Our whole existence is a progress and an advance to death. Paul spoke of himself as "dying daily." In the heyday of our youth and vigor, as in the late evening of existence, we have "the sentence of death in ourselves" (1 Cor. 15:31; 2 Cor. 1:9). From the day that we are born, we die; even as Adam, cut off in the day he sinned from the tree of life, died on that day. And here then is the reason why Paul will not apply the terms "quicken" and "make alive" to the resurrection of the lost. It is not a resurrection of man's true life, which is everlasting life, and he will not call it life at all.

And in denying it this title he agrees with all Scripture which confines the "*resurrection of life*" solely to the resurrection of the just.

But besides all this, there are parts of this chapter (1 Cor. 15) which utterly forbid the idea that it includes in its idea the resurrection of the unjust. If we will accept its description of the persons whose resurrection it speaks of, they are only "Christ the first fruits, afterwards them that are Christ's, at his coming." (v. 23). We cannot include the unjust here unless we suppose that Christ being the "first fruits," they, equally with the just, are the wheat, which in the tune of ingathering, the time of the second coming of Christ, are to be gathered into the barn. But even the Universalist does not claim this. He allows long periods of suffering to elapse subsequent to the second coming ere the unjust are restored. Christ Himself utterly rejects the idea (see Exod. 23:16; Matt. 13:30). The Augustinian, just as much as we, refuses to allow that the unjust are described here as "them that are Christ's." In fact, if the resurrection of the unjust is spoken of, we are forced to comprehend under the term "them that are Christ's," not merely all professing Christians, but all mankind—heathen, Jew, infidel, Atheist, as well as Christians; for all such shall rise with their bodies to give account of their deeds.

Later on in the chapter are descriptions given which forbid the idea that the resurrection of the unjust is so much as hinted at. *The resurrection of the dead,* of which Paul speaks, is *only a resurrection of glory. All the dead of whom he speaks receive such a resurrection.* The body of whose quickening he speaks "is sown in corruption, is raised in incorruption: is sown in dishonor, is raised *in glory*: is sown in weakness, is raised in power: is sown a natural body, is raised a spiritual body" (vs. 42-44). This is "the resurrection of the dead" of which Paul speaks. Our opponents, both Augustinians and Universalists, would and do apply much of his description to the resurrection of the unjust. They claim for them a resurrection to "incorruption" and to "power;" but they cannot, dare not, claim a resurrection to "glory;" because Daniel has, unfortunately for them, described the resurrection of the unjust as a resurrection to "shame and contempt."

We have established then that 1 Corinthians 15 does not describe the resurrection of the unjust. With this established we again ask the Augustinian for proof of that *change* which he asserts to be essential to enable their risen bodies to endure an eternity of pain. We answer for him that he has no proof that the Scripture says they will be "changed." This term is only used once in Scripture, in 1 Corinthians 15. And we have just seen that this chapter speaks *only* of the resurrection of the just.

But while the expression "changed" is only once used, we freely admit that the *nature of the change* is frequently spoken of in Scripture. It is minutely described in this chapter, and is mentioned in many other places. We have already seen the nature of the change which the Augustinian requires in order that the risen wicked should be able to sustain an eternity of anguish. They are, in the words of one whom we may fairly call the poet of our popular Protestant hell—

"Changed, *corruptible to incorrupt,*
And *mortal to immortal.*"—POLLOK

Now we ask for *proof* that the resurrection of the wicked is *ever* thus described in Scripture. It cannot be proved from 1 Corinthians 15; for that chapter does not speak of the resurrection of the unjust at all. If it is to be proved, proof must be sought elsewhere. We give you the range of Scripture. Look at every passage in it winch speaks of resurrection, with a microscopic vision. Remember, the credit of your terrible hell rests upon the success of your search. Yet we have no fear, not a flutter of apprehension. We deny that the resurrection of the unjust is ever described as a change from corruption to incorruption and from mortality to immortality, save in the poetry of Pollok and the prose of a false theology, whether it be that of the fathers, or of the schoolmen, Protestant, or Roman Catholic.

Where then is the proof of such a change?

Was it Job's faith when he said: "The wicked is reserved to the *day of destruction:* they shall be brought forth to the day of wrath?" (21:30). Does "destruction" signify "incorruption" and "immortality?" In your change discernible in Daniel's description of the wicked as rising to shame and everlasting contempt? What dictionary gives "immortality" as a sense for "shame," or "incorruption" for "contempt?" Will you find it in the faith of the "seven brethren" who endured death, sustained by the hope of the resurrection of the just, but who warned the persecuting Antiochus—"As to thee, thou shalt have *no resurrection unto life?*" Will you find it in the words of the Lord of Life, who describes the resurrection of the wicked as "the resurrection of *damnation*" while he describes that of his people as the resurrection of those who "can die no more?"* We know of no text of Scripture which speaks in any other way of the resurrection of the unjust. If our opponents do, let them bring it forth. The above texts do not describe a change from corruption to incorruption, or of mortality to immortality. To us they speak the opposite language. To us they describe a resurrection of persons raised in the natural body of corruption, dishonor, and weakness. If there are other texts let them be produced. If there are no other texts let our opponents set to work at these, and show that the words "destruction," "shame," and "contempt," mean "incorruption" and "immortality." Their theory has over and over involved them in verbal quibbles not one bit more candid.

Deprived of all support from Scripture, to what place will they resort? Will they say "*the change to incorruption is essential to our theory and*

---

* See Job 21:30; Daniel 12:2; 2 Maccabees 7:14; John 5:29; Luke 12:36.

therefore it is true?" We would rather allow the premise but draw the opposite conclusion. We would say, "This change *is* essential to your theory; but, since there are no grounds for holding this change, your theory which requires it falls to the ground." Or perhaps they will urge that this change, which is essential to their theory, though it is not *revealed* in the Bible is yet there *assumed!* They are at home in argument of this kind. They have used it pretty generally on the kindred subject of the "*immortality of the soul.*" They are very docile disciples of good old Archbishop Tillotson, who lays down the pleasing Augustinian *axiom (or fiction)* that "The immortality of the soul is *rather supposed, or taken for granted, than expressly revealed in the Bible.*" Pleasant easy way, no doubt, to end disputes! It is, however, troublesome to be *assuming so many disputed points,* and we would venture to point out a simpler, if not more effectual way, to our Augustinian friends. *Let them assume their own infallibility;* all their other requirements will follow as matters of course. They need not be startled at the suggestion. They need not give us credit for an imagination equal to that of the celebrated Baron Munchausen. The idea is quite beyond our moderate powers of fancy to originate. It was they who produced it in our minds. For surely they may assume their own infallibility with just as much reason as they assume the immortality of the soul!

As we cannot, however, without proof, admit of the infallibility of our opponents, and are therefore also unable to admit without proof their assumption either of the immortality of the soul or the incorruptibility of the body of the unjust at resurrection, we are compelled to reject the latter as unceremoniously as we have done the former. The unjust are not raised in incorruption; they are not raised in immortality. And therefore their resurrection is another of the accumulating proofs that our theory of destruction is the theory of Scripture, and that the theories of our opponents, whether of the Augustinian or Universalist schools, are unscriptural and false. For, the bodies of the unjust are raised only in then old mortality. They are thus raised for punishment. Raised in their old mortality, the pains of hell will again, must again, reduce them to a second death, from which there is no promise of resurrection.

The objections usually urged against our view of the resurrection from the time of Tertullian to the present day will be considered in a subsequent chapter.

9

The Divine Justice

We now approach a very solemn question—the question of Divine Justice. We approach it with the deep reverence that becomes a creature when he scans and judges the conduct of his Maker; but also with the confidence which becomes one who is invited by his Maker to this inquiry. It is indeed said that we are not able to judge of God's ways; and this, no doubt, is often true. It is true, however, only of those dealings of His with which we are imperfectly acquainted; or which, from their nature, are above our comprehension. The present subject belongs to neither of these categories. Future punishment is a matter fully placed before us. No question occupies a more distinct position than it does in divine revelation. We are clearly told its cause and its nature; we are told to ponder on and study it. We are not treated as children incapable of forming an opinion of what is just or unjust in God. If we were thus incapable, a large portion of Scripture would be useless and meaningless. Called upon in God's Word to love, respect, and confide in Him, and *having His entire conduct towards men,* whether just or unjust, *brought to our view, in order to produce these feelings in us,* we are thus *viewed by God Himself as capable of judging of His character,* of His love, His mercy, His wisdom, His justice, and His judgment. He does not thus merely regard us as capable, but He has directly appealed to us to judge His conduct towards us, admitted His creature's scrutiny as the exercise of a right, and this not merely in the case of His faithful people but even of those who were alienated from Him. Abraham was not rebuked when he judged a certain supposed line of conduct unworthy of the God in whom his trust was placed. Rebellious Israel, misjudging God's dealings from ignorance and prejudice, are invited to look fairly at it and see if indeed God's "ways are not equal." Christ allows to the generation of His day the power of judging rightly, and only on such a supposition could they lie under their deep guilt (see Gen. 18:23-25; Ezek. 18:29; Luke 12:57).

"The law of justice in our hearts," it has been well observed, "is only a reflection of God's perfect justice."* In the human breast there is a true sense of what is just, and God not only allows it, but insists upon its exercise towards Himself. He has told us His character. He challenges us to bring any line of conduct attributed to Him to the test. In the question of future punishment we have the highest case on which any tribunal shall have ever sat; and we may be sure that the Judge of all the Earth will do right, not merely in His own eyes, but in those of all His intelligent creation; of the angels who stand round His throne; of the redeemed who rejoice in their acceptance; of the very damned who listen to their sentence.

But we are often told that, while no doubt God's conduct towards sinners will one day appear to the redeemed and even to the lost to have been just, yet that we must be content *to wait* until it shall so appear. This life is to pass away, the hour of resurrection must come, the throne of judgment must be set, the guilt of the lost be displayed, the everlasting sentence be passed, *and then,* the redeemed and the lost alike will see that God's ways were just. Not so, we reply. God appeals to us *now* to judge. He places before us His character *now,* in order that we may judge. It is *now*

---

* R. B. Girdlestone, *Dies. Iræ.*, 170.

that our conduct is to be affected, our fears aroused, our respect gained, our love won, for the God and Father of our Lord Jesus Christ. It is *now* that misapprehension of Him will tell with power: it is now that a correct judgment is to save the soul. When the judgment is set, and the sentence passed, *it is too late.*

But they who tell us to *wait in faith* wholly miscalculate the real position of the question before us. *They suppose faith in God is to sustain the mind against the appearance of injustice in God's dealings with men.* They reverse the mode of God's own proceeding. They suppose faith first to exist, and this faith is to withstand and subdue all that may appear unjust. The exact opposite to this is the way in which God deals with man. *He has come to an unbelieving and alienated world and put his character before them to win their fear, their repentance, their love.* We judge from our little stand point, taught from infancy to believe in God, to believe that He can do no wrong, to attribute any appearance of wrong on His part to our ignorance, to put down all injurious judgment of Him as unbelief and sin. With all our training at our mother's knee, from our teacher's lips, from that pulpit where man claims to speak in the name of God, we yet know how the *Christian heart and judgment* mourn, stumble, are perplexed, stand aghast, at the *justice* which is proposed to them as *the justice of God.* But it was not thus that the question was first presented, or that the human mind was won to submission. *It was to a world of unbelievers* that God was proposed as a God of justice, as well as of pity and of love. To this world, which had no faith, God was proposed for acceptance. God's character and conduct were placed before it *to win* its faith and its love. So it is even now. So it is to a great extent even in so-called Christian lands: it is so wholly in heathen lands. God's character and conduct are to win faith; not to be sustained by faith against appearances. The missionary tells the unbeliever what kind of God the God of the Christian is, to convert the unbeliever to the faith. Can we wonder that the answer of the heathen to our messages should be, "We cannot, and will not, believe in a God of whom you affirm such outrageous wrong."

We arrange the matter as God has arranged it. God's conduct, whether past or future, is *to win* man's respect, faith, and love, and not to be hardly and with difficulty palliated, excused, defended, *tolerated,* through man's faith. We are to come not merely to the truthful child at our knee, to the modest youth in our school, to the admiring disciple listening to our words; but we are, and may, and ought, to come to the incredulous skeptic, the profligate sinner, the hard stern man, to the poor heathen outside our pale, the outcast Pariah, the cultivated Brahmin, the followers of Confucius, and say to one and all, "Here is *our God,* the God and the Father of our Lord Jesus Christ: give Him your love: give Him your faith, give Him your obedience and your fear: *His character demands it at your hands.*" It is thus we will propose the grand question of the Divine justice in the treatment of sinners. We will not wait for the Day of Judgment to propose it. We propose it, when it ought to be proposed, in the day of salvation. We ask the human heart for its verdict. We say that judged by human judgment, and that the judgment of believers and unbelievers alike, the punishment which the theory of Augustine supposes that God will inflict is *infinitely too great,* and we are therefore to reject it as untrue, because wholly unworthy, not merely of a Merciful Father, but a just God.

Before we put our question of just or unjust, we must first refer plainly to the punishment itself. We will not attempt to describe it in our own words. We will merely give a few passages descriptive of it from writers who hold the view.

Here is an extract from a little book entitled *The Child's Path to Glory,* published at Birmingham, and which has passed through at least seven editions:

"There is nothing but misery in hell. You would never more have one moment's ease; for there is nothing but pain and torment there. Put together all you can think of that is miserable, and painful, and terrible, and it is all nothing to what is prepared for those who go there; and that not for an hour, or a day, or a year, but *for an eternity.* The lost souls who live in that horrible pit *wish to die,* but they are not able; for God says, 'Their worm dieth not.' The frightful and cruel devil may torment them as much as he pleases—they are made strong to bear it."

Here is the description of hell by the Christian Father Hippolytus:

"The fire which is unquenchable and without end awaits the unrighteous, and a certain fiery worm which dieth not, and which does not waste the body, but continues bursting forth from the body with unending pain. No sleep will give them rest: no night will soothe them: no death will deliver them from punishment."

Here is the celebrated Bishop Jeremy Taylor's account:

"We are amazed to think of the brutality of Phalaris, who roasted men alive in his brazen bull. That was a joy in respect of that fire of hell. What comparison will there be between burning for a hundred years' space and to be burning without interruption as long as God is God!"

Here is the account given by the famous Jonathan Edwards of America:

"The woes of sinners in hell will not be a cause of grief to the saints in heaven but of rejoicing. Though they hear you groan, and sigh, and gnash your teeth, these things will not move them at all to pity you. After your godly parents have seen you lie millions of years, or ages, in torment, day and night, they will not begin to pity you then. They will praise God that His justice appears in the eternity of your misery. The torments in hell will

> be immeasurably greater than being in a glowing oven, a brick kiln, or fiery furnace."

Here is the way in which the Roman Catholic Church describes hell. It is taken from a book written by the Rev. J. Furniss, and published with the approval of the authorities of his Church:

> "The fifth dungeon is the red-hot oven. The little child is in the red-hot oven. Hear how it screams to come out; see how it turns and twists itself in the fire. It beats its head against the roof of the oven. It stamps its little feet on the floor. God was very good to this little child. Very likely God saw it would get worse and worse, and would never repent, and so it would have to be punished more severely in hell. So God, in his mercy, called it out of the world in early childhood."

Here is the description of hell by the celebrated preacher Mr. Spurgeon:

> "Only conceive that poor wretch in the flames, who is saying, 'Oh, for one drop of water to cool my parched tongue!' See how his tongue hangs from between his blistered lips! How it excoriates and burns the roof of his mouth, as if it were a firebrand! Behold him crying for a drop of water! I will not picture the scene! Suffice it for me to close up by saying that the hell of hells will be to thee, poor sinner, the thought that it is to be forever! Thou wilt look up there on the throne of God, and it shall be written 'For Ever!' When the damned jingle the burning irons of their torment they shall say 'For Ever!' When they howl, echo cries 'For Ever!'
>
> "'For Ever' is written on their racks,
> 'For Ever' on their chains;
> 'For Ever' burneth in the fire,
> 'For Ever,' ever reigns."

We will close our series of "horrible extracts" with a quotation from Pollok. He thus pictures one of the damned:

> "Like a cinder that had life and feeling seemed
> His face, with inward pining to be what
> He could not be. As being that had burned
> Half an eternity, and was to burn
> For evermore, he looked. Oh! sight to be
> Forgotten, thought too terrible to think."

The poet's picture of the damned would not be complete if we did not add his picture of God throughout all eternity looking on it as one who

> "Hears unmoved the endless groan
> Of those wasting within, and sees unmoved
> The endless tear of vain repentance fall."

These are very horrifying descriptions. *We* turn with unmitigated loathing from the idea that a scene such as is depicted above by Hippolytus, and Jeremy Taylor, and Father Furniss, is to go on to eternity. But others, who do not agree with us in our view of future punishment, are almost, if not altogether, as much disgusted with them as we are. The ablest and purest minds, that still cling desperately to the Augustinian theory, cannot endure such descriptions, and will not allow that they represent the hell in which they believe. They gravely reprobate the horrors which were so dear and familiar to the middle ages, and which are still urged in all their minute and terrible detail by preachers and writers, Protestant and Catholic. They do not think them *true* descriptions of hell. They think that they exaggerate its terrors. Dr. Salmon, of Trinity College, Dublin, a man widely known, and respected wherever he is known, rejects with indignation the idea "that all who hold the eternal existence of the wicked, must believe in the demonology of Dante, and in a hell such as is described by Father Pinamonti." He thinks such descriptions too harrowing, and in fact only suitable to an age characterized by "general callousness to human suffering."[*] He takes refuge in the idea that the *descriptions of Scripture* which such men as Bishop Taylor and Father Furniss and Pinamonti have taken as the groundwork of then more minute and circumstantial accounts, are probably not literal, but figurative. He evidently does not believe in a *literal* fire, or *literal* worm in hell.

While we honor the *feeling* of such men as Dr. Salmon we do so at the expense of their *reasoning ability.* We do not ourselves enter into the question whether the descriptions of future punishment in Scripture are literal or figurative, because we do not think the solution of the question to be really *of any consequence.* Scripture tells us there will be a worm, a fire, darkness, and so on; but it does not seem to take any trouble to explain whether it speaks literally or figuratively. But, whichever view be taken of its language, it must commend itself to reason that *the punishment signified is in either case equally terrible though different in character.* If there be a literal fire consuming, and a literal worm gnawing, we know the exact pain produced; if the fire and the worm be figurative, they are figurative of a pain and suffering such in intensity as would be produced by the literal agents. Nothing then is really gained by rejecting the literal view of Dante and Pinamonti, or by changing the *bodily pains* of which they chiefly speak *into suffering and anguish of the mind.* If the descriptions of Scripture are figures they are at the same time *true figures.* If they are not to be understood literally they must yet be understood as giving us the *truest and best ideas possible of the real anguish and misery of hell.* On no hypothesis can we understand hell as other than a scene where pain and anguish, mental or bodily, or both, of the most intense and terrible nature, are endured by all who have any existence there. Hell cannot by any artful handling of words, by any skillful manipulation of phrases, be toned down into a place other than of the most fearful kind. If Dr. Salmon and others

---

[*] Salmon, *Eternity of Future Punishment*, vii. 22.

object to literal pains of the body forever, they can only substitute for them pains of the mind that are just as bad. *They gain nothing by the exchange.* While, by removing from the mind the picture of hell and its pains which Scripture undoubtedly presents, they remove, so far as in them lies, a very leading motive which God has Himself placed before the mind of man. We doubt not that Fathers Furniss and Pinamonti are more scriptural than the *men of feeling who* are trying to whitewash bell to render it more endurable to the mind. Descriptions such as Christ has given are not to be by us withdrawn as too terrible. He has spoken of "unquenchable fire" and the undying "worm," and we may not, and ought not, to withhold these terrible images from the mind. The real question is, not whether they are literal or figurative, but whether the pains they point to and portray are pains to be endured forever; or are pains which sooner or later produce a destruction of the sentient being, from which there is no recovery. We take the mental conflicts of such minds as those of Dr. Salmon, of Albert Barnes, and others, to be *unconscious* rejections on their part of the Augustinian hell as a punishment which *could not* be inflicted by a merciful and just God. We hail these attempts at explaining away the awful terrors of biblical description as harbingers of the day when no man will dare to stand up and say that any man or fallen angel however guilty is to endure pain and agony throughout that eternity in which the unfallen and the redeemed enjoy their endless life.

Literal or figurative then, the descriptions which we have above quoted from various Augustinian writers are substantially true, if the Augustinian theory is true. Father Furniss did not invent his "red-hot oven," he only took it ready to hand from Malachi. Hippolytus did not originate his gnawing worm, or Jeremy Taylor his fire of hell, they only copied from the words of Christ (Mal. 4:1; Isa. 66:24; Mark 9:44). Between them and us there is a wide difference indeed; for we hold that these are *consuming and destroying agents,* reducing the living to death, and removing even the appearance of that which has become dead and loathsome. But between those who hold the descriptions of Scripture as literal, and those who hold them to be figurative, there is no difference of any material kind. Both believe in anguish of the most terrible nature as continuing throughout eternity: nor can we well see how they can refuse the additional idea that this anguish must go on increasing throughout eternity as the despair of any end grows blacker and blacker.

Such then, according to the Augustinian theory, is to be the eternal future of myriads of creatures framed and fashioned by God. Such descriptions, be they literal or be they figurative, are, according to their teaching, *true of every being placed in hell.* They picture the eternity not only of fallen angels and men who rejected the Gospel, but of the multitudes who never heard the name of the Father and the Son. If the "second death," and "everlasting destruction," and "perishing," of the wicked, be what the theory of Augustine teaches, the ignorant heathen endure it as well as the rejecter of the Gospel; for they who have sinned without law shall perish as they who sinned in the law; and the men of Tyre and Sidon and Nineveh must appear in the judgment as well as the generation which listened to the words of Christ (Rom. 2:12; Matt. 11:22; 12:41). Eternal agonies are the "*few stripes*" which Augustine's theory has provided for the most ignorant offender. Are eternal agonies a just punishment for *any,* be they servants who knew or were ignorant of their Master's will? We will take the latter case first.

We will take the case of some poor islander of a remote Pacific isle. Steeped in densest ignorance was his mind from the day he was cast a helpless infant upon this dark world, to the time he sunk back still more helpless in death. No lesson of virtue, of moderation, of purity, had ever cast its light on him. What should he know of justice who only saw the strong oppressing those who were weaker than they? What should he know of purity who in the women of his tribe or nation had never seen one who had even a faint idea of woman's highest grace? How was religion in his case to give him some higher, holier, lovelier notions than he could learn from his fellow man? Religion! The gods whom he worshipped—if indeed he worshipped any—were gods to whom rites of cruelty and impurity were a pleasing incense!

We do not say of such a man that he has *no* guilt. We do not believe that any one gifted with reason has ever lived *a life free* from guilt. Even where no revelation of true religion kept fully before the human mind the sense of right and wrong as in the sight of God—even where no distorted ray of tradition still kept up some rude sense of the essential difference of some from other actions—even in the darkest age and the remotest corner where a degraded humanity sees only a society as degraded as itself, even there the pain and suffering which evil inflicts through one man upon another keeps alive in the lowest type of the human mind the sense of a right and of a wrong.

The savage has indeed never heard such divine lessons as the gospel teaches in its every page—of a God who loves His enemies, and so urges upon His children, to be "tender-hearted, forgiving one another, even as God for Christ's sake hath forgiven you" (Eph. 4:32). The savage has never, in his experience or in the dim tradition of his tribe, conceived of such a man as Jesus of Nazareth, who, in all his aims, had none for self, but all for His Father and His brethren. But, in his smoking homestead, his slaughtered children, his wife carried captive to another's lust—in scenes such as these, and by acts such as these, some sense of right and wrong, produced by the sense of injury and loss, is kept alive, and where there is the sense of right and wrong there is the capacity of offending and the claim for punishment from God.

But how is such a man's guilt to be estimated to be weighed in the scales of justice, to be adjudged its fitting recompense? We have the Divine words for saying that this man's guilt is *small.* The judgment of reason is confirmed by that of God. A favorite proposition of our Augustinian opponents, though by no means so favorably regarded now as it used to be, is that "All sin is of an infinite nature, and requires endless conscious suffering as its only suitable punishment."

But what says God, and God's Son, of the sins of heathen men? Do we find Jesus Christ, who came down from heaven to tell us His Father's mind, talking the scholastic jargon which our modern preachers have learned from the ingenious brain-twisting of the Middle Ages?

We do not.

What does He say of sins such as we have spoken of?

Speaking even of Jews, who had so much fuller light than heathen men possess, He yet declared that if He had not "come and spoken unto them they would not have had sin" (John 15:22). While of the dark heathen sinner He said, "He that knew not his Lord's will, and did commit things worthy of stripes, *shall be beaten with few stripes*" (Luke 11:48). And thus we find from the highest authority that the sins of the heathen are light, and that the punishment which they shall feel shall be also light—*a few stripes.* They are the words of Christ. And is hell, according to Augustine's theory, a place of few stripes to any placed therein? Is a life of endless agony, of despair growing more despairing as eternity rolls, on and still brings no relief, no prospect of a close—is this a just punishment for the offences of heathen? Is this the Christian man's explanation of the "*few stripes*" of Christ his Master? A few stripes! Why if Methuselah had been multiplying the figures of arithmetic from the time he could calculate till he reached his 969th year he could not have arrived at any appreciable part of the sum of the stripes which the Augustinian theory would inflict on the sinners of the heathen.

Away then with this diabolical doctrine which shocks all our sense of justice and casts bitter contempt upon the merciful words of Christ. Is a life of endless agony, ever increasing, what Jesus meant by a "*few stripes?*"

God forbid that we should dare thus to tamper with his words. The heathen offender will know of no such hell as Mr. Spurgeon, and Father Furniss, and President Edwards, and Bishop Jeremy Taylor have depicted. When the Indian of the American forest, or the dusky child of the remote Pacific isle, wakes up at the solemn resurrection and hears judgment pronounced against him for willful offence against such dim light as he possessed, it will not be condemnation to a place where he is to suffer agony while the redeemed of Christ enjoy their endless life. The Lord has told us so, and we believe Him.

A word, before we pass on, upon the important bearing of this on the real nature of future punishment. *An eternal life of misery* we reject for heathen offenders not merely from our sense of justice but also from the express words of Christ. But from hence it follows that the terms descriptive of future punishment in Scripture *have no such meaning.* Heathen offenders are said to *"perish"* (απολλυμι, *apollumi*) in the coming judgment (Rom. 2:12). It does not mean here to endure endless misery. It can only then mean its usual meaning when applied to men treated as criminals, that is to say, *to have existence taken from them.* We have thus determined the scriptural use of this word—one of the most important and most frequently used in reference to future punishment. What "perishing" means for one lost sinner it means for all. The process indeed may, nay, certainly will, widely differ; so as to bring time the words of Christ, "for some many stripes, for some few," but the end is the same for all; it is the loss of the eternal life which Christ came to give back to man.

But we will not stop at the case of the sinners of the heathen. We will take the case that makes most strongly for our opponents' theory. We will ask if pain inflicted through eternity, endured without any hope of an end, no nearer to its close when numberless cycles have passed than when the first groan was uttered, is such *a just punishment* for any conceivable amount of sin committed by the worst of men? Man did not ask for life; it was given him without his knowledge or consent. Can any abuse of this unasked-for gift justify the recompense of an existence spent in everlasting agony?

We must put this question on its proper grounds. The ablest modern defenders of everlasting misery have put it on *a false issue*. They have done so in two main respects, urged on by their conscious inability to justify their theory in its naked light. The first of these we will give in the words of William Archer Butler, whose view is adopted by Dr. Salmon, Professor Mansel, Dr. Angus, and many others.* "*The punishments of hell,*" says Butler, "are but the perpetual vengeance that accompanies *the sins of hell. An eternity of wickedness* brings with it *an eternity of woe*. The sinner is to suffer for everlasting; but it is *because the sin itself is as everlasting as the suffering?*"

We must fairly and fully look at this *astounding* proposition. Our readers will first remark how it is an attempt to *change the ground*, on which the justice of everlasting misery is sought to be defended. The plea used to be that "sin being committed against *an infinite Being* was itself on this account infinite, and therefore deserved to be punished with pain and misery as long as the infinite Being Himself existed." This plea now justly does not satisfy Augustinian theorists.† Some of them, indeed, seem to consider it what it truly is, an argument worthy of the malignity of a devil linked with the ingenuity of a schoolman. On this ground, a single sin against God must be met by the punishment of agony as long as God lived. So the ground *must be changed*. Our opponents are now busy executing a flank march to take up their new ground. Instead of the old cry, "Sin is

* See W. A. Butler, *Sermons*, 2nd series, "On Everlasting Punishment;" Dr. Salmon's *Sermons*, p. 10; Mansel, *Bampton Lectures*, pp. 22-23; Dwight's *Theology*, sermon clxvii; Pollok, *Course of Time*, b. x.; Dr. Angus, *Future Punishment*, p. 47; Jonathan Edwards, quoted by Blain, *Life and Death*, p. 115; R. W. Landis, *Immortality of Soul*, 395.

† Dr. Salmon, *Ser.* p. 9; Abp. Tillotson, *Eternity of Hell Torments.*

infinite, and deserves unending suffering," we now hear, "The sinner will commit *an infinite number of sins,* and so will deserve suffering as infinite and endless."

We will first remark that this is a complete, if not conscious confession, *that the sins of the present life,* however aggravated and numerous, *do not deserve to be punished by everlasting misery.* This is exactly what we contend for. This is now conceded by every man who adopts the view just mentioned. Dr. Salmon, Dr. Angus, Professor Mansel, and their sympathisers, confess, that *to punish the sins of this life with endless misery would be the grossest injustice.*[*] "*Continued punishment*" says Dr. Angus, "*means continued sin.*" Says Dr. Salmon, "If the wicked suffer it is *because* they are still rebels against God." Both of these gentlemen agree with us that to go on inflicting suffering through eternity for the sins long, past of this present life, no matter what then character, would be to be guilty of inconceivable injustice:

> "Charge not a God with such outrageous wrong."

For endless suffering there must be, in this judgment, a course of sin just as endless.

But, good God, what a prospect do these men hold out to our view! Says Professor Mansel,

> "In that mysterious condition of the depraved will compelled and yet free—the slave of sinful habit, yet responsible for every act of sin, and *gathering deeper condemnation as the power of amendment grows less and less;* may we not see some possible *foreshadowing* of the yet deeper guilt and the yet more hopeless misery of the worm that dieth not, and the fire that is not quenched?"

[*] See final note on previous page.

This is one of Dr. Angus' *alleviations* of hell! This is one of those *lights* which are to relieve the terrible blackness of the place of doom! Sins throughout eternity increasing in number, in magnitude, and in guilt! Condemnation and punishment throughout eternity gathering force and falling more terribly upon the wretched sufferors! Talk of Fathers Furniss and Pinamonti giving descriptions too horrible to be heard! Talk of Jeremy Taylor's or Mr. Spurgeon's accounts as too harrowing to the mind! They are almost merciful in the face of a theory which describes eternity as entering down an endless course of increasing sin calling for endlessly increasing punishment.

And do not these fearful reasoners see that their theory obliterates that marked distinction which Christ has drawn between the sin and the punishment of heathen men and willful offenders! No distinction of *knowledge* can continue between one man and another after the judgment day. And then they place the sinners of a once greater or lesser knowledge side by side, and suppose that *both* will go on through eternity adding to the number of *willful sins*. Any difference that existed in this life from ignorance or knowledge would soon be imperceptible in that ever-increasing catalogue of fresh willful sins which both alike would and must add to their account. The comparative ignorance on which Christ rests so much, the comparative guilt which He so strongly marks, the wide difference of punishment which He speaks of, would all vanish in that awful vista of an eternity in which all the lost alike were ever adding to the number and magnitude of known and willful sins. Thank God, we have a Word which sweeps away this vision of terror from our sight.

It may very fairly be questioned whether, according to any principles of divine or human law, the lost in hell are *capable of sinning*. We deny that that they are. "Sin is the transgression of the law," St. John tells us; and Paul lays down this great principle of equity, "Where no law is, there is no transgression" (1 John 3:4; Rom. 4:15). We deny that those who are denied all the benefits of law and subjected to its greatest and final penalty, are ever considered as under the law, or capable of incurring any fresh guilt from its infraction. We call upon our opponents to produce any authority for their terrible theory: to produce from any code of human law any justification of it. Scripture, from first to last, says not one word of the sins of hell. Let them listen to the just words of a man who agrees with them in their view of future punishment but denounces their idea of the possibility of sinners adding to their sin in hell. "'Sin is the transgression of the law,' says Mr. Girdlestone,

> "but what law will be laid down for the guidance of those who are bound hand and foot, and cast into outward darkness in Gehenna? 'To him that knoweth to do good and doeth it not, to him it is sin' (Jas. 4:17); but what knowledge of good will there be among those who will have had all their talents taken from them? In a word, as the saved will be raised above the possibility of sinning; so the lost will be sunk below it."

Elsewhere he says,

> "Is there anything in the nature of eternal punishment which makes an eternity of sin certain, probable, or even possible? We think not. What does the Scripture say on this subject? Turning to the various texts which set forth the future and eternal punishment of the wicked, do we find anything to justify us in accepting the conclusion here suggested? Are there any intimations in God's Word that men will go on sinning forever in the world to come? Does not the whole spirit and tenor of the Scripture go the other way? Can any single verse be pointed out which show that the lost will continue in sin hereafter? No; we see neither the authority of the Scripture, nor the voice of reason, in favor of this idea, which appears to be absolutely without foundation."[*]

---

[*] R. B. Girdlestone, M. A., *Dies. Iræ.*, 165-67.

But, altogether independent of the question as to whether the outlaws of hell are capable of transgressing law, it is sufficient to say of the view that the punishment of the future is entirely, chiefly, or in the smallest degree, inflicted for the sins of the future, that it contradicts the teaching of Scripture, and is therefore to be rejected as a lie. Not once or twice, but over and over again, it tells us that *the punishment of the future is for the sins of the present life.*[*] The ablest defenders of the theory of everlasting misery are forced to confess this. "The justice of God," says Archbishop Tillotson, "doth *only* punish the sins which men have committed in this life." "The evil done by man in this life," says Mr. Paley, commenting on Paul's description of the grounds of future punishment in Romans 2:9, "is what is spoken of, *no other evil* was in the apostle's thoughts." And Mr. Landis, referring especially to the texts above referred to, says, "In all these, and in multitudes of other passages, there is a clear retrospective reference to sin perpetrated here as the *sole ground* of the judicial decision and succeeding punishment."[†] If we think this punishment too great, we are not at liberty to throw in the sins of the future, real or imaginary, to justify the punishment of the future. If we cannot defend man's future treatment as a just award for his present conduct, we cannot justify it at all. Do we not put ourselves into the exact position of the false prophets of Israel to whom God sternly says, "Have ye not seen a vain vision; and have ye not spoken a lying divination: whereas ye say, the Lord saith it; albeit I have not spoken?" (Ezek. 13:7). It is indeed a piece of impious effrontery for us to present as a reason for God's conduct what God has not Himself presented when explaining to man His judicial action. Just fancy an earthly judge sentencing a criminal to a punishment too severe for the offence

---

[*] See Matthew 25:41-24; Romans 2:6; 2 Corinthians 5:10; 2 Thessalonians 1:6-9.

[†] Tillotson's *Sermons*, "Eternity of Hell Torments;" Archd. Paley's *Sermons* on Matthew 16; R. W. Landis, *Immortality of the Soul*, 395.

committed, and then gravely justifying his sentence by the observation that *the criminal would be sure to deserve it all by his conduct in gaol!* Yet such is the judicature, unworthy of a Jeffreys, which professors of theology and doctors of divinity take upon them to ascribe, without any authority from Him, to the Judge of the whole earth!

Another very favorite refuge for the Augustinian theorist, in defending his fearful view of future punishment from the charge of cruelty and injustice, is that it only follows that natural law which inextricably links together sin and misery. They represent God as though he did not directly interpose in the matter, but left things to take their natural course. As this course would, from the very nature of moral evil, lead certainly and irresistibly to misery, they imagine that such a view of hell shields their theory from its apparent harshness and injustice. They suppose that God just banishes the wicked to a place where they are kept from doing further injury; that in this place they of course go on indulging in all evil passions, and that the indulgence in their evil passions involves misery, and is in fact the terrible hell of the future. They would thus shield God from the awful aspect of directly inflicting pain upon His creatures throughout all eternity. Future punishment is thus, with them, allowing things to take their natural course. The only part God takes in it is that He allows this course, originally ordained by Himself, to go on, and does not interfere with it.

We do not say that Bishop Butler *originated* this view of future punishment; but certainly more modern thinkers have eagerly followed his lead, and have gladly sheltered themselves under the authority of England's greatest theological reasoner. We apprehend that the present controversy on the eternity of evil will reveal the weak points in the armor of the great Bishop of Durham, and that chapters 1 and 2 of part one of the famous "Analogy" will be seen to be those parts which show that even Butler's marvelous reason had its imperfection and its flaw. In chapter 2 he defends future punishment on the ground that it may be the natural effect and consequence of sin.[*]

Later thinkers, who will scarcely deem it an injustice to be ranked as inferior in intellectual power to the Bishop of Durham, have followed out the idea of Butler. "May we not," says Professor Mansel,

> "trace something not wholly unlike the irrevocable sentence of the future, in that dark and fearful, yet too certain law of our nature, by which sin and misery ever tend to perpetuate themselves; by which evil habits gather strength with every fresh indulgence, till it is no longer, humanly-speaking, in the power of the sinner to shake off the burden which his own deeds have laid upon him? In that mysterious condition of the depraved will, compelled and yet free—the state of sinful habit, yet responsible for every act of sin, and gathering deeper condemnation as the power of amendment grows less and less; may we not see some possible foreshadowing of the yet deeper guilt, and the yet more hopeless misery of the worm that dieth not, and the fire that is not quenched?"[†]

Dr. Salmon shows a very evident inclination to give the same view, though he carefully and very prudently guards himself from being supposed to assert that there is no other punishment to be apprehended than such as follows in the way of natural consequence.[‡]

But the writer of our day, who has put forward this view with a minuteness and circumstantiality that equals in its tremendous power the descriptions of Roman Catholic and Protestant preachers in their details of the material torments of hell, is Dr. Pusey. "Gather in your mind," he says,

---

[*] Bp. Butler, *Analogy*, p. 1, c. ii.

[†] Profess Mansel, *Bampton Lectures*, vii.

[‡] G. Salmon, D.D., *Eternity of Future Punishment*, p. 9.

> "an assembly of all those men and women, from whom, whether in history or in fiction, your memory most shrinks (no fiction can reach the reality of human sin), gather in mind all which is most loathsome, most revolting, the most treacherous, malicious, coarse, brutal, invective, fiendish cruelty, unsoftened by any remains of human feeling, such as thou couldest not endure for a single hour; conceive the fierce fiery eyes of hate, spite, frenzied rage, ever fixed on thee, looking through and through and through with hate; sleepless in their horrible gaze; felt, if not seen; never turning from thee, never to be turned from, except to quail under the like piercing sight of hate. Hear those yells of blasphemy and concentrated hate, as they echo along the lurid vaults of hell; every one hating every one, and venting that hate unceasingly, with every inconceivable expression of malignity; conceive all this, multiplied, intensified, reflected on all around, on every side; and amid it, the especial hatred of any one whose sins thou sharest, whom thou didst thoughtlessly encourage in sin, or teach some sin unknown before—a deathlessness of hate were in itself everlasting misery. Yet a fixedness in that state, in which the hardened, malignant sinner dies, involves, *without any further retribution from God,* this endless misery."*

Such is the idea of future punishment which many of our modern Augustinians would substitute for the material torments of Messrs. Spurgeon and Furniss: and which, in attributing the misery of the lost to the operation of what they call *a natural law,* seems to them to shield God from all imputation of cruelty or injustice. Between the amount of misery of Dr. Pusey's hell and that of Mr. Spurgeon, it seems difficult to decide. Mental agony is known to equal, if not sometimes to exceed, the keenest agony of our bodily frame.

We object however to this theory on two grounds. In the first place we deny that future punishment is the mere result of a natural law now in operation. In the second place we say that even if it could be

---

* Rev. Dr. Pusey; Henry W. Beecher, *Sermons on Future Punishment*, Plymouth Pulpit, 1870, p. 100.

incontrovertibly proved to be so it would not in the smallest degree serve the purpose for which it is brought forward.

We do not think that any unprejudiced person could read the general scriptural accounts of future punishment and suppose that they mean nothing more than leaving the wicked to the operation of those natural laws which are now actually in full force. The connection of sin and misery is an established connection. It has always been at work. Men see it and know it. The drunkard knows to what his excess will and is leading him; the profligate man knows the same. The natural results of hatred are obvious to us all. What effect this knowledge has in restraining from sin, let every one judge.

"Virtue is its own reward and vice its own punishment" is an adage perhaps more familiar to heathen than to Christian ears. We wanted no revelation to be made of such punishment as this. The sinner, with the full knowledge of it, is found from experience to prefer vice with its natural punishment to virtue with its natural reward. To be told that hell is merely the continuation of the state of things which he has here deliberately chosen is scarcely *to him* a warning. But certainly no specious philosophy, about natural laws will ever lead us to suppose the *hell which is now only in preparation* (Matt. 25:41), to be identical with the punishment which has, from the operation of a great natural law, been in execution from the entrance of sin. Neither do the fallen spirits who have been, for we do not know how many thousands years, under the operation of this natural law, binding together sin and suffering, consider this punishment to be in the smallest measure identical with the punishment to which they know themselves doomed. They have had full time to judge of the connection between sin and misery. Their sin, being of the most aggravated kind, must have produced all the natural punishment which it is capable of producing, yet still they cling fondly and desperately to even such a life as they now possess.

The fearful cry of the devils, "What have we to do with thee, Jesus, thou Son of God? Art thou come hither *to torment us before the time?*" ought surely to dissipate the picture which is drawn by human theorists of the punishment of hell as being simply the result of a natural law (Matt. 8:29).

But there is one grand fact in connection with the future punishment of wicked men which removes it altogether from the sphere of mere natural law. Whatever might be said of the fallen angels as being removed from the power of doing further injury by their being confined in hell, and of their being left there to the punishment produced by a law which must operate in their case as well as in that of man, *the resurrection of the wicked* is a full proof that God *directly interferes with future punishment,* and does not merely leave it to the operation of natural law. To carry out this theory of *natural punishment* our opponents must be consistent. If God were to leave things to their *natural course,* there would be *no resurrection of the wicked,* for surely the resurrection of the wicked is not the operation of a natural law. If our theorists were consistent they must teach that God would leave the wicked forever in their graves. But this is not at all the case. Without here entering at all into the enquiry as to whether the *human soul,* separate from the body, is properly capable of pain or pleasure, or of life at all, it is undeniably the case that God does directly and immediately interfere for the purpose of future punishment. It is His voice and direct act, not the operation of a natural law, which calls the wicked to resurrection. They would else have slumbered on forever. *And he thus interferes directly for the purpose of punishment.* "We must all appear," St. Paul tells us, "before the judgment seat of Christ; *that every one may receive the things done in his body, according to that he hath done,* whether it be good or bad" (2 Cor. 5:10). The idea of future punishment then, as being merely the result of natural laws, is overthrown by Scripture. God does not leave things just to follow their natural course. He puts forth what we call miraculous power to bring about the punishment of the wicked. We cannot deny this without denying the resurrection of the unjust.

But we also reject this view of future punishment on the ground that it *violates every known principle of law and its sanctions.* The very notion of a punishment announced for the violation of a law implies *some infliction different from that unpleasantness* or wretchedness which *the infraction of the law itself produces.* To tell a child that if he does wrong his conscience will upbraid him and he will be unhappy is quite a different thing from telling him that if he does wrong you will punish him. To make the sanctions of any law, divine or human, to consist in the amount of dissatisfaction and misery which its infraction naturally produces is really to render the sanction nugatory and useless. A creature yet unfallen, as Adam was before transgression, could not possibly know in the remotest degree to what he was about to subject himself. He could see the supposed *advantage* of transgression, but he could not possibly judge its *pain.* Experience alone could teach him this.

The theory of natural punishment fails in the first grand primary object of punishment, that is, *the prevention of* transgression. Nor, after transgression, could it have much more effect. Universal experience testifies that *sin is pleasant at the outset.* "Stolen waters" are not bitter the moment they are drunk: the sinner will tell you they are "sweet." Also, "Bread eaten in secret" does not at first grate upon the teeth: the sinner will tell you it is "pleasant." How are all the advice, and warnings, and testimonies of experience accepted by youth and inexperience bent upon the pursuits of unhallowed pleasure? They are treated as the passing wind. The beautiful figure of pleasure smiles and beckons on to follow in her train. The road is strewn with roses; the air filled with perfume. After her eagerly follow the crowd, and think the few who hold aloof are fools to lose the substance of life. Not till they have followed long does the scene change. The road is rough and weary; the perfume is gone; the flowers are withered; the fair soft cheek is yellow and withered. And then! And then it is *too late.* In the long wild pursuit, *the memory of good has been forgotten.* The figure of grace, of virtue, is *austere, hateful,* to the debased follower of harlot vice. He confesses to himself no doubt that a fair appearance deceived, but the adage "*virtue is its own reward*" seems to him more supremely ridiculous than when he set out in the train of her rival. Evil has become his only good. To tell him that the punishment of sin is only the result of natural laws producing wretchedness, is only to tell him all he knows already, and has made up his mind to accept and hold by. We must then in the Divine, as well as in all law, have a punishment distinct from the natural effects of transgression, if we would have a punishment effectual either to prevent transgression or to induce to amendment after sin has been entered upon.

Dr. Salmon, in one place, seems to think very favorably of that view of future punishment which makes it consist in the lost being miserable because they are wicked.* When however he comes to reason with an opponent who carries out this view to its full and natural conclusion, who does not toy with it as Dr. Salmon does, but holds it, and manfully uses it without apprehension, then Dr. Salmon undertakes its refutation, and refutes it, we must say, in a very pleasant and logical way. "*There can be no greater misery than to be a sinner*" is what Dr. Salmon gives us as "the substance" of Mr. Maurice's view. We should have supposed this would fall very much into Dr. Salmon's own idea; but it is not so. Dr. Salmon remembers the pleasant Roman satirist who tells us that there is no objection in the world to our stating truth in a pleasant or even a jocular way, and so proceeds to direct against Mr. Maurice some very pleasant and telling banter. "Imagine," he says,

* *The Eternity of Punishment,* p. 9.

> "Mr. Maurice's house attacked by burglars, and think of the effect of this remonstrance: *'Consider, my good friends, how your consciences will sting you for this by and by.'* And if you find a sinner, trembling under the denunciation of judgment to come, you will give him immediate relief if you tell him that the sting of conscience will be the only punishment he need dread. He will say, 'Is that all? I think I can bear that.'"*

But we reject this view of future punishment on the ground that it gives a view of the highest law, of that which is the model and pattern of all law, the Divine Law, which is inconsistent with, and contrary to *the nature of all law.* We should not fear to oppose to the authority of Bishop Butler the authority of John Locke. On a question of this kind, indeed, we should prefer the authority of the latter. Besides, Bishop Butler, in his chapter on "The Government of God by Punishment," while he with the most perfect correctness insists that in evil actions leading as their natural result to misery we have God actually punishing such actions in the ordinary course of nature, nowhere denies that there may be, either in this life or in the next, other punishment of a direct and immediate kind inflicted by God for sin. The nature of Bishop Butler's argument did not lead him *at all* to enquiries of this kind. They were *wholly foreign* to his purpose. When he speaks therefore of the *natural results* of ill conduct here as pointing to the probability of similar natural results hereafter; and as in both cases being truly and properly a Divine punishment for transgression; he does not in the smallest degree contradict the idea that there may be *other punishment,* of a kind different from that which is the natural result of ill doing, in store for unpardoned sin. They who would quote Bishop Butler as teaching that the natural evil results of ill doing are its *only* punishment do not understand *the fundamental idea of his "Analogy."* We

* *The Eternity of Punishment*, p. 59.

have then the authority of Locke, wholly undiminished by any contrary authority of Butler.

What is the testimony of Locke on this question of law and punishment? "Since it would be utterly vain," he tells us,

> "to suppose a rule set to the free actions of man, without annexing to it some enforcement of good and evil, to determine his will, we must, *wherever we suppose a law, suppose also some reward or punishment annexed to that law.* It would be in vain for one intelligent being to set a rule to the actions of another, if he had it not in his power to reward the compliance with, and punish the deviation from, his rule, by some good and evil, *that is not the natural product and consequence of the action itself:* for that being a natural convenience or inconvenience, would operate of itself, without a law. *This, if I mistake not, is the true nature of all law, properly so called.*"[*]

But even if it could be established—which it cannot—that future punishment was solely and entirely the result of that *natural law* which binds sin and suffering together, this would not, in the remotest degree, remove this charge of injustice from God, if the punishment thus naturally following were too great for the offence. A natural law must be as just as a special law. In fact, if possible, it should be more so; since it has a wider and more permanent operation. To account for the injustice of an infliction by saying: "Oh, it is the effect of a natural law," is the highest slander against God. Let us call the law which produces any effect by what name we please, natural, or miraculous, or special, it makes no difference. The law must in each case be just in its operation, in order to be justifiable. The laws of nature, as any other law enacted or executed by Him, are the laws of God. For all their consequences, after they have worked their

[*] Locke, *Human Understanding*, b. 2, c. xxviii.

uniform work for ages, He is just as responsible as when He first ordained them, or as when He departs from them by an alteration of law or a miraculous interference. If the laws of nature were to bring on the sinner a punishment greater than his sin deserved, it is God Himself who would be doing so. They who quote Bishop Butler for future punishment being the result of a natural law must also take the remainder of the great reasoner's view on the subject. "We are at present," he says,

> "actually under God's government, *in the strictest and most proper sense*—in such a sense as that *He* rewards and punishes us for our actions. Whether the pleasure or pain which follows upon our behavior be *owing to the Author of nature's acting upon us every moment which we feel it, or to His having at once contrived and executed His own part in the plan of the world, makes no alteration as to the matter before us.*"*

But God, by one special act of His, takes in the great day of reckoning on Himself the whole responsibility of future punishment, be it of what character it may. *God raises the wicked for the very purpose of this punishment.* It matters not then what *is* its source. If it be a special punishment then specially inflicted; and, different from the mere result of the natural law now in operation, we have God immediately and specially inflicting it. If it be wholly and entirely the result of natural law, producing the fearful hell which Dr. Pusey has pictured with such tremendous power, and which would seem to equal any natural suffering, *we have God directly and specially interfering*, in the resurrection of the wicked, *in order to subject them to this punishment.* God assumes the entire responsibility of their punishment, just as much in one case as in the other. We cannot separate the God of nature from the God of revelation. They are one and the same.

* *Analogy*, part 1, c. ii.

The simple question then is, "Could man by any conduct here deserve to suffer through eternity pain and torment to which only the worst pain we suffer here can afford a true parallel? Would the agonies to which the martyr was subjected for an hour be only sufficient for the sinner if drawn out through the eternal age? Would it be just in God to inflict this on any single creature of His hand, on any being who would never have had life at all if the Maker had not called him from his clay?"

The verdict of the human heart, in its fierce denial, in its secret recoil, answers "No."

"Eternal pain," says Augustine, "seems harsh and unjust to human sense." And, "With the majority of men of the world," says Archer Butler, "this doctrine seems, when they think at all about it, monstrous, disproportioned, impossible." It seems so, in the same writer's mind, to others besides men of the world, to men who do not fear the doom for themselves: "Were it possible," he says,

> "for human imagination to conceive the horror of such a doom as this, all reasoning about it were at an end; it would scorch and wither all the powers of human thought. Human life were at a stand, could these things be felt as they deserve. Even for him who can humbly trust himself comparatively secure in faith and obedience, were the thin veil of this poor shadowy life suddenly withdrawn, and these immortal agonies, that never-dying death, made known in the way of direct perception: and those, it may be, that such a one, with the keen sympathies so characteristic of the Christian, loves and values, seen to be at last among the victims of that irreparable doom—can we doubt that he would come forth with intellect blanched and idealess from a sight too terrible for any whose faculties are not on the scale of eternity itself? It is God's mercy that we can *believe* what *adequately to conceive were death.*"[*]

---

[*] Augustine, *City of God,* xxi. 12; W. A. Butler, *Sermons,* 376, 383.

Thus does a writer, who himself believed this doctrine, describe it. He attributes *the possibility of believing it to a special act of grace.* If God were now to ask man whether his conduct on this hypothesis were just, man with one voice would reply that, according to all His conceivable ideas of justice and judgment, conduct such as this would *be most unjust.*

The history of human religious thought shows man's ineradicable sense of the burning wrong of this fearful theory. If Plato, deriving his inspiration from Egypt, taught a Tartarus with its fiery streams, whence none could come forth, he taught it for an infinitesimally small portion of men. For most, even for the homicide, the parricide, and the matricide, he had his Acherusian lake, whence, after a purgative process, they issued forth again to the upper air. If Augustine adopted his great master's abode of unending pain, he adopted also his purgatory, whence there was a way to heaven. If the Church of Rome has sanctioned the theory of Augustine, she practically holds out its terrors only to those without her pale of safety: for her own millions she has the fires of a finite period. The assertion of Augustine's hell by Tertullian and his contemporaries did but drive the gentler mind of Origen to the notion of a far vaster purgatory than Rome's or Augustine's, where even devils should be prepared to resume their place in heaven.

The Churches of the Reformation have generally followed Augustine in his hell, and denied his purgatory; but, at all times, within their bosom has been a struggle against the dominant doctrine, and even from those who maintained it it has only commanded a sullen, uncheerful assent. Such men as Burnet, Whitby, Hammond, Law, Sir Isaac and Bishop Newton, Locke, Bengel, Foster, Birks, have rejected it with abhorrence. Such men as Tillotson, Hermann Witsius, Robert Hall, Dr. Watts, Isaac Taylor, William Butler, Albert Barnes, Bishop Ellicott, while they accepted the theory, loved it not. "I should be very glad," says Dr. Salmon, "to see it proved that I was wrong." Also, "*Who would not?*" groans out Mr. Grant, laboring under the terrific weight of a theory ho yet felt himself bound to maintain. Let these men reason as they would, the black look of injustice lurked about the ugly thing. Let them allow their minds to dwell upon the reality of what eternal evil and eternal misery meant, and their hearts would grieve that man had been made at all; that the feelings of pity were implanted in the human breast, and cherished by the gospel of Christ. Darkness and anguish settled down and brooded over their spirit; yea, the very light of reason would almost abandon them for madness, when they conceived even in the far-off future the horrible hell of Augustine. We constantly find them, even when they are struggling hard to defend the monstrous thought before a reluctant world, candidly confessing that with all their hearts they could wish that it was a monstrous lie.*

The modern mind, shaken in religious conviction, denies the inspiration of a book which is supposed to teach this creed of cruelty. With those who will not throw away their faith in man's future, the theory of Origen, with all its consequences, bids fair, if only confronted with the fearful nightmare of Augustine, to take the place which the authority of the latter father has so long imposed upon the Church. The ablest modem defenders of the theory are shrinking back from putting forward a vindication of it in its plain and hideous aspect. One after another of the arguments on which it has heretofore been defended they are abandoning as unworthy of their reason or abhorrent to their sense of justice, while those they are striving to substitute are to the full as unreasonable and unjust.†

---

* Abp. Tillotson, *Sermons*, "Eternity of Hell Torments;" Dr. Watts, *The World to Come*; Isaac Taylor, *Restoration of Belief*, 367; W. A. Butler, *Sermons*; Albert Barnes, *Practical Sermons*, 123; Professor Rogers, *Greyson's Letters*; Dr. Ellicott, *The Church and the Age*; Dr. Salmon's *Sermons*, Preface; J. Grant, *Religious Tendencies*, i. 219.

† Abp. Tillotson's *Eternity of Hell Torments*; Magee, *Discourses on the Atonement*, note 13; Dr. Salmon's *Sermons*, pp. 9, 47; W. Sherlock, *Future Punishment*, introduction; Edward

Listen to the low, sad wail of Foster, as he passes in review the great subject of future punishment. His powerful mind believed in the Platonic view of the immortality of the soul, and therefore he knew not *what* to believe of the future of the wicked. He would turn to Origen's conception of a universal restoration, until driven from it by passages of Scripture too plain to be mistaken. He would turn to the theory of everlasting destruction, until repelled by his belief in the immortality of the soul which forbid him to imagine that it could be destroyed. But *one thing* he would not and could not admit into his faith, the notion of the eternity of woe. He set *God's character,* everywhere revealed in its justice and its love, against what appeared to him the *apparent meaning of some of God's words,* and the character of God led him to the true and logical conclusion that the theory of eternal misery was a slander against his Maker. "Think of *man,*" he says,

> "his nature, his situation, the circumstances of his brief sojourn and trial on earth. Far be it from us to make light of the demerit of sin, and to remonstrate with the Supreme Judge against a severe chastisement, of whatever moral nature we may suppose the infliction to be. But still, what is man? He comes into the world with a nature fatally corrupt, and powerfully tending to actual evil. He comes among a crowd of temptations adapted to his innate evil propensities. He grows up (incomparably the greater proportion of the race) in great ignorance, his judgment weak, and under numberless beguilements into error; while his passions and appetites are strong, his conscience unequally matched against their power—in the majority of men but feebly and rudely constituted. The influence of whatever good instruction he may receive is counteracted by a combination of opposite influences almost constantly acting on him. He is essentially and inevitably unapt to be powerfully acted on by what is

---

Beecher, *Conflict of Ages*, b. v., c. i.; Professor Mansel, *Bampton Lectures*, pp. 22, 225-26; Dwight's *Theology*, Sermon clxvii.

> invisible and future. In addition to all which, there is the intervention and activity of the great tempter and destroyer. . . . Now this creature, thus constituted and circumstanced, passes a few fleeting years on the earth, a short, sinful course, in which he does often what, notwithstanding his ignorance and ill-disciplined judgment and conscience, he knows to be wrong, and neglects what he knows to be his duty; and consequently, for a greater or less measure of guilt, widely different in different offenders, deserves punishment. But *endless punishment! Hopeless misery, through a duration to which the terms above imagined will be* absolutely nothing! I acknowledge my *inability* (I would say reverently) *to admit this belief together with a belief in the divine goodness*—the belief that 'God is love,' that his tender mercies are over all his works."[*]

The struggles of two such minds as those of John Foster and William Archer Butler may well weigh strongly on this question. Both were men of powerful mind, sincere piety, deep trust in the truth of Scripture, educated alike from childhood to believe in the eternal misery of the lost. They both accepted as an indisputable axiom the inalienable immortality of man. But they will give their mind to understand as much as they may what this doctrine of endless woe and evil in which they have been educated *means.* It is too important, too prominent, to be overlooked. They cannot accept it and then lay it by. They cannot be satisfied with an occasional mention of it when professional decency compelled them, and then to hide it as unsuitable to ears polite. If it is true, they truly felt it should be proclaimed in all its terrors, as with the blast of a trumpet. *They look at it, and stand aghast!* They see *a little part of its woe,* and horror seizes on their minds. Wild questionings of God, strange, thoughts of Him which are blasphemy almost to conceive, suspicions which it is anguish even to entertain, bitter wails over the creature called into a life that was to have such an end, rush into their thoughts and cannot be shut out. Foster looks at it and rejects it,

[*] Letter of the Rev. John Foster, "On Future Punishment."

though he knew not where else to turn. Butler looks at it with half-closed eyes and accepts it, and his faith all but sets him mad.

Our view needs no vindication, does not compel us to keep it discreetly in the background, reduces us to no subterfuge to escape its consequences. It does not force us to advance arguments which we feel to be unworthy of a child, or faintly to defend the justice of a procedure which our heart whispers to us is only worthy of a devil's conception. By it, the next life's dealings with the sinner will but follow the analogy of this. He who scans the course of nature may from it anticipate that future course which revelation opens to our view. *According to it God's ways with the sinner are equal.* They are severe; but they are just. They are full of awe; but they can be contemplated with calmness. They show the award of a justice in whose consequences we can rejoice. Its issue is eternal death. If it brings the sigh of sadness over a lost soul, it brings also the deep full breathing of infinite relief. "The wicked," says Locke, "had no right to demand their existence, and so no right to demand its continuance." We require neither the "purgatory" of Augustine, nor the "universal restoration" of Origen—man's desperate refuges from the hell he has himself conceived. Looking on the calmed face of death, we will say, "It is well." The woes, the agony, the despair, of life, are passed away from its features with the sin that produced them.

10

The Extinction of Evil

IN THE PREDICTED EXTINCTION of evil we have another conclusive proof of the truth of our theory as opposed to that of Augustine. Evil is not to be eternal. We are told in God's Word that it had a beginning, and will have an end. Neither the Manichæism of Manes, asserting for evil an eternal past and future, nor the Semi-Manichæism of Augustine, asserting for it an eternal future, is true; God has pledged His Word and His power that it shall be abolished and destroyed. He has promised a "*restitution of all things*" by the mouth of all His holy prophets since the world began. A time shall come when all things will be once more very good; when iniquity shall have an end; when the pure eyes of God shall no more be offended by its sight. A time shall come when they who would not glorify God shall be silent in darkness; and when everything that has breath shall praise the Lord (Acts 3:21; Matt. 3:12; Ps. 5:4-5; 37:10; 150:6; 1 Sam 2:9; Hab. 1:13).

So plainly is the end of evil insisted on in Scripture that men of the most opposite opinions on the question of future punishment are forced to maintain that according to their system evil is truly and really brought to an end. It is one of the fundamental bases of the theory of universal restoration. It also forms one of the grand supports for our theory of destruction. "The day is at hand," says the Epistle of Barnabas, "when all things shall perish with the evil one;" when "he who chooseth other things [than the judgments of the Lord] shall be destroyed with his works."[*] Says Irenaeus, "At the end of time, Christ shall come to do away with all evil, and to reconcile all things, in order that there may be an end of all infirmities."[†] Even the maintainers of eternal evil are happy to teach that their system brings evil to an end. Thus Tertullian reasons against Hermogenes, that for God "to bear with evil instead of extirpating it" would "prove Him to be the promoter thereof; criminally, if through his own will; disgracefully, if through necessity:" and he lays it down as beyond a question that "there is to be *an end of evil.*"[‡]

But the system of Augustine, let its defenders argue or assert as they may, is here at direct issue with Scripture. The theory of eternal life in hell contradicts the whole tenor of the Bible upon this point. It denies the restitution of all things; it asserts that evil shall be eternal in God's world; and that iniquity shall never have an end. It tells us that God's eyes shall throughout eternity be offended with the sight of evil, and His ears pained with the sounds of blasphemy. It denies that the wicked will ever be silent in darkness, and that everything that has breath shall praise the Lord. It sets apart a portion of God's universe, not for the destruction of evil, but for its everlasting preservation. According to many of its advocates, evil will go on increasing throughout eternity in the continued sin and blasphemy of fallen angels and men; and according to others these will receive constant accession to their numbers from the ranks of other races; so that it may become doubtful whether good or evil predominates in a

[*] Apostolical Fathers, *Epistle of Barnabas*, c. xxi.

[†] Irenaeus, *Fragments*, No. xxxix.

[‡] Tertullian, *Against Hermogenes*, c. x., xi.

world over which an omnipotent and holy God is allowed by these men to reign.*

For the theory of Augustine does not in any true or intelligible sense put an end to evil. It merely removes it from one part of God's world to another, and, as a direct consequence of this removal, intensifies it in its new habitation. "There is to be an end of evil," says Tertullian, "when the chief thereof, the devil, shall go away into the fire which God hath prepared for him and his angels." Strange end of evil! As if evil was terminated by its change of locality, or as if evil was no evil when it was in hell! This is no restitution of all things. It is not true that all things are once more very good while any portion of God's creatures are in rebellion against His will. Hell, wherever it be, is as much a part of God's world as earth or heaven; and all would not be very good in God's world, if there were in any part of it, however remote, such a hell as Augustine has pictured—a fearful place filled with its teeming myriads of fallen spirits and men throughout eternity blaspheming the God of the whole universe.

Our theory fully answers the requirements of Scripture. It teaches a restitution of all things and an extinction of evil. To us it seems to do even more than this. It appears to afford a reason for what, after all, is the grand mystery in connection with evil, that is, *its permission for any period in God's world. The origin of evil* is accounted for by the freedom of will which belongs to all creatures of loftier nature and nobler destiny than the brutes; for wherever there is freedom of will there must be the possibility of a fall. On this point, the best thinkers have agreed. Again, *the obliteration of evil* is provided for in the restoration of some in their day of grace and the eternal death of all who have not thus been restored to God. *The permission of evil* for the period of time from the angelic fall to the final

* Dr. Salmon's *Sermons*, p. 10; Mansel, *Bampton Lectures*, pp. 22-23; Letter of C. H. Waller, *The Rock*, December 29, 1868.

consummation of all things, is therefore the great problem to be solved in the history of evil. Faith in such a God as we have tells us that the permission of evil must have some wise gracious end in view:

> "Oh, yet we trust that *somehow* good
> Will be the final goal of ill."

We will now endeavor to show that such is the goal of ill, though our theory leads us to a different conclusion from that which Tennyson would fain arrive at in his exquisite "In Memoriam."

We must ever keep in mind *the great object of punishment.* With a just ruler, this object is never pain inflicted in a spirit of hatred, or pain greater than the offense deserves. With a just ruler *retribution,* no doubt, is *an end;* but it is the *least end of punishment.* His great end is *prevention.* In the punishment of offenders, he always has more regard to the law keepers than to the law breakers. Protection to the former in their lawful callings; warning to them against the imitation of crime; these are the great ends aimed at by wise and just rulers in the punishment of actual crime. Regard to these will be the great ruling motive in the regulation of punishment. Regard to these will operate *most powerfully* on the treatment of the criminal. At one time it will demand a sternness in punishment all but productive of actual injustice to the individual punished. Regard for society may, in another aspect, mitigate to a most serious extent the punishment justly due to his crime. But regard to society, in all its branches and all its interests, is the grand aim in all wise human legislation on crime; and that legislator has shown the highest wisdom who, while never transgressing the limits of justice, has so arranged his penal code that it has had the greatest possible effect in protecting the law—respecting community in their minutest rights, and providing that they shall never degenerate into the condition of the law-breaking classes. All severity, short of injustice, is not only wise, but is *most merciful*, that has this effect.

Now it is in this light that we are to view future punishment, together with that long permission of evil, with all its attendant circumstances—its glitter, its pleasures, its supposed advantages, its delusiveness, its pains, which we have seen in the history of our own race; and which will doubtless in all their real bearing remain an eternal record in the annals of God's great world. To say that what we call the fall of angels was the first appearance of moral evil is to say what cannot with certainty be affirmed. All we can say with certainty is that it was the beginning of that outburst of moral evil with which we are connected, and in which, as regards us, the redemption of Christ has interposed. Our opinion is that the outburst of evil which began with the angelic fall, and spread on to the fall of man, is positively the first appearance of moral evil in the universe of God. But we cannot here dogmatize. What we are much more strongly persuaded of is that, if not the first, it will be the last. We know from Scripture that this outburst of evil will be obliterated and become extinct. We think we see, with almost equal certainty, that evil will break out no more.

But God, in dealing with the higher order of His creatures, is not dealing with lifeless matter, not with living things walking by a law of necessity, but with living creatures walking under the high and elevating, but also *most perilous condition of a free will.* No doubt there are difficulties connected with this question of free will; but men of the most opposite views elsewhere concur in admitting that it is the ordinance of God in His creation of the higher creatures, and that through it there is among them a possibility of the entrance of moral evil.* Free to choose the good, and to rise on the wings of goodness to God its source, and to enjoy the

* Irenaeus, b. iv. c. xxxvii.; Tertullian, *Against Marcion*, b. ii. c. v. vi.; Stillingfleet, Or. Sac. iii. iii., xiv.; R. Baxter, *God's Purpose in Judgment*, 64; R. W. Landis, *Immortality of the Soul*, 446.

immortality of God. *As free,* to choose the evil, and to sink beneath its weight to depths of utter darkness. Nor is this an imaginary evil, a theoretical possibility, to be discussed as a school problem, but never to be met with in reality. Angels, we know not how many, but we know that they are many, who once walked in holiness, used their free will to range themselves in opposition to God. Man, a weaker and a lower creature, yet inexperienced and unsuspecting, also uses his free will to depart from God. And so, in these various ways, in these various shades of original guilt, sin entered into God's universe, and produced evil effects, of which we know something from what we daily hear and see, but whose full consequences are only known to God.

But this is not all. There is the very same possibility and danger of further fall that there ever was. It may be that the angelic world of a past creation are so fortified and strengthened by what they have already seen of the evil of sin that with them there is no moral possibility of further fall. But we have no reason for supposing that among the spheres are no creatures such as we. Nor have we the smallest reason for supposing that God has come to the limit of His creative energy and will. He is not the inactive God of an Epicurean philosophy, reposing in dreary self-satisfied contemplation. He is a God who delights to be at work; and the spirit He breathes into all is a love of work (John 5:17). Look at the earth; it affords innumerable evidences of His busy hand and brain. Look at the stars; doubtless they show the same ceaseless energy of God. But we know that He is not content with the creation only of the lower organizations. He delights to form creatures that know with a conscious love their Maker, and in this knowledge rise higher and higher, nearer and yet more near to their Source. Who can say, with any faint shadow of probability, that God will close His creation with man? Even while we write, or while we read, there may be reproducing in some distant planet, whose geological changes have come to their required perfection, the facsimile of the scene in Eden six thousand years ago. Nor can we say that it may not be ours as the ages of our blessed future roll on—our own days of marrying and giving in marriage existing only in the memory—to see what angels once saw here, a figure of noble front and faultless form rising from the earth in the majesty of perfect manhood, and God placing in his thrilling grasp the hand of woman, as lovely in face as she is innocent in mind, and saying in words that should cover with shame all who derogate from God's holy ordinance of marriage, "Increase, and, multiply, and replenish the world I have given you."

But these races are made under free will. It may be that some of them in their beginning are no higher than we were in ours. Eve does not seem to have been before the fall much wiser than she was after it. A woman without guile, without suspicion, loving, curious, credulous. Do you reject the picture? It is not ours: it is what we see on the canvas of Scripture. Adam was apparently in much resembling many of his sons. Irenaeus calls him in the hour of his creation "as yet an infant." Ardent, hasty, impetuous, at a beautiful woman's solicitation, he threw away, with open eyes, duty and loyalty: without her he will not live; with her he will die. And what were the consequences? We read them—outside Eden, in the deluge, at Sodom, in Potiphar's house, in the wars of Canaan, on the hill of Calvary, at the siege of Jerusalem, in the shouts of the Goths and Vandals, in the Crusader's wars, in the massacre of Bartholomew, in the snows of Russia, in the glittering scenes of heartless vanity, in the morbid passions and stunted affections of conventual imprisonment, in the gambling tables of Baden, in the lust markets of Paris and of London. We read them in our world's history of crime, and sin, and sorrow, and death.

Now the divine code of punishment—from the expulsion from Eden and the growth of the thistle down to the closing punishment of hell—has regard to the various, complicated, and universal interests of the higher creation, wherever it may now or will hereafter exist. It is not solely, we say it is not chiefly, for those to whom it will be said, "Depart into everlasting fire." We are by no means prepared to say that if fallen man, aye! and even fallen angels, had alone been in question, their treatment by God might not have been widely different. Had they alone been in question, we dare not confine the efforts for their recovery to those which have actually been made. Christ might in that case have taken hold of angels, instead of putting forth redemption only for the sons of Abraham. Man's day of grace might not in that case have been confined to his life here from the cradle to the grave, but grace might have followed him on from age to age, and world to world, before it ceased to strive to win back those who had once offered to God the pure incense of a creature's praise, who had once felt the ennobling emotion of the heart's love and worship of God.

So it has not been. Angels fell. No saving hand was stretched from the throne to raise them up; no Son of God went forth to war for them. Man fell. The Son rose up from the place of honor, and said to His Father, "Here am I, send Me;" and He laid aside His majesty, and He emptied Himself, and He became a man, and for humanity He bore shame, and rejection, and the death upon the cross. "Not in vain" sounds forth the voice of grateful love, which has been growing and swelling from the small voice outside the gates of Eden, to the voice of many waters within the gates of the New Jerusalem. But, how many left behind! How many voices silent! How many pulsations of life stilled for evermore!

Our thoughts revert to Wellington as he saw the army of Spain crossing the Bidassoa after the retreating armies of France. By him went the flowing plumes, by him rolled the heavy guns, by him marched with dauntless breast the matchless infantry of Britain; in nobler array, in denser bands than had marched under their leader's eye at the great soldier's opening victory at Vimiera. But, *few of those first soldiers are crossing into France under Wellington's eye.* At various intervals they are left behind. On the first battle-field of the Peninsula, on the heights of

Busaco, in the bloody struggle of Fuentes de Onoro, by the towers of Salamanca, on the breach of St. Sebastian, at Vittoria beneath the shadow of the Pyrenees, along the whole line of the victorious march, lie the bones of those who never gazed on French ground from the slopes of the mountains, or saw the spray of the waves as they broke in foam on the bar of the Bidassoa. So it will be in the great muster-roll of heaven. Many are called, few are chosen to eternal life.

Now, what we say is this. Doubtless with a merciful view to others—to others, perhaps, as far exceeding the number of the lost as the sands of all old ocean's shores exceed those of its smallest strand—has the punishment of those consigned at the judgment to hell been decreed. In that of angels will be seen the *danger of one irrevocable step,* where no hand was put forth to save; where, perhaps, no wish was ever felt to return. As regards men, some in all ages, even the darkest, were saved from the effects of a step which, in their case, was not irrevocable; but how various the degrees of guilt and opportunity among others, all of whom yet endured one irrevocable sentence! To some, Christ was preached with all the circumstances that could win back the heart, with all the earnestness that could secure the love. No response came from that willful heart; it closed up all the avenues that could lead to repentance, and went on resolutely to perdition. "But," it might be suggested, "at least there will be such an effort made; we shall not, if we fall, find ourselves ushered into a doom of which we know little beyond what some faint indistinct fears and misgivings may darkly insinuate." Yet even such, God's dealings with our race show us, may be the case. For ages, He left the generations of the world *to themselves.* A glimmering tradition, a darkened conscience—nature's indications of a Great Being in whom love, and justice, and judgment, and power, had each a place—these were all myriads had to guide them to the brink of that last step which each one must take, for himself and by himself, into the dark world beyond. We do not affirm or believe of the heathen that all are lost; but we do know from Scripture that *as a rule* their future is without hope. Light sufficient to condemn where it did not save; light so little as to reduce their guilt to its minimum, but not to make them guiltless; and yet, with this small amount of light and of guilt, they endure the second and endless death. And who dare say, with Christ's words in his ears, that none of these lost ones would have heard and hailed to life eternal the words of Christ's gospel if they had been addressed to them by Him who spoke on the shores of Gennesaret and in the synagogues of Galilee? From Sodom and Gomorrah, from Tyre and Sidon, He tells us, souls would have sprang forth to the living call which was heard and unheeded by the callous hearts of Chorazin and Capernaum (Matt. 11:21). But no such call was heard amid the vice of Sodom: no such call mingled with the din of the mariners of Tyre, or with the beating of its waves. They sinned without law, and they perish without law: for them it will be more tolerable than for others when they rise up to judgment; but they will not for all that escape its endless sentence.

We acknowledge that there is *severity* in this. Augustine's sentence against such is one of the blackest tyranny and injustice. Even in the scriptural sentence of death, there is *severity.* God tells us that He sometimes acts with severity (Rom. 11:22). If He had not told us so in His Word we should have known it from His other great Book of Nature, whose pages have been open to all eyes, and in which lessons of severity are read as it enters each age's records on its tablet of stone. Severity in the future world, if it be not unjust, is no argument against any religious theory. If anyone will say it is, he must take his stand *on atheistic ground.* And poor, after all, is the assurance which atheism can afford! Impotent to promise good, it is equally impotent to avert evil. To tell us that we are the children of blind, unreasoning, unfeeling, unhealing *chance,* is no gospel. The blind power that flung us, without consent from us, on the bleak shores of this world's ocean, may fling us on bleaker shores in more inhospitable climes. If we live here without a God we may live elsewhere without one. Atheism cannot guard us from life, from misery, from evil. If here on earth are, as no doubt there are, places which may almost vie with any pictures of a future hell in their guilt, their misery, and their despair, will the Atheist tell us that such may not exist in the hereafter as well? Even for him, it is better to come back to a belief in God. But with the *Theist* we will allow of no argument against a theory which has in it the element of severity. Let him first eliminate severity from his Book of God, his inspired record, his infallible interpreter of Divine secrets—the roll of Nature through her mighty annals—before we will hear one word of complaint from *him,* that in the Christian man's book of God there is the record of severity past or to come.

And may we not even here see mercy beaming forth? In all judgment, we believe that God remembers mercy; and that mercy is kept full in mind in the judgment of fallen angels and reprobate men of every shade of guilt. God's higher orders of creation have all to walk along the perilous course of free will in order to attain each the end of their being. There are rocks, shoals, quicksands, in their way. Each rock has witnessed the wreck of some gallant ship; each shoal is strewn with fragments: each quicksand has swallowed up brave beating hearts. But straightway has risen up the beacon on the headland, the lighthouse on the reef, the deep-toned bell floating over the sands and sending its solemn warning across the treacherous waves; and fleets traverse in safety where now one and now another noble vessel had been dashed in pieces and gone down. We feel satisfied that we are not drawing on imagination for what we say. We know that in the path which race after race has to tread there is danger of falling. We know that called to go up higher, even to the top of God's mount, they may fall headlong. We are satisfied that in the Divine jurisprudence the welfare of the greatest number is its paramount consideration.

We see the important bearing of future punishment, as it is revealed in Scripture, on this widely stretching interest of unbounded space, of eternal duration. We see how every shade of severity tells on some vast destiny of the future, from the severity which punishes where the hands had been vainly stretched out all the day long, and the pleading voice had been mocked at, to the severity which punishes where no clear voice had ever spoken, and where, if such a voice had spoken, it would have been heard. To none, no, not the least guilty, is wrong done, when God withdraws from the dim child of savage nature, or the as dim child of the dark circles which lies within the surrounding of our most vaunted civilization, the life He withdraws from the angel above Him, as from the beast scarce below Him. But to numbers without number may this act, to us bordering upon injustice, but never entering one hair's breadth within its domain, be an act of supreme mercy, love, and wisdom; for, surely, that conduct of God is most wise, most loving, most merciful, which, through a severity which the lost have ceased to feel, has made to countless others the ennobling path of free will to be as safe as to the lower creatures is their ignoble path of necessity.

Milton, in his *Paradise Lost*, relates what he supposes may have passed in conversation between angels and our first parents before the fall. The mind of our great poet was traversing here the very line of thought which we have been endeavoring to pursue. He contemplated man, without experience, yet of necessity placed in the post of danger. Eden had its joys, its peace, its progress: *it must have its peril.* Among the trees yielding fruit, whose seed was in "themselves," which the earth brought forth, there were two trees of a peculiar kind. They grew together, side by side, in the midst of the garden. By the "tree of life," the emblem and pledge of safety, grew the "tree of knowledge of good and evil," the sign of a possible ruin. We know that this must be so; since man was made higher than the brutes, only a little lower than the angels. That tree of life, conferring God's immortality, could not be hung with its precious fruit unless the deadly fruit of its neighbor tree hung close by. It is only saying that Eden was to man the land of free will, and therefore of a possible immortality and of as possible a death. Under such circumstances, Milton brings before us Raphael relating to Adam the angelic fall.[*] It was the angelic architect building up before the sailor's eye the beacon on the rock. It was the ministering spirit telling one child of free will of the pitfall into which another and yet brighter child had fallen. It was without avail. As one race fell, so fell another: and down from that day to this, and from this day to the closing scene of earth's history, it has been seen, and will be seen, that the pathway of the higher creation is beset with danger. In life restored through Christ; in death incurred without Christ; this history of evil, in which the angelic and the human race are so blended and mixed up together, is concluded.

It may be part of our office in the coming age to point the moral of the marvelous parable to ears that will hear it with more benefit than Adam listened to the tale brought from heaven by Raphael. We can then follow out to its close what the angel could only begin. We can then intertwine with the history of the higher race the fortunes of the lower, and carry on both to their common termination. We can tell of a race that in its fall had no redemption. We can tell of a redemption that visited another fallen race, of its miracles of grace and its final victory; but also of its utter failure to save in unnumbered instances. We can tell them that not only obstinate guilt has its danger, but negligence also, inexperience, ignorance, descending as an inheritance from generation to generation, and all this is told to races rejoicing in the first flush of that life which beats tumultuously in the new created. If the sinner's rain is their safety, and his destruction their safeguard against loss, then even the sinner's ruin was not in vain:

[*] *Paradise Lost*, b. v.

even his devious footsteps have not been aimless: and we can find a great and precious truth in a Scripture at which we are sometimes inclined to stumble, that "The Lord hath made all things for Himself; yea, even the wicked, for the day of evil." The great stumbling-block, the existence of evil, will be a stumbling-block no more. Evil is seen to exist, not with Augustine to be perpetuated forever; but to be, under the providence of the Great Sovereign and loving Father, *its own eternal destruction.*

And this conclusion of the matter will exhibit to us the limits of that free will into whose bounds we have ventured with hesitating step to enter. We do not think we have done so without a guide more trustworthy than led Virgil through the realms of the shades or guided Dante through the regions of the lost and the saved. *The free creature can defeat divine goodness for itself, but no further.* His own good he may refuse, his own evil he may choose; and yet there may be designs in the great scheme of Divine Providence which in so doing he has unconsciously or unwillingly worked out. Such we know to be the case here. God maketh the "wrath of man," his sin, its end, "to praise Him."

The sinner has, no doubt, defeated God's goodness for himself—thrust back the proffered hand that was full of blessing—like the sullen child retired into the darkness from the cheerful room where the fire blazed brightly, and brothers and sisters played and laughed; but he saw not a good glorious end which God brought about by this very conduct. Other worlds hear of us. Earth's drama—its gladness and its sadness, its sin and its holiness, its life and its death, its redemption embraced and rejected—is not an unconnected episode of a great poem, but is a mighty transaction of time, in which all worlds and all beings take a share—God, and angels, and men; and which is to bear with a mighty bearing upon the ages of the future. So it is represented in Scripture. The puny skeptic, blear-eyed and short-sighted, may sneer at the thought of the trouble which our world is said to have occasioned in the councils of heaven. Not so they who stand near the throne.

Angels desire to look into these things: the conversion of a sinner is joy throughout their ranks. Here, in this remotest sphere, things are doing and will be done which will tell on intelligences whose names and abodes will never reach our knowledge here. That fall of angels and men which free will made possible—that death among angels and men which the power of choice effected—may, working only by moral means, make in the glorious realms of freedom another fall and another death *morally impossible.* The loss of life to some, possible from their place in creation, just in the dealings of God's jurisprudence, may be pure unmitigated mercy to the greater number. The permission of evil—of evil leading to one sad result in death—may issue in another result, *the eternal and undisturbed establishment of good.*

11

Examination of Particular Texts

IN OUR SURVEY OF SCRIPTURE heretofore, we were unable to give to some individual texts that attention which from their prominent place in this controversy they deserve. We now proceed to do so. The texts we refer to are texts which are most commonly and most boldly advanced by Augustinian theorists in proof of their view. We think a fair and candid examination of them will show that instead of supporting they condemn their view.

We will first consider Mark 9:44. Speaking here of hell, and of those who will be consigned to hell, our Lord most solemnly, and with threefold repetition, pronounces their doom—"Their worm dieth not, and the fire is not quenched." It is on this text that Augustine, in his "City of God," mainly relies for his view,* and this is perhaps the text of all others which is most boldly put forward as establishing it. Instead of supporting, however, it contradicts it plainly. This solemn declaration of Christ is not an original saying of His, but is quoted *word for word* from Isaiah 66:24. We will give it *with its context.* Speaking of the redeemed of the earth, Isaiah says, "They shall go forth, and look upon the *carcasses* of the men

---

* *City of God*, xxi. 9.

that have transgressed against Me; for *their worm* shall not die, neither shall *their fire* be quenched; and they shall be an abhorring unto all flesh." A moment's glance shows us that both the worm and the fire are alike external to and distinct from the subject on which they prey; and also that what both prey upon are *not the living but the dead.* "The allusion," says Bengel, "is to *dead bodies* which are the food of the worm and the funeral pile." Isaiah frequently uses the image of "the worm;" but it is always in connection with *death.* What he means in 51:8, "The moth shall eat them up like a garment, and the worm shall eat them like wool," is what he means when he speaks in 66:24, of the fire and the worm consuming the carcasses. This fearful image conveys the idea, not of life, but of its opposite—death, and of hell, as the cleanser of God's world by the utter and eternal destruction of the wicked. These most solemn words of the prophet, so solemnly endorsed by Christ, assert a state of eternal death and destruction, not one of eternal life in hell, as the destiny of transgressors in the world to come. They are fatal alike to the theories of Augustine and Origen.

Next is Isaiah 33:14. "Who among us shall dwell with the devouring fire? Who among us shall dwell with everlasting burnings?" This is very often brought forward in proof of the eternity of future misery. Many have doubted whether this refers to future punishment at all. For our part we are satisfied to suppose that it does. If it does, it affords very valuable proof that the eternity which it affirms of future punishment does not refer to any eternity of life in misery; but to the *eternal extinction of life,* the *irrevocable loss* which the wicked will bring upon themselves. This is seen from the context of the passage. They who are spoken of in the 14th verse are the people of the 12th verse, who "*shall be as the burning of lime: as thorns cut up shall they be burned in the fire.*" The "everlasting burnings," then, are burnings *whose effects are endured throughout eternity. They have cut off a life which shall never be restored again.* They are God's solemn warnings, repeated throughout Scripture, that Origen's theory of a restoration at some future period from hell is a false and delusive dream.

Poole's comment on this passage *ought* to be a very instructive one. It shows us, on the testimony of an opponent, that the interpretation we put on such phrases as "everlasting burnings," "unquenchable fire," and so on as signifying a destruction and death from which there is no recovery, is readily accepted *by Augustinian theorists as a proper and natural interpretation.* Poole thus paraphrases this verse: "How shall we be able to abide the presence, and endure, or avoid the wrath of that God who is a consuming fire; *who is now about to destroy us utterly by the Assyrians,* and will afterwards burn us with unquenchable fire." Here Poole supposes the "everlasting burnings" of the verse to mean both the destruction inflicted by the Assyrians in this life, and that which God will inflict on sinners hereafter; or, in other words, he tells us that "everlasting burnings" *need not* suppose everlasting life in misery; but that they find a suitable sense in the utter cutting off from life which man inflicts upon his fellow man here. We are not, therefore, even in the judgment of own opponents, putting any forced or unnatural meaning upon Scripture, when we put *this very sense* upon such phrases wherever we find them: Poole puts upon them *two senses,* one of which is as different from the other as it is possible to be.

We now come to the famous passages in the book of Revelation. Driven hopelessly from the plainer parts of Scripture, the advocates of eternal life and misery in hell think that they have in this mysterious and highly-wrought figurative book at least two passages which authorize them to change numberless passages in the rest of Scripture, and some even in the book of Revelation itself, from their plain and obvious meaning to one that is forced, unnatural, and often false to all the laws of the interpretation of language. We would suppose that the natural way would be to interpret by the already-gathered sense of the great body of the earlier Scriptures one or two difficult and figurative passages in this, probably, the last-written of the books of Scripture. But this is not the way with our opponents. They take a text or two in the very end of the Bible, and by them interpret a thousand passages written long before. No matter what may be the apparent meaning of these earlier and far more numerous passages, they must all be made to square with the text from Revelation! The first written, the more numerous, and the plainer Scriptures, must be interpreted by one or two last-written and figurative passages! Unless this extraordinary canon of interpretation is rigidly enforced, the Augustinian hell must be abandoned as a myth.

The passages in question are these. Of the worshippers of the beast, we are told in the former of them, that, "They shall be tormented with fire and brimstone in the presence of the holy angels, and in the presence of the Lamb: *and the smoke of their torment ascendeth up for ever and ever*: and they have no rest day nor night:" in the latter passage we are told that, "The devil that deceived them was cast into the lake of fire and brimstone, where the beast and the false prophet are, *and shall be tormented day and night for ever and ever.*"

We will not dwell upon the fact that it is a very disputed question even among Augustinian theorists, whether the former of these passages *refers at all to future punishment.* Elliott has no hesitation in referring Revelation 14:10-11, together with the kindred passage in Revelation 19:3, *to a temporal judgment,* that is, the swallowing up by volcanic fire of the territory of Rome in Italy.* We only refer to this to show our readers how readily Augustinian theorists admit that our interpretation of such passages is a natural and proper one. We are not insisting that Elliott is correct, or otherwise, in his application. We will here take the passages in their usual application, as indicating God's judgments hereafter upon fallen spirits and wicked men. For our part we are persuaded of the perfect

* Horæ. *Apoc.* iv. 212; iii. 443; iv. 5.

propriety of applying the very same terms to judgments inflicted in this world and the next, because those judgments are essentially the same in their character. All through the sacred writings judgments here and hereafter are described by the same expressions (Luke 13:3; 1 Cor. 10:9-11). It is for those who suppose these judgments to be essentially different in character to explain how they are properly represented by identity of phrase.

The sense we would put upon the passages in Revelation is, that they convey in highly-wrought figures suitable to the character of the entire book, only the old idea which we have already gathered from the rest of Scripture, namely, that the punishment of all consigned to hell will be of an eternal nature, and that its fearful effect—the plunging of its subjects into death and destruction—will ever remain visible to the redeemed and angelic worlds. We will not try to establish this sense by examining the force of each word. We deny that language so highly figurative is *capable* of any such dialectical analysis, *or that such is the manner in which we ordinarily interpret language of the kind.* We will rather turn to *similar language elsewhere* and show that the interpretation put upon it even by our opponents both justifies and demands the interpretation we put on the passage from Revelation.

We will first turn to a passage in Isaiah from which there can be little doubt that the imagery of Revelation is borrowed. Dean Alford calls it its "fountain head."* Isaiah is describing the judgments brought by God upon the land of Idumea. He says: "*The land thereof shall become burning pitch: it shall not be quenched day nor night; the smoke thereof shall go up forever.*" Here, as in Revelation, we have the smoke of God's judgments described as going *up forever.* But will the advocates of Augustine's hell tell us that if we went to Idumea we should see people who had been suffering pain from

* Alford, on Revelation 14:11.

some period subsequent to Isaiah's prophecy to the present time? The poetical figure of a perpetual furnace of burning pitch and ever-ascending smoke conveys the idea of perpetual desolations, but not at all of endless life in pain. The present condition of Edom is the explanation of the poetic figure: its cities have fallen into ruin: the whole land is a desert.[*] Here is Poole's comment on the text: "*It shall be irrecoverably ruined, and shall remain as a spectacle of God's vengeance to all succeeding ages.*" The "burning pitch," the "unquenchable fire," the "smoke ascending forever," *is reduced to this sober hue in the language of prose.* As Poole, the Augustinian, interprets Isaiah, so do we interpret those passages in Revelation which are borrowed from Isaiah. We interpret Scripture by its own analogy.

We next turn to Jude, verse 7: "*Even as Sodom and Gomorrah,* and the cities about them in like manner, giving themselves over to fornication, and going after strange flesh, *are set forth for an example, suffering the vengeance of eternal fire.*" Here is another passage of Scripture, of equally strong language and very similar terms to those found in Revelation. In what does the suffering of the Sodomites here spoken of consist? It certainly does not in the first place refer to anything they suffer, or may be supposed to suffer, in *Hades;* for the condition of the Sodomites in *Hades* is never alluded to in Scripture, and is therefore no warning example set before man to learn from. It does not, in the second place, refer to any suffering of theirs in *hell;* for hell is to them, as to all sinners, *a future thing;* whereas what the text speaks of is something which they were suffering when Jude wrote, and had suffered before he wrote, and which had long been a plain and palpable warning to the ungodly of this earth. Not referring to these, it is very evident what it does refer to. It means that punishment, open to human sight, which began when the fire from heaven

[*] Smith's Dictionary, art. "Edom."

descended on the guilty cities, and which has remained in force through all the succeeding generations down to our own time, and will continue while the earth remains. *It is their overthrow in the days of Lot, and their abiding condition ever since,* which are here placed before the ungodly as an example of what hereafter awaits them if they imitate Sodom. This view is not first presented by Jude. It is frequently met with in the older Scriptures, and we are therefore guided *by Scripture itself* in putting this interpretation upon it (Isa. 1:9; 13:19; Jer. 49:18; 50:40; 2 Pet. 2:6). Many indeed of the ablest of our opponents, led by the natural force of the passage, and apparently unaware of the force of their own admission, put on it the same interpretation that we do. They say that the fire which consumed Sodom and Gomorrah was an *eternal one, "because it was eternal in its effects."* Neither of the two cities ever was, nor ever will be, built.* We could only wish that they who give so just an interpretation of the "eternal fire" of Sodom would give the same explanation of the eternal fire of hell. Let both be eternal, as being "eternal in their effects."

What then, has been and is the state of Sodom? In the days of Abraham, four rich and populous cities flourished in the plain of Jordan. On a sudden, fire descended from heaven, and, after a period of terror, regrets, and pain, the inhabitants were deprived of life. They and their works were burnt up; and this ruined, lifeless, hopeless condition has remained to the present time. "The smell of the fire is still over the land," says Tertullian. The whole transaction conveys the idea of conscious pain for a time, followed by nun and death forever. This is, according to Scripture, to "*suffer the vengeance of eternal fire.*"

We have then as our first use of the passage of Jude a *scriptural* guide to the interpretation of all similar language, and in especial of those passages in Revelation which we have been considering. "The smoke of

---

* J. Grant, *Religious Tendencies*, i. 270.

torment ascending up forever," and the being "tormented forever," applied to the subjects of future punishment, are phrases not more indicative of endless life and pain in hell than is the phrase "suffering the vengeance of eternal fire," applied to the punishment of the Sodomites, indicative of their having lived in pain from Abraham's day to ours. Even that word "to torment," βασανίζω, on which so much stress is laid, does not carry out the requirements of our opponents. It is as applicable to things without life as to living things. It is the same Greek verb which describes the "tossing" of the boat in Matthew 14:24; and the "torment" of the lost in Revelation. It is used, according to Schleusner, not only for actual pain inflicted, but *for death produced by such pain.* In this sense it is peculiarly applicable to future punishment, and carries out the idea, common to the kindred passages we have considered, of pain severe and terrible for a time followed by the destruction of life.

But this passage from Jude serves another purpose of equal value in this controversy. It lays down the great principle that the *judgments of God upon individuals or nations, in destroying them here for sin, is the pattern and example of that destruction which He will inflict on them hereafter for sin.* If we had indeed but this one passage, we might perhaps hesitate to draw so important a conclusion from it; but it is the teaching of many other Scriptures. It is our Lord's teaching where, speaking of the Galileans, whose blood Pilate mingled with their sacrifices, and of the eighteen upon whom the tower in Siloam fell and slew them, he adds the warning: "Unless ye repent, ye shall all *likewise perish,*" *i.e.*, perish in the same way. And St. Paul enters largely into the history of the sins of and judgments upon Israel in the wilderness, in order to tell us that *those very things which happened to them are examples of what will happen to us hereafter* if we imitate them in transgression (Luke 13:1-5; 1 Cor. 10:8-11). And this accounts for a large portion of Scripture which would otherwise be unintelligible, but which on this principle is intelligible and plain; namely, the inextricable blending together of judgments, some of which appear to refer to this life and some to the next, while all are spoken of in similar language. On our theory, this is quite natural and explicable. The slaying of the Galileans by Pilate essentially resembles the death of the wicked in hell. So does the falling of the three and twenty thousand in the wilderness, and the destruction of others by the bite of the serpent, resemble the destruction of the sinner hereafter. The *circumstances* of the future doom will of course vary from those "examples," just as they vary from one another; but in all its issues it will be identical, specifically, the destruction of life. How these are "examples" of the doom of sinners on the Augustinian hypothesis we leave it to Augustinian advocates to settle. How the loss of existence resembles endless existence, and falling resembles never falling, and being destroyed resembles never being destroyed, is for our opponents to justify on some peculiar theory of Augustinian interpretation which would enable us to put on every word of Scripture the exactly opposite sense to that which it bore in ordinary language.

Before concluding this chapter, it will be well to say a few words on the term "unquenchable fire," so often applied to the fire of hell. It is a most significant phrase, and deserves attention; but it does not signify what the Augustinian theorist imposes upon it as its meaning. It signifies the very reverse. It is a word in common use now, and was a word in common use both in Scripture and profane writings. If the reader will look into a dictionary he will find that an unquenchable fire is a fire which cannot be extinguished until it has consumed all on which it preyed and it then goes out of itself for want of fuel. The classical scholar will remember the famous passage of Homer where the Trojans hurl "unquenchable fire" upon the Grecian ships. Eusebius calls the fire which had been kindled around a martyr's body and burned on till it consumed him to ashes an "unquenchable fire." *Unquenchable fires* constantly break out among us; but none of them go on burning forever.

Their simple meaning is that they do not go out and cannot be put out till they have thoroughly done their work of destruction. It is in this very way that the term is constantly used in Scripture itself. When God in one place declares that His anger would be poured out upon man and upon beast, and upon the fruit of the ground, and "shall burn, and *shall not be quenched,*" and in another that He will "kindle a fire in the gates of Jerusalem, and it *shall not be quenched,*" He means that His wrath was to continue till man and beast were destroyed, and the fire was to continue till the gates of Jerusalem were consumed.* Then wrath ceased, because it had fully spent its force; and the fire went out, because it had eaten up all on which it could prey. So we are to understand that "unquenchable fire" which is the terrible fate of the lost. *Their fire is never quenched.* It preys upon them with ruthless force. No cries on the part of the damned arrest it: no prayers ascend from the redeemed for the sin which they know to be unto eternal death. No feelings of pity on God's part interfere to check its course. It burns on, consuming, preying, reducing, until it has consumed and burnt all. When it has spent its force, it dies out for want of food, leaving behind it the endless sign of the destruction which it has brought on fallen archangel, and angel, and man. *This is the second death.* But we can bear to look upon it *because it is death.* We are not looking upon a picture which would overturn reason and banish peace from all who beheld it. Life has left the realms of the lost. The reprobate felt, but do not continue to feel, the consuming flames. These prey upon the dead until dust and ashes cover the floor of the furnace of hell (Mal. 4:3).

In Origen's view of the future, a view far more widely spread than many suspect, we see the real cause of the emphatic, repeated, awful declarations of the *eternity* of future punishment. That view, so pleasing to

---

* Homer, *Illiad.* xvi. 123, 194; i. 599; Eusebius, *Eccles. History*, vi. 41; *Scripture Revelations of a Future State*, 7th ed., 234; Jeremiah 7:20; 17:27; Ezekiel 20:47-48; Eccleus. 28:23.

human nature, so cherished in the sinful heart, was the view against which the Spirit of God laid down in Scripture the warnings of an everlasting destruction and an unquenchable fire. Even in the face of these Scriptures, men are found who dare to teach that there will be a restoration from hell. Far more than Augustine's theory does the view here advocated root out this false delusive hope. So long as men believe that life is not extinguished in hell, so long they will nourish hope. Milton pictures such a hope as visiting in hell the hearts even of the fallen angels—

> *"Suppose God should relent,*
> *And publish grace to all!"*

Impossible indeed it is to shut out such thoughts from the mind on the theory of the immortality of the lost men will cherish the idea that somewhere down through the ages, when the groans of hell have been beating sadly, ceaselessly, at the gates of heaven, the message of mercy and deliverance may be sent down, even as He used to send it of old to Israel, groaning beneath the bondage of Egypt, Philistia, and Canaan. "*We are the clay, and Thou our potter; and we are all the work of Thy hand,*" would—men *will think* when they think what God is—rise up from hell to the throne a plea of power some time in that eternal age during all of which life must last. Death extirpates all such hopes. "Corruption has a hope of a kind of removal, *but death has everlasting ruin.*"*

---

* Apostolical Fathers, Pastor of Hermas, Tim. vi., c. ii.

12

Distinctions in Future Punishment

WHILE WE SEE ONE UNIVERSAL result, death, to arise from future punishment, we are also told in Scripture of varying circumstances attendant on it, which are necessary to be considered, in order to enable us to form an adequate conception of its nature and variety.

Hell is not to all a sudden cessation of existence. There is life in that fearful prison, though it does not continue forever. This is shown by those numerous texts which speak of weeping and wailing, of regrets and anguish, on the part of the damned. As here, life goes before death, and as here, regrets and pains precede and produce death; so we find it to be, on the part of many, at least, in the scene of future doom. The children of the kingdom, cast into its outer darkness, gnash their teeth when they think of those who have come from east and west, and enjoy what they have lost.

The unworthy guest at the marriage feast of Christ is in despair that he is not suffered to continue there. The despisers of the offers of redemption, be they Jews or Gentiles, behold their astounding folly, and marvel at its greatness. The unfaithful servant has time to bewail his want of fidelity, and the hypocrite to see that the part he has chosen is a bitter and a hard one, ere all—sooner or later—sink into that state where wonder and remorse and pain and shame are lulled in the unconscious sleep of the second death (Matt. 8:12; 22:13; 24:51; Luke 13:48; Acts 13:41).

And here we must remark that all the warnings of "weeping and gnashing of teeth" are addressed *to the rejecters of proffered grace.* Not one of them is addressed to such as the men of Sodom and Gomorrah, Nineveh and Babylon were in old times; to such as the men of Cabul and Bokhara, Teheran and Timbuktu are at the present day. The same holds good, we believe, of every especial warning found in Scripture.

Now it is doubtless in these circumstances that we find room for that great distinction in guilt and consequent punishment which Scripture repeatedly insists on. Its cities of Chorazin and Bethsaida; its children of the kingdom; its refusers of an apostle's message; its hypocrites trading on a false profession; its men aware of their Master's will; are held up as exceeding in guilt the ignorant offender, the undesigning sinner, the rejecter of an unauthenticated messenger, the uncovenanted transgressor, the men of Tyre and Sidon (Matt. 8:12; 10:15; 11:22; Luke 12:48; 20:47; John 9:41). For the former are the many stripes: for the latter the few. Our theory affords ample room for that great distinction in punishment which God will hereafter make.

The circumstances of the first death show us plainly how this can be. This world is a world of death. All here are doomed to die, and all suffer death. In this there is no distinction. But in the circumstances of dying there is infinite variety. One man lives close upon a thousand years before he yields to death: to another the first breath he breathes in the world is his last. Between Methusaleh and the infant of a moment's life lies every variety of duration. Again, one dies as though he were going to rest in deep; another is racked with pains, year after year, by day and by night, which make him curse the weary life that is so hardly parted from. Between these deaths lies every variety of comparative unconsciousness, uneasiness, weariness and anguish. A like distinction we are positively told will exist in the second death, and our theory affords for it perfect scope. To some, this death may be an instantaneous process, a momentary transition from one state to another, like the infant who opens his eyes on this world and then closes them forever. Here may be the amount of conscious pain for the myriads upon myriads of young and old, who, in heathen and even in Christian countries, from the inevitable moral darkness with which their circumstances had surrounded them, scarce knew wrong from right. To others, the process of the second death may be more or less lengthened, until we arrive at the case of the greatest human offenders, or that more aggravated one of the angels who fell from heaven and drew weaker men along with them in their fall. Without presuming to say that such must be, or will be, the *manner* of God's dealing, we yet see how by our theory such a result *may be* arrived at: how, while stripes many and sore fall on some, on others they may fall so few and so light as scarcely to be felt at all.

It has doubtless been remarked from several expressions of ours that we hold that the ultimate fate of devils will be the same as that of the reprobate. We have no doubt that such is the case, and all Scripture tends to that end. They share in that judgment which awaits the ungodly. The everlasting fire which consumes the wicked is that which has been prepared for the devil and his angels. They themselves look forward to their being destroyed in hell. The pains which they dread are those which the ungodly will endure, and which result in death. The final extinction of evil to which God has pledged Himself in His Word compels us to hold their destruction (2 Pet. 2:4; Jude 6; Matt. 25:41; Mark 1:24; Luke 4:34). Nor can one single reason be advanced why God should not do this. And we have thus in Scripture a far more satisfactory and reasonable view of the state of final retribution than is afforded us by popular theology or poetic imagination. Devils are not the tyrants of hell. Devils do not exercise there an endless power over the victims of their fraud. This were poor retributive justice on God's part. They are only punished in hell with a severity proportioned to their guilt. With fearful reason they look forward to it, not as a scene of fearful triumph, but of unmitigated woe. They see, in all probability, the world whom they had seduced from God—the greater part of it speedily, all of it at one time or other—reduced to the original unfeeling elements of their being, while their stronger nature retains that vigorous life which makes it but the more susceptible of pain. The last being that retains the misery of existence may be that arch-fiend, Satan, the leader in heaven's rebellion, the prime mover in earth's falling away. When the last race of man has long ceased to feel; when his fellow angels have, one by one, been reduced to the state of death; he may still survive, longing for the time when he too shall lay aside a life which is only one of pain.

The view here advocated derives powerful confirmation from its being in complete analogy with nature, *i.e.*, with God's ordinary working. While those who seek God find Him, and in finding Him find life, and through His gracious plan of redemption are advanced in place and glory, we also find, with regard to others, lives innumerable lost, and in the case of angels an entire race blotted out of life. God and nature are not here at strife.* We find in nature that death and destruction are God's usual agents in removing from their place things animate and inanimate as soon as they cease to discharge the part for which they were intended. Throughout the wide domain of nature the law of death is in ceaseless operation. Of fifty seeds but one may bear fruit. Of the lower animals, death after life is the universal law. Whole races of living things have long ceased to exist.

> "From scarpéd cliff and quarried stone,
> She cries, a thousand lives are gone."

* Tennyson, *In Memoriam*, liv.

In our view, God does but apply to higher races for their sin that which He has applied to lower races who knew no sin. The grand distinction between them and us is, that we may see and know God who is life and the source of all human life. If we turn from Him, we turn from life. We deny and renounce our real distinction, and are treated as that which we have made ourselves to become. *Mere life is not precious in God's sight.* If He scatters it with a prodigal hand, He withdraws it with a hand that is just as free. In the myriads of human beings reduced in hell to death, in the extinction of the fallen angels, we do but find a particular application of a great natural law. Lower creatures know not God, and fade away out of life. Higher intelligences knew Him, turned from Him, made themselves like beasts, and like beasts are treated. Hell will add its fossil remains to those of the quarries of the earth.

13

Theories of Punishment and Christian Missions

THE QUESTION OF FUTURE punishment cannot be considered at all adequately without giving marked attention to its influence on the question of missions to the heathen—the duty and the privilege of the Christian Church. The religious world is much indebted for having its attention drawn to this feature of the question by the Rev. Edward White, in a very able paper on "Missionary Theology."* We will endeavor to follow out the line of reflection which he has initiated.

It strikes us almost immediately that the natural influence of the general acceptance of the theory of Origen would be to put a total stop to missionary effort as needless and positively injurious to those whom it was meant to benefit. The guilt of the heathen for sins here committed we are taught in Scripture to be small, and their punishment to be proportionally light. There appears therefore to be little occasion to send the Gospel to them for the purpose of saving them from suffering hereafter. That, at the

* *The Rainbow*, July, 1869.

worst, will be light; while their rejection of the Gospel offers would expose them to many stripes.

Nor can it be said by the Universalist that the future and eternal bliss of a single one of the heathen depends in the remotest degree on his here hearing and accepting the Gospel of Christ. His immortality is, with the Universalist as with the Augustinian, already secure. He is one of a deathless race. His soul is immortal: his body will be raised incorruptible at the resurrection. If he has not in this life heard the Gospel of Christ he will hear it in the intermediate state. He will hear it then, apparently, under far more favorable circumstances than he could possibly hear it here. It will not be preached to him by men themselves stained by sin and full of imperfection, but by men from whom all the stains of sin shall have been purged away. There will not then be the thousand difficulties of one kind or other which here so effectually hinder the progress and the force of truth. In that coming age, of which the Universalist dreams, it is difficult to see how a single being could hesitate for a moment to embrace that Gospel of Christ which is to bring him from the realms of pain to the realms of joy. We see not any imaginable motive with the Universalist to send Christ's Gospel to the heathen, save only his Master's command, which to him comes enforced by no apparent reasons which make it urgent and pressing. We enquire whether Universalism has ever afforded a zealous missionary to heathen lands. If it has, we think he must be a man of different passions from those of other men. If Universalism had been the creed of Christ and His apostles, we do not believe that the command "Go, teach all nations," would either have been uttered or obeyed. The deadening, dispiriting influence of this theory on Christian missions is in itself enough to overthrow it.

The objection which lies in this respect against the theory of Origen, does not, we fully concede, lie against that of Augustine. The advocates of the latter have, no doubt, a great, powerful, overwhelming, motive to obey their Master's command and send the Gospel to the heathen. But their theory contains within itself an element fatal to its success. They offer the Gospel of salvation mixed up with a theory that necessitates and almost justifies its rejection. They present the God of justice, love, and mercy, in a light which makes Him appear devoid of every one of these qualities. And they themselves by their line of argument upon this question *virtually confess that they do so.*

For it will be remarked by those conversant with this controversy that whenever Augustinian advocates come forward with the smallest show of argument in defense of the *justice* of their theory of eternal agony, they sedulously confine their argument to the case of those who *have sinned against light and grace.* One would imagine from their writings that there were no men in the world who had not had the offers of mercy made to them over and over again, and pressed upon them with all the earnestness of love, as Christ Himself, with His heart of love and His words of earnestness, pressed it upon the men of his generation.

Bunyan, in his *Visions of Hell*, pictures the lamentations of a lost soul:

> "I know I cannot, must not die; but live a dying life, worse than ten thousand deaths; and yet I might once have helped all this, and would not. *O, that is the gnawing worm that never dies!* I might have once been happy; salvation once was offered me, and I refused it: had it been but once, yet to refuse it had been a folly not to be forgiven; *but it was offered me a thousand times, and yet* (wretch that I was) *I still as oft refused it.*"

And such is the general tone of Augustinian theorists. They speak, as the cause of endless misery, of sinners, amid God's wondrous long suffering and pleading with them, still persisting obstinately in rebellion.*

---

* Bunyan, *Visions of Hell*; Robert Baxter, *God's Purpose in Judgment*, 4.

These men ignore the vast majority of mankind. They forget that in the times before Christ revelation was confined to a petty race in a corner of Syria. They forget that in the times since Christ salvation has not been offered to or heard of by one in one hundred of mankind. Now there can be no doubt that *the end* of the ungodly, be they heathen, Jew, or Christian, is the very same. It is death, destruction, perishing. In the circumstances attendant on this there will be a marked distinction, but the end of all will be the same. If death then be, as many tell us, eternal misery, they represent eternal misery as inflicted upon countless myriads who never heard the Gospel of Christ, who never heard the very name of that God against whom they ignorantly sinned. With such a creed, how are they to present the God and Father of Jesus Christ to the heathen mind.

A Christian missionary proceeds to India to preach there the Gospel of Christ. It is the old story of Paul at Athens, disputing with Jews and devout persons and all coiners, be they philosophers or illiterate men. At Lucknow, or Delhi, or Benares, our modern missionary meets the Brahmin. He addresses him as Paul addressed the Epicureans and Stoics of Athens: "Whom ye ignorantly worship, Him declare I unto you."

Brahmin: "What is your message to us?"

Missionary: "Life from the dead to all who believe in and obey Jesus Christ, the Son of the Father."

Brahmin: "That sounds well. What is this life you offer in Christ? What is this death from which you promise deliverance?"

Missionary: "The life I offer you in my Master's name is spiritual life—a new heart, loving God, and all that is good, and consequent happiness forever. The death from which Christ will deliver you is spiritual death, *i.e.*, moral pollution, its consequent misery, and the eternal anguish and suffering which God will inflict on all who believe not the Gospel of His Son Jesus Christ."

Brahmin: "When and where will your God inflict this death upon unbelievers?"

Missionary: "It is already begun through the sinner's own sin; but God has prepared a place where He will complete what is here only begun. That fearful place is hell, where all unbelievers shall suffer throughout an eternal existence pain inflicted for their sin and unbelief."

Brahmin: "You say, '*for their unbelief*.' Then this hell of yours can be only for those who reject the Gospel of Christ."

Missionary: "No. Hell is for all your fathers of the past times; at least for all of them who sinned against such light and knowledge as they were possessed of."

Brahmin: "That would include, I fear, the vast majority of my fathers. If this is true, it is a terrible message that you bring us. You say that all the past generations of India will suffer pain as a punishment from your God for all eternity! Tell me plainly *for what they* must suffer a punishment infinitely beyond all the punishment that has ever been inflicted by the cruelest tyrants of earth?"

Missionary: "They will certainly thus suffer for eternity, but their sufferings will be much lighter than are inflicted upon those who refuse God's offer of salvation."

Brahmin: "Greater or less, you speak of a punishment which, if inflicted on but one person for all eternity, would exceed in amount all the punishments which have ever been inflicted in this temporal life upon all the criminals against human laws."

Missionary: "Yes. If we consider what eternity is, I must confess that it is so."

Brahmin: "I ask, then, *for what* will your God inflict this most appalling punishment?"

Missionary: "We are sprung from one father, the first man, Adam. God made with him a covenant which included his posterity. Adam violated this covenant; and thereby involved all his posterity in the death he brought upon himself."

Brahmin: "You say, then, that because Adam sinned, his children, who had nothing to say personally to his sin, will suffer pain for all eternity, and this by your God's arrangement!"

Missionary: "Yes."

Brahmin: "Then those who have died before they could know the difference of good or evil are all to go to this fearful hell! You include the infant as well as the adult! Is this the God whom you tell me to love and adore?"

Missionary: "I do not think that infants will be included. At least I cannot affirm positively of them. It may be that God will exempt them, and save them through Christ, though they never heard of His name."

Brahmin: "Then you must allow that you do not think the mere fact of being descended from Adam sufficient to justify the awful punishment of which you speak!"

Missionary: "I should rather omit this matter as one on which sufficient light has not been shed to justify me in speaking positively. I would rather speak of such heathen as have come to years of understanding, and in those years have sinned against their knowledge of what was right. You cannot deny that there have been multitudes of such."

Brahmin: "I deny it not. Nor do I deny that punishment is due to crime. Nor do I deny that if crime has gone unpunished in this world it would be but just to punish it in another."

Missionary: "You are coming over to my view. That is what my God will do. No sin has met with sufficient punishment here, therefore He will punish it, if unforgiven, hereafter."

Brahmin: "I quarrel not with *punishment.* I only speak of its *amount.* I do not see that any fault of my father that could merit the amount of punishment you speak of, and therefore I ask you to tell me particularly *for what* it is they are thus to suffer? You do not surely say that your God will inflict *more* punishment on the sinner than he deserves!"

Missionary: "No. My God is the judge of all the earth and He can do no injustice or wrong."

Brahmin: "It is well. Then for what is He to condemn my ancestors to unending pain?"

Missionary: "For those sins of which you allow them to be guilty."

Brahmin: "Yes; but I affirm the punishment to be too great."

Missionary: "They sinned against my God, who is infinite, and no punishment for sin against such a God can be too great."

Brahmin: "But they never heard of His name: they never knew His laws; their offence, *as against Him,* was purely one of ignorance!"

Missionary: "Yes, but He placed within them a conscience which should condemn them when they did what they knew to be wrong, and their going against conscience was in fact going against His voice within them."

Brahmin: "But they did not know it was His voice!"

Missionary: "That I allow."

Brahmin: "And you affirm that your God will punish men with pain for all eternity for an offense against His voice, when they did not, and could not, know it to be His voice!"

Missionary: "I do. This is the arrangement of His world, with which no creature of His hand may dare quarrel."

Brahmin: "I was not taught from infancy to believe in your God, and what you now tell me of Him makes me resolve never to believe in Him. You come to reason with me about your God, and you thereby allow that I am capable of forming a just opinion of Him. Indeed, if I were not capable, there would be no use in your disputing with me. I have formed my opinions of Him from what you, His servant, have told me of Him. I reject Him as a monster of injustice and cruelty. You tell me of the cruelties of what you call this heathen land! There are, it may be, and have been, with us many cruel men, but none so cruel as your God. You speak to me of the cruelty of Juggernaut's worship! I regard it not from your point of view; but, say the worst you could of it, it compares not with the cruelty of your God. What! To inflict endless agony on myriads of men who never heard of Him, or of His laws! With us the worst of crimes is thought sufficiently punished with the loss of life. But your God thinks that the smallest crimes against His laws—for surely sins of ignorance are small—can be punished with no less a punishment than endless existence in misery! Justice! No; but the foulest injustice, with which no injustice of any of the old rulers of our land, whom you Christians have displaced, can compare. Your God has no excuse. Could he not remove out of life those who have ignorantly sinned?! That were easy for Omnipotence to do. Then He does not choose to do to so. He prefers to sustain them in an endless life of pain! You tell me of His love! But His love I cannot see while this black stain rests upon His character. You tell me He has doomed all the past millions of India to eternal agony either for Adam's willful sin, or for their own sins of ignorance, or for both together! Then I will have naught to do with such a God. I prefer mine to yours."

Conversations such as this do not rank among imaginary "Dialogues of the Dead:" they are dialogues of living men. In Siam, a priest came to an American missionary and asked him how long His God tormented bad men in a future state. When answered, "Forever," he replied, "Our God torments the worst of men only one thousand years, so we will not have your American God in Siam."*

Have not the Brahmin and the Siamese priest the best in such an argument? How can minds like theirs judge in any other way? Yet the theology which they reject is the current theology of Christendom! This is

* Jacob Blain, *Death not Life*, p. 116.

part of the Gospel we send to heathen lands. Can we wonder at its rejection? Is it not the wonder that our missions should have met even with the small success they have? Is their success not proof of the Divine power of that religion which, weighted with the Augustinian hell, can make any progress at all? No other religion but Christianity could sustain itself for a generation with such a load upon its back.

Give to the millions of India and of China the Gospel which was preached by Christ, and Paul, and John—*Life from the dead.* Give to life and death the only senses which these poor heathen have ever attached to them. Life is to them precious—the most precious of all things: even for a year of this poor life they would give all they have. Put before them eternal life in Christ. Tell these poor perishing creatures who have no hope, that "God so loved the world that He gave His only begotten Son, that whosoever believeth in Him should not perish, but have everlasting life." Tell them that in a world over which God rules the ungodly can have no abiding place, but that the very vilest are invited, just as they are, to come to Jesus Christ, and to His and their loving Father, and through the Spirit of grace to receive a new heart and a new spirit to qualify them to enjoy the endless life which Christ bestows. Tell them this, and you tell them of what shocks no sense of justice, and of what appeals to the innermost chord even of their degraded being.

Life! Life forever! No more to die! No more to dread the approach of that death from which human nature shrinks with dread and aversion because it was not made for death!

Here is a prize for a poor heathen offered him in Jesus Christ! Here is a message of love from the God of heaven! Here is a token of affection that shows that the Judge of all the earth is its Father too, and has a Father's heart even for the poor outcast of India and China! The heathen of the day may sigh, may be even perplexed at the thought, why God did not send to his fathers the message of peace He sent to him. But, in His not having sent it, he can see no injustice; for no terrible future, such as the Augustinian missionary summons up from the depth of his hell, looms before his forefathers, rude or civilized, of the ages, that have gone before. The Creator withdraws the life He gave. No man can say that is unjust. Man takes life from the creature he gave no life to: much more may God take what He bestows. But to him and to his age has come the message of life from God, and he can hail it as to him a message of pure love and mercy which may well touch his heart, fire his intellect, nerve his purpose, make him feel what he never did before, the heir of immortality, through the Savior of the world.

Here is something, we think, for us to lay to heart. Here is a solemn question for our missionaries and our missionary societies. The Brahmin of India has condemned the theology of Augustine. Let us condemn it too; and take and send to the dark places of the world the theology of apostolic times. We may then speak boldly to the heathen ear. The Christian missionary need no more stand rebuked by the sophist of India.

14

Some Objections Answered

DOCTRINE OF DESTRUCTION such as we advocate would, we may be certain, draw forth many objections. Subversive of theories cherished and taught in Christendom for fifteen hundred years: subversive of man's boast of his natural inalienable immortality, handed down from Egyptian priestcraft to Christian fathers: subversive of man's clinging to the fond hope that somewhere in the hereafter, no matter what may have been here his conversation, life, or faith, he will find life and peace: we might well expect that from every point of the atmosphere of human thought the storm of objection would blow fiercely against a doctrine which rebuked the hideous cruelty of the Augustinian, exposed the delusive hope of the Universalist, and told the Theist that his system of natural religion, sufficient for the unfallen but not sufficient for the sinner, is of no avail whatever. From all such quarters we are blown upon. The Augustinian rails and gnashes upon us with his teeth. The Universalist dreads the putting forth of a theory which robs him of the plea on which most he rested. The Theist hates a doctrine which rests all human hope of blessing upon that Gospel of Christ which he disdainfully rejects. To some of these objections we will briefly reply. We could not hope here to reply to them all. Our reply will chiefly confine itself to the objections of that

Augustinian system which has enrolled so vast and heterogeneous a body in defense of its faith: which summons the priests of Egypt and the philosophers of Greece to side with fathers of the Christian Church: which calls forth the subtle cruel schoolmen of the middle ages, in union with the religious orders of the Roman church and the bishops and pastors of the churches of the Reformation, to do battle for its hell.

One objection which constantly meets us is this, that in denying eternity of being to the wicked we diminish the certainty of everlasting life to the redeemed, or remove the ground for the latter altogether. Dr. Salmon thus states the objection: "In no system which disposes of the wicked by annihilation will it be long possible to maintain faith in the immortality of the good."[*] A more groundless objection we think it scarcely possible to make. The Universalist who denies the eternity of future punishment is open to this objection: we, who hold its eternity, are not. Dr. Salmon rests his objection upon two grounds. The first is, that "Scripture in many passages leads us to attribute co-extensive duration to the *happiness* of the blessed, and *the pains* of the lost." This is precisely what we wholly deny. We hold that Scripture attributes co-extensive duration to the *life* of the blessed and to the *death, punishment, destruction,* of the lost. We deny that there is in Scripture one single passage which tells us that the pains of the lost are co-extensive in duration with the happiness of the blest. To say that the lost will wail in hell is not saying that they will wail forever. To say that their punishment is everlasting is not to say that it consists in an everlasting life of misery. If we will be satisfied with the scriptural definition of everlasting punishment we will find it to consist in a destruction and death which remain in force forever. According to our theory, *the life* of the righteous is co-extensive in duration with the

---

[*] Salmon, *Eternity of Future Punishment,* Preface, 2nd edition.

destruction of the wicked. *Both are eternal.* How does this militate against the "immortality of the good?"

The second ground on which Dr. Salmon rests his objection is, that,

> "If human souls enjoy no exemption from the lot which ordains that all things eventually become the prey of death, it is hard to believe that self-love is not deceiving us when we flatter ourselves that we can escape the doom which overhangs not only all other created things, but also multitudes of our fellow men."

Dr. Salmon's argument here appears to us to be this, that, unless the souls of all mankind possess within themselves an essential or inalienable immortality of which they cannot be deprived, we can have no good reliance that the blessed will live forever! Dr. Salmon tells us that our only *sure hope of immortality rests upon the nature of the soul itself! He throws us on Plato for our hope!* We think that we have in our theory drawn from Scripture a far surer ground for hope. It is that immortality is brought to us through Christ: that it is the believer's heritage resting on the sure promise and almighty power of the only Being who hath life in Himself or can bestow it upon others. If this is not enough for the Augustinian, it is enough for us. Elsewhere we see no good hope at all.

Another objection brought against our view is, that, if annihilation be the end of the ungodly hereafter, it seems a pitiless and uncalled-for act of severity on God's part to raise them in judgment and expose them to any pain or suffering whatever in a future state of being.* It is very amusing to hear an *Augustinian* objecting to our system on the score of its severity, but nevertheless it is frequently done. We however do not fear scrutiny on this account. The common principles of justice, as recognized among men, demand some such procedure as Dr. Salmon and his fellow theorists affect

* Salmon, *Eternity of Punishment*, 5.

to condemn as vindictive and cruel. This present world does not present to view Divine rewards and punishments attending men according to their deserts. This is universally acknowledged. It is asserted in the Bible. It is confessed, deplored, wondered at, among men who believe in a Moral Governor of the world. It is used as a favorite argument by the Atheist to prove that there is no God. It is accepted by the Theist as a sure ground of belief that there will be a future life and retribution. It is laid down in Scripture as the reason why there will be a future judgment (Eccl. 11:9; 12:14). God means to show Himself a rewarder of every man according to his works. He does not do so here; therefore He will do so hereafter. Therefore there will be, and ought to be, such pains and penalties as we, following Scripture, teach. And for this we are condemned, even by such men as Dr. Salmon, as holding a cruel and pitiless theory! If we taught that God would raise up the wicked to endure *eternal pain* in the way of retribution, we should be teaching what, according to them, would be logical, just, and merciful: when we teach that God will raise them up to suffer *such pains as their evil deeds deserve,* we are illogical, unmerciful, and unjust! Such is Augustinian reasoning! A bad cause can only present a weak defense.

Another argument brought in favor of the Augustinian theory and against ours is, that the "perpetual exhibition" of the everlasting agony of the lost may be essential to keep unfallen races from transgression, while temporary pain, followed by destruction, would not have this salutary effect.* We differ wholly from such reasoning. We think that the "perpetual exhibition" of agony would make the unfallen regard God as unjust and tyrannical. Nor do we think so meanly of the races whom God has brought, or may hereafter bring, into being, as to think that they will require such a picture to be ever before their eyes to keep them from sinning (Josh. 4:5-7;

* Salmon, *Eternity of Punishment*, 6.

Exod. 12:24-27). The consciousness of their own happy life, the knowledge perpetually kept in mind by that hell where myriads such as they lost an eternal life, would seem to us sufficient to prevent them from falling, without their requiring to have ever before them a scene which, unless their hearts were harder than the nether millstone, must rob their own life of its joy and peace.

Perhaps the most usual objection to our doctrine is, that it removes from the sinner the dread of the consequences of his sin. It is often said that if the common view of hell, with all its imaginable terrors, is yet insufficient to deter man from transgression, what would the effect be if we removed from the mind the fear of this hell, and substituted for it a punishment which, however severe, was yet infinitely less?

Now we allow that the Augustinian theory of punishment is infinitely more terrible than ours. Between the two there is and can be *no comparison.* It is idle to compare them—as idle as to compare time with eternity. Read our view of punishment. You can bear it. Read the accounts of punishment as given by Tertullian, or Jeremy Taylor, or Father Furniss, or Mr. Spurgeon. If you dwell on them, and try to realize them, they will set you wild. Now it is just *because* of this infinite difference between the Augustinian hell and ours that we say that, taking the principle of fear into calculation, the Augustinian theory is *less capable* of deterring from sin than ours. We ground our assertion on a well-known and universally acknowledged principle of legal jurisprudence. Moses Stuart, who held the Augustinian theory, thus admirably expressed it: "If a penalty is enormously disproportioned to an offense, it loses all its power as a penalty, and produces reaction and disgust, if not indignation." Moses Stuart has here given the text on which may be preached the grave homily of the failure of the Augustinian theory of punishment to deter from sin, and the cause of its failure. We will try and draw out a short homily on the Professor of Andover's text.

The threatening of a penalty felt to be excessive defeats its own end. It has done so in the present case. The theory of eternal agony, as the punishment for the sins of this life, has long been held as the view taught by Scripture. Tatian, and Tertullian, and Athanasius, and Augustine, led the way, and Christendom as a body accepted their view, and has held it for centuries. What was *one* of its immediate results? *A refuge from it in Purgatory!* Rome tells you that purgatory is a very ancient doctrine. So it is. It dates from the inculcation of eternal misery in hell. Rome tells you it is and has been very commonly held. So it has. It is and has been the belief of nine-tenths of professing Christendom. The partial purgatory of Tertullian, Augustine, and Rome, has not been enough. Origen fled from eternal misery to a universal purgatory, and has been followed by multitudes of the most thoughtful minds in every century, and especially in our own. Eternal agony has *no terrors* for those who have substituted for it a purgatory of cleansing and purifying pain.

Let us take another large class of men—the profane, the irreligious, and the skeptical. You tell them that everlasting misery is the doctrine taught in Scripture. They willingly accept at your hands this comment on Bible teaching. It is just what they want. You put the weapon into their hands and they proceed to knock you down with it. They do not love the Scriptures: they do not love God: they want to live without any sense of responsibility and control. The God of the Bible is the only God wicked men of any intelligence fear. So they willingly accept your account of this God. He is one who dooms to eternal agony myriads who never heard of Him, and who would have never had this miserable life if He had not given it unasked. He dooms to eternal misery others who did hear of Him, and disobeyed Him. As death was the only punishment that could satisfy an ancient Grecian lawgiver for every offence against his law, so eternal misery is the only punishment that can satisfy this God of yours for disobedience to Him. What is the consequence? You put into the mouths of these men a plea, a most powerful plea, for their infidelity. They reject your God and your Bible altogether. They reject your God as a monster: your Bible as a foul lie. Their whole nature, their reason, their conscience, their heart, tells them that punishment such as you speak of is unjust. Theodore Parker is at one with Mr. Spurgeon in his premise; but he differs from him in his conclusion. "I believe," says the infidel, "that Jesus Christ taught eternal torment: I do not accept it on His authority."* Of what avail is your theory of punishment upon Theodore Parker and his great school? They are not afraid of your hell, because your hell has given them their best reason for not believing in your God.

It is almost as inoperative as a motive of fear with others who neither take refuge in purgatory or infidelity. They think of *your hell, and its unspeakable endless agony.* They do not perhaps reject it: they probably imagine that they believe it: at all events they argue for it as though it were the corner stone of faith. But they secretly think that God will scarcely inflict it *on them.* There may be great multitudes for whom it is in store—heathens, Mohammedans, Papists, Schismatics, Destructionists, and such like: *but surely not for them.* Something or other will avert it *from them.* A change of life, a word of penitence at the end, a sigh of sorrow for the past as the spirit leaves its tabernacle, *something,* will surely avert *from them* a fate too terrible for a merciful God to inflict on such as they. So the very transcendent terrors of the Augustinian hell defeat the object of threatened penalty; for few, if any, believe in it *for themselves.* We will not be suspected of summoning an unfair witness when we summon the modern poet of Augustine's hell to testify to the sinner's universal disbelief in it:

> "But say, believing in such woe to come,
> Such dreadful certainty of endless pain,
> Could beings of forecasting mould, as thou

* Theodore Parker, *Two Sermons,* p. 14.

Entitlest man, deliberately walk on?
  Thy tone of asking seems to make reply,
And rightly seems: *they did not so believe*:
  Not one."[*]

And now what comes of the outcry against us, that in overthrowing the terrors of Augustine's hell we are removing the salutary effect of fear as a restraint, or as a motive to repentance? Why the very people who are mythically supposed to be living under a constant dread of the Augustinian hell do not believe that they are in any danger of it. To use the words of Archer Butler: "When they think about it at all, it seems to them monstrous, disproportioned, impossible." The Augustinian theorist, in his study or his pulpit, fancies men are trembling at his hell when they are only laughing at it.

Our theory is credible, and does not remove from the sinner the salutary dread of punishment. Even if we taught that the first death would be for the sinner an eternal sleep, we should be laying before him the awful deprivation of that eternal life which Christ offers him. But this is not our teaching. We affirm for the sinner a resurrection, a judgment, a sentence to the realm of hell, where he will suffer the due reward for his deeds in passing under the sad irrevocable sentence of eternal death. Are there no terrors here? Is there not here enough to terrify any soul whom mere fear may lead to fly from the wrath to come? And all this is *credible*. It may be carped at; but it cannot be reasoned down. Here, in God's world, is pain: here, in God's world, is death: here, pain is the token, the premonition, produced by and producing death. The man of natural religion cannot object to finding pain and death in a life following this. We are but making the God of Nature and the God of Revelation one and the same Being. And are they not one and the same? We hold up before the human mind those

---

[*] Pollock, *Course of Time*, b. viii.

"terrors of the Lord" which Paul held up before the mind of Felix when he reasoned of "judgment to come;" that death which Paul declared would be the end of sin and sinners, and which minds such as that of Felix feel and acknowledge to be the worthy award of evil deeds (Acts 24:25; Rom. 1:32). Accept our theory, and Atheism has no weapon, infidelity is robbed of its sneer, pious and holy men can preach and teach with authority of a terrible judgment to come, sinners may tremble at the prospect and fly through dread even where they are not drawn by the stronger voice that tells them that the God of righteous judgment is also the God of love.

Another frequent objection to our view is that it detracts from the value of the atonement of Christ. To us it adds to it. The way in which it is sought to establish that the Augustinian theory imputes a greater value to the atonement than ours is this. The Augustinian punishment of endless misery is a greater punishment than that which we teach; therefore an atonement which delivers from the greater punishment is more to be valued and thought of than that which delivers from the less. Arguments of this land are to us very valueless things. They are the old scholastic reasoning of the middle ages which largely taints our Protestant theology. They are appeals to reason to determine the course of God's proceedings. We might well leave them unanswered, except that we are told that we must sometimes, "Answer a fool according to his folly, lest he be wise in his own conceit." We will therefore say a few words to show that our view of future punishment magnifies the grace of God far more than the Augustinian theory, and stamps a greater value upon the atonement of His Son.

If the Augustinian theory of punishment were true, we could scarcely think it possible for God to avoid making the most strenuous efforts to save man from it. *We cannot imagine a man,* we can scarce even imagine a devil, who would not pity and seek to save *from such a doom.* To say that God would send His Son to redeem mankind from endless agony is only to say of Him what we would say of any being who was susceptible of the most ordinary feelings of compassion. It certainly does not magnify His grace to say that it was exerted for such a cause. It magnifies it infinitely more to say that it sought to save *from death.* Surely God's love, and pity, and grace, shine with brighter luster when we believe that it was from consideration for a creature who had once known Him, and whose existence was endangered by transgression, that He planned salvation. He had been less than man, we would think, if He had made no effort to save from Augustine's hell: He is God, His ways higher than our ways, His love stronger than ours, His pity purer and deeper, when He sends His Son that "whosoever believeth in Him should *not perish, but have eternal life.*"

Again, the atonement of Christ is itself magnified by our view. According to the Augustinian theory, Christ came to *alter the condition of life* from being miserable to being happy: according to our theory, Christ came to bestow *life itself.* This latter is the greater work. It involves the happiness of which the Augustinian speaks, it adds the grand gift of an immortal life. It brings forward Christ once more in His old part of *Creator.* It attributes to Him as Redeemer the part He took in man's opening as Creator. It makes us owe our life, our being, our existence, to our Redeemer, and not merely the happiness of our existence. This latter follows as a matter of course from the former. To say that *God* gives *life,* is to say that he gives with it all that can make life happy. To say that he would bestow life without those circumstances that render it delightful is to attribute to the Universal Father what we would not attribute to one of us who had a son. It is therefore that Scripture, in speaking of the effect of the atonement of Christ, generally calls it simply *the gift of life.* That is enough. That involves all the pleasures that are at God's right hand to give. And the view which attributes to the atonement the gift of eternal life magnifies that atonement more, infinitely more, than the view which only attributes to the atonement the alteration of the condition and circumstances of life.

Once more, we are commonly charged with *endangering the faith* by our theory. General charges of this kind have considerable weight with ignorant people: with others they have none. If they are not substantiated they only deserve contempt. In such a charge we only say, "Not guilty!" and demand *proof.* Remember what our view is. It is an eternal life of joy for the redeemed: eternal death, after they have suffered as God judges right, for the lost. What is there here to endanger any article of faith? Does it imperil our *faith in God?* What attribute of His is attacked? His love! Is it the part of love to inflict eternal pain if it can be helped? His mercy! Is it the part of mercy never to be satisfied with the misery of others? His holiness! Is it essential to holiness to keep evil forever in existence? His justice! Can justice only be satisfied with everlasting agonies? No; we do not endanger faith. We strengthen it, by allying it once more with the divine principles of mercy, equity, and justice. It is the Augustinian theory which endangers faith, and has made shipwreck of faith in the case of multitudes, by representing God as a Being of boundless injustice, caprice, and cruelty.

15

The Apostolic Fathers: St. Clement of Rome

IT HAS BEEN SO OFTEN asserted that the theory of Augustine was the theory *always* held in the Christian Church, that our treatise would not be complete if we did not show that such was not the case. We wholly deny it. The doctrine of the Apostolical Church was on this question in perfect agreement with Scripture. We see this from those "Writings of the Apostolical Fathers" which have been preserved to our time, and which are now readily accessible to the English reader in the admirable issue of the "Ante Nicene Christian Library," edited by Rev. A. Roberts, D.D., and James Donaldson, L.L.D. From beginning to end of them, there is not one word said of that immortality of the soul which is so prominent in the writings of the later fathers. Immortality is by them asserted to be peculiar to the redeemed. The punishment of the wicked is by them emphatically declared to be everlasting. Not one stray expression of theirs can be interpreted as giving any countenance to the theory of restoration after purgatorial suffering. The fire of hell is with them, as with us, an unquenchable one; but its issue is with them, as with Scripture, "destruction," "death," and "loss of life."

We could not, within a moderate volume, attempt to examine the writings of all these several fathers. We must content ourselves with the general view we have given above of their teaching. We beg to refer our readers to the volume which contains their writings from which they can judge for themselves.

We challenge our opponents to controvert our view of them in a single particular. In our present chapter we propose to give at some length the views of one of these fathers, Clement of Rome. We select him, because his first epistle is a work of whose authenticity there is little doubt. If genuine, it is the work of a man who was a contemporary, and highly-valued friend of the apostle Paul (see Phil. 4:3).

It would thus rank in authority of statement next to the testimony of an apostle. It was in fact "read in numerous churches" of the apostolic age "as being almost on a level with the canonical writings"* In the succeeding chapter, we propose to exhibit the views of two of the principal fathers immediately following the apostolic age—Justin Martyr and Irenaeus. We will after them give a sketch of the rise of the theory of eternal life in hell; and of that doctrine of universal restoration which was man's indignant revolt from man's cruel hell.

The first thing we will notice in Clement is his *silence* on certain points. He very often speaks of future punishment. It is a theme upon which no Christian teacher can with fidelity be silent. Yet Clement never speaks of *the immortality of the soul* which is so indissolubly bound up with the theory of punishment as taught by Tertullian and Augustine. Nor is there throughout his epistle (we speak only of his first epistle as the authenticity of the second is generally doubted) a single passage descriptive of future punishment which can be paralleled in expression

* Writings of the Apostolical Fathers, edited by Rev. A. Roberts, First Epistle of Clement, Introductory Notice.

with passage after passage from every writer who holds the Augustinian theory. In Tatian, and Tertullian, and Hippolytus, and Athanasius, and Augustine, we find expressions which have no parallel in the epistle of Clement.

He differs from them just as much in what he says as in his silence. His descriptions of human nature are quite unlike the lofty descriptions of Plato copied by his Christian imitators. With Clement, man is a *material being*, made out of that *matter* which from the time of Aristotle downward was distinguished from the intelligent principle, the mind. With him man has come *out of a sepulcher, from utter darkness.* So far from being an immortal, he is, in Clement's phrase, *a mortal* creature, consisting only of *dust and ashes—his life as but the life of one day.*[*] Such is Clement's general description of man with which we will find his particular accounts in perfect harmony.

We believe that for the Greek word ἀθανασία (*athanasia*), translated "immortality," there is but *one* meaning. We have never seen but one meaning given to it in any dictionary we have used, no matter what were the theological bias of its editor. Its root, θανατος (*thanatos*), has acquired new figurative senses; but this derivative has but one sense, showing emphatically the original and proper sense, of the root from which it sprung. *Immortality, or eternal existence, is its only sense.*

Clement tells us that this immortality is one of God's gifts to the redeemed: that if we would gain it we must "earnestly strive" for it: that if we do not thus strive for it we shall not obtain it.[†] He distinguishes it expressly from the moral qualities that make up the believer's character, his righteousness, truth, faith, holiness. Clement did not believe that the lost were possessed of, or should ever obtain, any immortality at all.

---

[*] Epistle, para. 17, 38, 39.

[†] Para. 35.

We come to another word Ζωη (*zoe*), "life," and will see how Clement uses it. The meaning of this word is not so undisputed as that in the last paragraph. Many people suppose it means "happiness," "well-being," and so on. We will however confine ourselves to Clement's use of it. In one place he speaks of it as that *life of Christ* which was taken from the earth. It can here have no meaning but existence. In another place he describes it as that *life of man* which may last but for a day. Here too existence is its only sense.

In another place he expressly distinguishes it from that "righteousness," or moral well-being of man, with which so many confound it: with him *righteousness is not life, but the way to life.* And lastly he tells us that *this life when joined to immortality* is God's gift to His people, for which they must strive.[*] Clement did not think that there was any everlasting existence for the lost.

One of Clement's descriptions of what will happen to the wicked hereafter, is that they will suffer "death" (*thanatos*). He probably took this from the epistle to the Romans where it is the usual expression of Paul. The ready definition of this phrase by Augustinian theorists, whence derived we cannot see, is that it means death temporal, spiritual death in sin, and everlasting misery. This was not Clement's sense of it. In the first place he expressly distinguishes it from spiritual death or the ill-being of the moral condition of man. *Death, he tells us, results from this.* In the next place he identifies the death which sinners will hereafter endure with that death which Enoch was exempted from, which certainly was only the death which men, whether good or evil, ordinarily undergo. And he also identifies it with the death which Abel, Christ, and the martyrs endured.[†]

---

[*] Para. 16, 17, 35, 48.

[†] Para. 3, 4, 5, 8, 9, 16.

When Clement tells us that death is the ultimate fate of the wicked he means that they will be deprived of their existence.

While we do not know whether Clement ever *directly* uses the verb "to destroy," (απολλυμι, *apollumi*), in his descriptions of future punishment, he leaves us in no doubt what is his established meaning for it. He applies it to the death of the people of Jericho by the hand of Joshua, to the death of the army of Pharaoh in the Red Sea, to the death which has come on all, good and evil, through sin.[*] We also see what force he attributes to it, when we find him making it the equivalent for such verbs as αναιρεω, θανατaω, τελευταω (*anaireo, thanatoo, teleutao*).[†]

Our readers will see the force of this from the consideration of the force of one of these verbs, *teleutao*. This verb *never* has the meaning of bringing misery or moral ruin on a man. It meant originally "to bring about," "finish," "accomplish," "end," and hence it came absolutely to signify *"to die," as the end of human existence.* We thus see Clement's meaning for that word *apollumi,* one of the most usual in Scripture for the end of the wicked. It meant, with him, their loss of existence.

There can be no doubt then of Clement of Rome's view of future punishment. By his silence and by his words he tells us what it was. With him there was no immortality for any but the redeemed of Christ. Endless life was, with him, only for those who would use it to the glory of the Giver. For all others there was, after resurrection and judgment, the sentence to a second death, the loss of existence forever, from which they were never to be recalled to another life, another probation, another opportunity of salvation.

What we have established in the case of Clement, we could with equal ease establish in the case of all the other Apostolical Fathers. Every one of

[*] Para. 12, 39, 51

[†] Para. 39

the men who were contemporaries of the apostles, and have left to our times any of their writings, agree with our view of future punishment as consisting in the destruction of the ungodly, their becoming as a thing of nought.

16

Justin Martyr

THE PERIOD OF THE APOSTOLICAL Fathers reaches down to the end of the first century and a half from the birth of Christ. During it, we find Barnabas, Clement of Rome, Hermas, Ignatius, and Polycarp, testifying to their complete unity of opinion with us on the future of the wicked. We are immediately after introduced to the writings of a father who has on this subject given rise to the utmost perplexity as to what were his real sentiments—we refer to Justin Martyr. We claim him among our supporters, and have ranked him as such. We have always however allowed that there were passages in his writings which apparently rank him as a holder of Augustine's views. We have no wish to claim what does not belong to us: but we are satisfied that we are right. We will endeavor in this chapter to present a view of those opinions of Justin which have hitherto perplexed all his commentators without exception. We hope to present a more satisfactory view of this eminent father than that he put forward two diametrically opposite theories upon a vital question: for to such a conclusion we must come if we reject such a solution as we offer here.

We will first show reason for concluding that on this question of future punishment Justin agreed with us. There is not, we believe, in language a more unambiguous word than "*existence*," or "*to exist*" (ἰμί, *eimi*). When applied to living creatures it only signifies their having life or animation, as, "Men cannot exist in water, nor fishes on land" (Webster). In several places, Justin expressly states his belief, that no wicked being will continue to have an eternal existence. In one place he points to the original transgression of Adam as having exposed man to this. "When God formed man at the beginning," he says, "he suspended the things of nature on his will, and made an experiment by means of one commandment. For He ordained that, if he kept this, he should partake of *immortal existence*; but if he transgressed it, *the contrary should be his lot.*" In another place he speaks of the soul's survival of the body in the intermediate state, and of the ultimate non-existence of the souls of the wicked.

> "I do not say, indeed, that all souls die; for that were truly a piece of good fortune to the evil. What then? The souls of the pious remain in a better place, while those of the unjust and wicked are in a worse, waiting for the time of judgment. Thus *some* which have appeared worthy of God *never die;* but others are punished so *long as God wills them to exist* and to be punished."

That in Justin's judgment a time would come when God would wish them not to exist appears from his positive declaration in another place where he includes the fallen angels in this doom of annihilation. "God," he says, "delays causing the confusion and destruction of the whole world, *by which the wicked angels and demons and men shall cease to exist.*"

We will now consider the important word "destroy," (*apollumi*), as used by Justin. No doubt there are various shades of meaning attached to this word in all its forms. It is used figuratively, as when men known to be alive are said to be destroyed, *i.e.*, to suffer injury of some severe nature. We also find it used hyperbolically, as when men say they or others are destroyed, meaning some hurt which has a tendency to utter destruction. But what we want to know is the sense which Justin puts on it as its full proper natural sense, the sense, in which he uses it when there are no attending circumstances to point out that it is used in other than its ordinary sense. Justin has left us in no doubt here. His meaning for this word is, to bring to an end, to cause to cease to exist.

In his address to the Greeks he is speaking of Plato's opinion of the gods of the heathen, that they are not truly eternal; but come at some time into existence, and at another time cease to exist. Commenting on some of Plato's words, which appeared to bear this sense, he says, "These expressions declare to them who rightly understand them, *the death and destruction of the gods that have been brought into being.*"* There can here be no doubt what is Justin's meaning for "destruction." The idea of endless misery does not enter into it at all. He means simply by it *the cessation of existence or being.* We will refer but to one other place to show his meaning. The Augustinian theorists would tell us that when the future punishment of the wicked, and of devils, is spoken of by saying they will be destroyed, what is meant is that they will be tormented and suffer pain. Justin expressly distinguishes "torment" from "destruction," with reference to the future punishment of devils: he says, speaking of Christ, "This shall be the strength of Him alone, whose name every power dreads, *being very much tormented because they shall be destroyed by Him.*"†

Here Justin uses "destruction" as distinct from "torment." He says that evil powers now endure the one, at the prospect of the other. When we know Justin's meaning for the word "destroy," which is also its usual meaning with every Greek writer, we can have no doubt what is his view of future punishment, when he constantly uses this word "destroy" to point it out, without the smallest intimation that he uses it in any but its

* *Address to the Greeks*, c. xxii.

† *Dialogue with Trypho*, c. cxi.

natural sense. The following is one out of numberless passages that might be quoted:

> "By whom (Christ) God destroys both the serpent, and those angels and men who are like him; but works deliverance from death to those who repent of their wickedness and believe upon Him."[*]

We will only advert to one other expression of Justin's in order to show reason for concluding that he held our view. We believe that, for the words "immortal" and "immortality," there is but one meaning, and that they describe a condition not subject to death, *i.e.*, to the loss of existence. In numberless passages, Justin tells us, that immortality will be the peculiar, exclusive, possession of the redeemed, and that the wicked *will not obtain it.* In several places he lays down the principle that immortality is a gift of God, not bestowed upon any as yet, but *promised at the resurrection.* It is true that he sometimes speaks of the soul as immortal; but he also tells us he condemns the Platonic theory of its essential immortality: that he only holds it immortal, as compared with the body, in that it survives in the intermediate state, while, if wicked, it will die with the body in hell: but of absolute immortality he has over and over declared that only the just will obtain it either in respect of body or of soul. "Those filthy garments," he says, "which have been put by you on all who have become Christians by the name of Jesus, God shows shall be taken away from us, when he shall raise all men from the dead, and *appoint some to be incorruptible, immortal,* and free from sorrow in the everlasting and imperishable kingdom."[†]

---

[*] *Dialogue with Trypho*, c. c., xxxix; *Second Apology*, c. vi.

[†] *First Apology*, c. xliii, lii; *Dialogue with Trypho*, c. iv, v, xlvi, lxix, cxvii; *Address to the Greeks*, xxiii.

We could easily add a great deal more to the same effect; but we think enough has been adduced to prove that Justin does in some parts of his writings teach a theory of future punishment which is identical with ours. This is all we as yet contend for. But in saying this we do not deny that in other parts of his writings there are *passages which apparently affirm the Augustinian theory.* We do not want to hide these. We only aim at truth. We will give the very strongest of these passages. We will then enquire what we are to do. Does Justin contradict himself? Some say he does. Does Justin write in a hazy, indistinct, ambiguous way, so that it is impossible to know what his meaning is? Very many scholars affirm this of him. Or, has Justin some philosophical theory which may appear to us and really be a very absurd one—which relieves him of the charge of ambiguity and contradiction? This latter in our belief. We will first give the strongest passages adducible from Justin's writings which are quoted in proof of his having held the Augustinian theory.

In his Dialogue with the Jew, Trypho, Justin has a very curious passage. He is speaking of the joy which the faithful, whether Jews or Gentiles shall have in God. He proceeds to say that he does not believe that all Jews, simply as descended from Abraham in the flesh, will partake of this joy. "We will not," he says, "receive it of *all your* nation; since we know from Isaiah that *the members* of those who have transgressed shall be consumed by the worm and unquenchable fire, *remaining immortal; so that they become a spectacle to all flesh.*"[*] In his first Apology, he has another striking passage. He is speaking of the resurrection. Christ, he tells us,

> "shall raise *the bodies* of all men who have lived, and shall clothe those of the worthy with immortality, and shall send those of the wicked, *endued*

[*] *Dialogue with Trypho*, c. cxxx.

> *with eternal sensibility,* into everlasting fire with the wicked devils. . . . And *in what kind of sensation* and punishment the wicked are to be, hear from what was said in like manner with reference to this; it is as follows: '*Their worm shall not rest; and their fire shall not be quenched*' (Isa. 66:24); and then shall they repent, when it profits them not."*

We will merely add that Justin here, and in many other places, appears evidently to give to the term "unquenchable," as applied to the fire of hell, a meaning beyond what we attach to it. We hold that an unquenchable fire simply means a fire which cannot be quenched until it has consumed all on which it preyed. It then goes out itself, leaving behind it the tokens of the destruction it has wrought. We think, at all events we admit, that Justin means by the unquenchable fire of hell what the Augustinian theorists mean by it—a fire which will never cease to burn throughout eternity. And now we have Justin's view of hell which he holds out as a solemn warning to the sinner. He holds that its flames will never cease to burn while God Himself lives: that it will have a perpetual fuel on which to feed, namely, the bodies, or members of the wicked: that these bodies or members will be endowed with immortality so as to be capable of boing thus endless fuel for endless fire; and that in the fire they will have a kind of sensation or sensibility. This is Justin's theory. Can we reconcile it with his substantial agreement with our view, or with his own declarations elsewhere that all life and existence will cease in the scene of future punishment? We can.

Justin Martyr, while a good and sound Christian, had a good deal of the philosophy, both in thought and word, about him, in which he had been educated. Of all the philosophers Plato was his favorite, though he repeatedly condemns some of his opinions. It was in his old philosopher's garb, as Eusebius tells us, that Justin was inclined to preach the word of God. It is in a philosophic idea, very absurd as it appears to us, but,

---

* *First Apology*, c. lii.

nevertheless, very commonly held at that time, and esteemed just as indubitable as we hold the principle of gravitation—it was in such a philosophic idea that we are to find what is to reconcile Justin Martyr to himself and to us. We may smile at the idea; but such men as Aristotle, and Pliny, and Tertullian, and Augustine, did not doubt it. If we had lived in their time we should not have doubted it ourselves. It is possible we hold as first truths what are far more unsound. What if the immortality of the soul may be one such!

There was then in Justin's time, and had long been, a strange philosophical opinion as to the nature and qualities of *a kind of fire,* which by some was called "secret," and by some "divine." It had the supposed property of reproducing the material which it consumed. Tertullian thus speaks of it: "The philosophers," he says, "are familiar, as well as we, with the distinction between *a common and a secret fire.* Thus that which is in common use is far different from that which we see in Divine judgments, whether striking as thunderbolts from heaven, or bursting up out of the earth through mountain tops; *for it does not consume what it scorches; but while it burns it repairs.*"[*] We have thus the idea, represented as a common one, of a fire which perpetually burned and perpetually reproduced what it fed on, and this fire was supposed by the Christian fathers in general to be identical in this property with the fire of hell. "A notable proof this," says Tertullian, "of the fire eternal! A notable example of the endless judgment which still supplies punishment with fuel!" It is in this philosophical idea, held by Justin as by others, that we see the reconciliation of his apparently conflicting statements. We suppose him to have held that life, as we have it now, would cease in hell, that the souls of the wicked would die and perish there; but that a fire would continue to burn there throughout eternity; that the limbs or carcasses would be ever

[*] *Apology*, par. 48; Augustine, *City of God*, xxi., iv.

consuming and ever being reproduced to supply it with fuel; and in reference to this eternal reproduction he calls those limbs "immortal," and in reference to their being perpetually scorched and consumed he calls them possessed with a kind of *sensation,* such as all animal or vegetable matter is possessed of and exhibits when submitted to the action of fire. All Justin's expressions are suited to this view; and this view makes him throughout consistent with himself in his descriptions of future punishment.

Justin's description of the *members of the wicked as immortal* he probably borrowed from Plato, with whose writings he was perfectly acquainted, and who describes some of the members of the human body, *after death,* by this very phrase "immortal" (αθανατα, *athanata*), in reference to their long continuance in their organization.[*] He supposes the fire of hell to burn on through eternity; and to be ever consuming and reproducing these "immortal members." As consuming, they must possess that sensitiveness to the action of fire which all consumable matter though devoid of animal life is possessed of, and without which it could not be consumed at all. And it is to be noted that the word *aisthesis,* which he puts for the sensation of the members, is the very word which his master, Plato, uses to distinguish the substance which he supposes distinct from "incorporeal and intelligent substance," *i.e.*, from the mind or soul. The latter he calls ουσιαν ασωματον or ουσιαν νοητην, in contradiction to ουσιαν αισθητην.[†]

That this is "*the kind of* sensation" with which he supposes them endowed, and not the sensitiveness of pain which the living animal feels when exposed to the heat of fire, is quite plain from his own words: for he refers his readers, in order that they may understand this, to the passage in

[*] Plato, *Phædo*, par. 29.

[†] *Ibid.*

Isaiah 66:24, which describes the *action of the worm and of the fire upon carcasses or dead bodies.* The dead body, exposed to the action of fire, exhibits a sensitiveness to its action. Such is "the kind of sensation" which Justin supposes that the members of the wicked will throughout eternity continue to exhibit under the action of the eternal fire. He supposes that God will continue to exhibit this spectacle through eternity as a warning. But it is a spectacle unaccompanied with pain. Pain departed when the soul ceased to exist in hell. That it is not absurd to suppose that Justin held such a view may appear from the fact that one of the ablest modern works which has appeared on our side of the question has advocated the view that the fire of hell will continue to burn throughout eternity;* and that Justin's view was in every particular that which we ourselves held for a time until we came to see the more simple and common sense of the term "unquenchable" as applied to fire. Justin did not see this, and hence the only difference, and that an unimportant one, from us. Imagining a fire burning on for eternity, he gathered naturally that it must have something to feed upon. Holding that animal life would not continue for eternity in hell, he laid hold of the idea, justified by the philosophical opinion of his time, that the members of the damned, devoid of animal life and therefore incapable of pain, would forever continue to grow and renew themselves. This he thought, and truly, a kind of life, such as vegetables have, and so he calls them immortal. And thus we have Justin consistent with himself. Thus we are free to give their natural force to his descriptions of the utter destruction of existence in hell, *i.e.*, of the existence of animal life. And thus we vindicate our claim to the testimony of Justin Martyr as holding our view of future punishment, in the age *immediately succeeding that of the apostles.*

---

* Denniston, *Perishing Soul.*

17

Irenaeus, Martyr and Bishop of Lyons

We will now draw our reader's attention to the opinion of Irenaeus on future punishment. He is, unquestionably, one of the soundest and most able of the early fathers. He was a pupil of Polycarp, who was himself a disciple of St. John. His martyrdom is usually placed A.D. 202. Of his five books against heresies, we unfortunately possess only the first in the original Greek. We possess the other four through a rude *Latin translation, made when the Church had all but universally adopted the Augustinian theory.* We might probably hence expect to see some expressions having a tendency in that direction, and should not rely too implicitly on the force of a word here or there. In spite of this drawback it is most satisfactory to find the clear emphatic testimony of this justly-valued father in favor of the scriptural theory of punishment.

Irenaeus sets out with views of human nature diametrically opposed to those of Augustine and his school. Indeed his views of our nature as it came from God's hands are such as we do not hold ourselves. He seems to have considered that man as he was at first created was *mortal as to his entire nature.** The *spirit* which is in the believer now he apparently

* iv., xxxix, 2.

considers not to have been bestowed upon Adam at creation: he was a being at the first only of body and of soul, and therefore mortal as to his entire nature. The spirit of the believer he evidently thinks is a part of the Divine Spirit imparted to the believer through Christ, and only given since Gospel times. Without this Spirit, he holds that there can be no such thing as immortality for man. He apparently considers that the union of this Spirit to the soul of the believer in this life renders the *believer's soul* immortal now, and that its union with the *believer's body* at the resurrection will render the body thenceforward incorruptible and immortal.*

We are not here vindicating these views of Irenaeus on what is unquestionably a very deep theme; neither are we here controverting them. We merely present a very brief abstract of them to show how diametrically opposite to Augustine's views of human nature were those of Irenaeus. Augustine makes a part of human nature to have been possessed from the very beginning of an essential and inalienable immortality. Irenaeus represents *the entire of that nature,* body and soul alike, to have been created mortal, and to have been as yet unjoined by an element which was essential to the possession by either of immortality. In order that *unfallen man* should obtain immortality, Irenaeus thinks that he must have obtained something which he had not at first. This something—this third part of man—the Divine Spirit, uncreated and eternal, he supposes not to have been given until the time of Christ, and then only to believers. They who were not believers never receive it, according to Irenaeus; *and must therefore be mortal,* and can by no means enjoy or possess eternal existence. Man in his first estate was but mortal: man in his fallen estate, and refusing to accept Christ as his Savior, cuts himself off from the gift of that Spirit which would have been essential to

* B. v., c. x., xi., xii., xiii.

the immortality even of unfallen man. Irenaeus' views of human nature, be they true or false, are absolutely irreconcilable with the idea that he could suppose that the wicked should possess an immortal existence. With this summary of his views agrees every particular which he gives us on the question before us.

We will first enquire what Irenaeus tells us of life, and of that eternal life which Christ bestows upon His people. With respect to "life," he gives it its literal and proper sense of "existence." While our Augustinian theorists are forcing upon the word as its proper sense "well-being," "happiness," and other senses of the kind, Irenaeus tells us over and over that with him it simply means *existence.* He tells us there may be life where there is no light, no joy, but only fear, perplexity, darkness, and sorrow. He tells us that our "flesh" partakes of life. Life eternal he defines to be never growing old. And he calls Christ the Prince of Life because he exists before all and goes before all.*

When he comes in particular to speak of life as bestowed by Christ upon His redeemed, which he sometimes, following Scripture, calls "life," and sometimes "eternal life," he not only never tells us that he supposes it to be in its nature different from that life which means existence; but he over and over tells us that he means by it the very same thing. He expressly defines "the life" which the Father bestows upon those who are saved, to be "*continuance for ever and ever,*" "*length of days for ever and ever.*" "Eternal life" he defines as identical with "immortality." He defines believers "living to God," to mean that they "*have not passed out of existence,*" but are children of that resurrection in which they will obtain the life now pledged to them. While he tells us that Christ has bestowed life now upon his people, he carefully teaches that it is given in faithful promise, not in actual possession, just as Canaan was given to Abraham

* B. i., c. iv., xviii. 5; i. xxix; ii., xxii. 4.

and his seed when they possessed in it nothing beyond a burial place. The "world of life," he tells us, is a world "*which is to come;* the elect are they who are *enrolled for this eternal life.*"*

While he thus explicitly defines eternal life to be "continuance forever," and "length of days forever," and the possession of an "existence" that was never to end, and "perpetual duration," he also explicitly tells us that none but the redeemed of Christ wall obtain it. It is with him the gift of Christ to His people. Receiving it as a gift from His Father, Christ "confers it upon those who are partakers of Himself." The unbelieving and the blinded "shall not inherit the world of life which is to come." They have forfeited this life, and "defraud themselves of this life" through their perverseness. Their "everlasting perdition" consists in "cutting them off from this life."† Thus, while a later school of theology, following Plato, taught for all men length of days forever, Irenaeus, following Christ, confined it to the redeemed.

We now come to a word, "immortality," (αθανασια, *athanasia*), which has, in its application to living beings, the singular advantage of having but one meaning. We need not therefore spend time in ascertaining what Irenaeus meant by it. He meant by it what everyone means by it: "exemption from death and annihilation; unending existence" (Webster's Dictionary). When applied to God, it means an existence of which He cannot be deprived; because He cannot change: when applied to a creature, it means an existence of which he cannot be deprived while he continues in the condition in which he was created.

With respect to immortality, then, Irenaeus plainly and repeatedly lays down the broad intelligible principle that it is lost by transgression, and cannot possibly continue to be the possession of the disobedient. For

---

* B. ii., c., xxxiv. 3; iv., v., 2; iv., xiii., 4; ii., xxxiii., 5; iii, vii., 2.

† iii., xvii. 2; iii., vii. 2; iii., xviii. 7; iii. xxiv.1.

disobedience, he tell us, man was "cast off from immortality." And again he asks: "How can he be immortal, who in his mortal nature did not obey his Maker?"* The immortality thus lost by sin, Irenaeus tells us, we can only regain by struggle. Commenting on Paul's admonition to the Christians at Corinth, "So to run that they may obtain," he says, "This able wrestler, therefore, exhorts us to *the struggle for immortality,* that we may be crowned, and may deem the crown precious; namely, *that which is acquired by our struggle*; *but which does not encircle us of its own accord.*"†

In a great variety of ways, and by every variety of expression, does Irenaeus continue to convey to us this impression of his views. That immortality which our Augustinian and Universalist theorists tell us is man's natural heritage, no matter what be his character, is, according to Irenaeus, a gift conveyed to the believer through the Gospel, which he describes as "breathing out immortality on every side, and vivifying man afresh." In no other way than through Christ, and our union with Him, does he allow that immortality can be gained at all. "By no other means," he says, "could we have attained to incorruptibility and immortality unless we had been united to incorruptibility and immortality." "The knowledge of the Son of God is," with him, "immortality." It is "the friendship of God which imparts immortality to those who embrace it." It is an honor not bestowed on all, but given as their high privilege to "those who have obeyed and believed on God."‡

Irenaeus' view of the resurrection, both of the just and of the unjust, further confirms us as to his opinion. We all know how unanimous Augustinian theorists are in their assertion that the bodies of the wicked will be raised immortal. This is essential to their theory; though whence they derive their knowledge of it, save whence the false prophets of Israel

---

* iii., xx. 2; iv., xxxix. 2.

† iv., xxxvii. 7.

‡ iii., xi. 8; iii., xix. 1; iv., xx. 2; iv., xiii. 4; iv., xv. 2.

derived their dreams, that is, "of the deceit of their own hearts," we cannot say. This was not the opinion of Irenaeus. As he confines immortality in general to the redeemed, so he restricts the immortality which is to be bestowed at the resurrection on the body to the bodies of the just. It is those "mortal bodies which preserved righteousness" which "God will render incorruptible and immortal."* The bodies of the wicked will be mortal in resurrection as the bodies of all men in this present life. With one observation, we will dismiss our inferences from Irenaeus' view of "immortality." Every one may know how loud and unanimous all the upholders of the Augustinian theory of future punishment are in their assertion of the immortality of the wicked. From its enunciation in the obscure and worthless forgeries of the first ages, through the fathers, and schoolmen, and divines of modern times, we ever hear repeated in every mode of speech the old insinuation and lie of Satan, that sin has not deprived the sinner of his immortality. Are we to suppose that a writer who confines immortality to the redeemed is of one mind with those who extend it to all men? By what strange law of language will Irenaeus be brought to an agreement here with the Clementine forgeries, and the writings of Tertullian, Augustine, Peter Lombard, Jonathan Edwards, Richard Baxter, Messrs. Spurgeon, Angus, Furniss, Grant, and others?

We next come to consider what Irenaeus means by "incorruption," and of whom he affirms it. We will find him using it in the sense in which any one may find it used in our standard dictionaries of every language. The English reader will find it in Johnson and Webster. Irenaeus leaves us in no doubt that he uses it in the sense common to all ages and all languages. Thus, in one place, he tells us that heretics "declare of all that is *material* that it must of necessity *perish,* inasmuch as it is incapable of receiving *any afflatus of incorruption.*" On this idea of the essential

* ii., xxix. 2.

corruptibility of matter, the heretics against whom Irenaeus directed a great proportion of his reasoning, denied bodily resurrection. "They disallow," he says, "the salvation of the *flesh,* and treat with contempt its regeneration, maintaining that it is *not capable of incorruption.*" Incorruption then, according to the common idea of Irenaeus and his opponents, meant incapacity of decay or dissolution. The heretics, in their opposition to the doctrine of the resurrection, *denied its applicability to matter:* Irenaeus, in his defense of the faith, asserted its applicability to matter.*

That he means by incorruption simply exemption, from decay, from a process of dissolution and ceasing to exist, is evident from his language throughout his work. Thus he reasons against the heretics in one place: "That *the flesh* can really partake of life, is shown from the fact of its being alive; for it lives on so long as it is God's purpose that it should do so. It is manifest, too, that God has the power to confer life upon it, inasmuch as He grants life to us who are in existence. And, therefore, since the Lord has power to infuse life into what He has fashioned, and since the flesh is capable of being quickened, *what remains to prevent its participating in incorruption, which is a blissful and never-ending life* granted by God?" Here he tells us that *flesh* in this present age partakes of a temporary life or existence, and that, consequently, there is nothing to prevent God from bestowing on it an eternal existence; *and this eternity of existence or life he defines to be incorruption.* The same idea he states farther on where he speaks of the new heavens and the new earth of the coming age, "when this fashion passes away, and man has been renewed, *and flourishes in art incorruptible state, so as to preclude the possibility of becoming old.*"† We can have no doubt, then, what Irenaeus means by incorruption.

---

* i. vi. 1; v., ii. 2.

† v., iii. 3; v. xxxvi. 1.

This incorruption Irenaeus expressly states will belong to the redeemed alone, and will not belong to the wicked. "Christ," he says, "has recalled fallen man to incorruption;" has "bestowed upon him the gift of incorruption." "By no means," he tells us, could "incorruptibility" be attained, save by the union with Christ: "unless man had been joined to God, he could never have been a partaker of incorruptibility." And lest we might think, as many now think, that the efficacy of the work of Christ procured incorruption for all mankind, believers and unbelievers alike, he tells us that Paul in 2 Corinthians 4:4, speaks of the unbelievers of this world, "because they shall not inherit the future age of incorruption." Incorruption, then, he confines to the redeemed of Christ, and denies to the wicked, *i.e.*, he held that the former would exist forever and the latter would not.[*]

If we wanted anything to explain Irenaeus' view, which we certainly do not, we should find it in the period when he supposes this "incorruption" to commence. Our Augustinian friends are always describing the primary sense of words as "low," "sensual," "materialistic."[†] Their principles carried out to their legitimate extent would overturn our belief in a bodily resurrection, in the personality of Satan and fallen angels, yea, in the very personality of God Himself. But Irenaeus was a thinker of a different stamp. That "incorruption" which the Augustinian would doubtless explain in a figurative way he explained in a material way. While the Augustinian would refer it to a mental and spiritual process *here begun,* Irenaeus plainly tells us that it has not commenced in this present life at all, and will not commence until the resurrection. We have, according to Irenaeus, incorruption *now in promise*: at the resurrection we shall have it *in possession.* The Holy Spirit now in the believer is, he tells us, "the earnest

[*] ii., xx. 3; iii. xix. 1; iii., xviii. 7; iii., vii. 1.

[†] Bartlett, *Life and Death Eternal,* 21-25.

(or pledge) of incorruption." He considers the indwelling of the Spirit to be God's security given to the believer that He will fulfill His promise and covenant of incorruption. But not until the resurrection of the just; not until Christ has set up that kingdom which is then to be established does Irenaeus allow incorruption to have actually begun: *"The kingdom"* he tells us, which dates from the resurrection, *"is the commencement of incorruption."*[*] Irenaeus had no idea of that figurative explanation of words which, introduced by Origen, and adopted in this whole controversy of future punishment by the Augustinian school opposed to Origen, finds its fitting end in the dreamland of Swedenborgh and the Spiritualists.

Irenaeus' opinion of the resurrection is also in agreement with our theory. He maintained that the wicked would rise in the flesh, to confess in this the power of God, and to suffer for their evil deeds. But between the resurrection of the just and the unjust he put a most marked distinction. We do not here refer to his making that of the just anterior in point of time to that of the unjust; for this difference belongs to another question of theology. We refer to the distinction which he everywhere draws between the condition after resurrection of the bodies of these two classes.

The eternal duration of the bodies of the wicked is essential to the Augustinian theory of punishment, which is so far scriptural as that it requires, for the consummation of punishment, the presence of that body in, through, and by which sin was committed. Its eternal duration can only be asserted by such terms as "immortal" and "incorruptible." Augustine and his school accordingly apply these terms to the bodies of the wicked as well as to those of the just at their resurrection. "All shall rise incorruptible," says Augustine, speaking of these two classes. But Irenaeus speaks in quite an opposite way. So far from supposing that incorruption to belong to both, he expressly confines it to those *"mortal bodies which*

---

[*] iii., xxiv. 1; v., xxxii. 1.

preserved righteousness." So far from supposing that the resurrection of Christ was the first fruits, or the pledge, or in any way connected with the resurrection of the unjust, he expressly tells us that it is only a first fruit "of every man who is found in life." They alone, he tells us, have the hope of that resurrection which is "to eternity." Of all the wicked, of all who remain in the bondage of the old disobedience, of all who have not received liberty through the Son, he tells us that "*they remain in mortal flesh.*"*

With all that has been advanced of the opinion of Irenaeus agrees what he tells us more particularly of the punishment of the wicked. We can only advert to a small portion of his teaching, but that we suppose will be sufficient after all that has gone before. Of those whom he describes as mortal: of those whom he denies to be incorruptible or immortal, or to have any hope of an endless existence; we will not deny to the terms descriptive of their punishment, their natural and ordinary sense. When Tertullian or Augustine speak of the perishing or destruction of the wicked, we know that their theory of immortality obliges them to put an unnatural and forced sense upon such terms. But Irenaeus has, we have seen, no philosophical theory which compels him to do so. Even on this fact however, we will not ask our readers wholly to rely. We will show them from Irenaeus' own mouth in what sense he uses his words.

To perish is one of the very strongest words in the vocabulary of Irenaeus. It is with him the synonym for non-existence, and apparently even for that philosophical annihilation of matter which, though so often and desperately charged against our view, is held by none of us. Thus, when he describes the grief of one of those imaginary Æons, whom Gnostic heretics introduced into the ecclesiastical discussions of the first centuries, in fear lest her imperfect generation "*should end her own existence,*" he describes this end of existence as "a *perishing* by being

* i., xxii. 1; ii., xxix. 2; iv., xviii. 5; iii., xix. 1.

absorbed in the universal substance:" and of the bodies of the just he says, that "*although they go to corruption, yet they do not perish.*" To perish, he tells us, will be the ultimate fate of all unrighteous souls.*

His general descriptions of future punishment are quite decisive of his opinion. No one of the fathers recurs more perpetually to it than Irenaeus does. In this he is a faithful disciple of Scripture which never allows us to lose sight of it. Nor is there one of the fathers who gives fuller descriptions of it. He evidently brought it forward in all the terrors he supposed to belong to it as a warning to escape from it. Yet in all his allusions to and descriptions of it, there cannot be found a parallel to numberless passages which we might quote readily from Hippolytus, Tertullian, Augustine, and others of their view. When these men mean to set forth beyond mistake what they considered the *nature* of that punishment which they rightly supposed eternal, they use a variety of phrases never found thus applied by Irenaeus. They are careful to tell us that the wicked in hell do not die, that death never comes to them, that they are both in soul and body incorruptible, eternal, and immortal. If Irenaeus agreed with them, we cannot but suppose that he would have used similar phrases when intending to place future punishment in all its terrors before the mind. But instead of doing so, he uses terms indicative of an opposite belief.

No doubt he describes it over and over as everlasting and eternal. The disciples of Origen can find no countenance in the pages of Irenaeus. The theory that future punishment is for a single soul of a purgative nature, and that after a certain period, more or less protracted, any sentenced in the judgment to hell will come forth and join the ranks of the redeemed, finds not one word in its support throughout the books of this scriptural father. The judgment is eternal: the punishment which it awards is eternal:

* i., ii. 3; i., iii. 1; i., vi. 1; Fragments, xii.; b. ii., xxix. 1.

the condition to which it dooms is an unending one. But if Origen's hope finds no support in Irenaeus, the hideous cruelty of Augustine finds just as little sanction. Irenaeus agrees with us in our view both of the duration and nature of future punishment. Its duration is eternal: its nature is death, destruction, perdition, annihilation.

The period of future punishment he describes as "a day of fire," in which God will be to sinners "a consuming fire." In this fire, in which the Augustinian tells us the wicked will remain forever alive and unconsumed, Irenaeus tells they "shall be burned up as were Nadab and Abihu" by the fire from the Lord. In it he tells us, that unrighteous souls will perish, that they will be "punished with everlasting death," that they will "pass away," and "will not endure forever." "Everlasting perdition" he explains to mean "cutting off the wicked from the life," which Christ will bestow upon His people. Their fate will be to be "deprived of continuance for ever and ever," "not to receive from God length of days forever." Perdition signifies with him "nonexistence;" and the death and eternal separation from God which sin entails means with him "the loss of all the benefits which God has in store" for His people.*

It is well to notice how Irenaeus makes his view of future punishment to consist in its being *eternal.* It is, with him, eternal because it is the loss of blessing which is eternal. It does not consist in eternally inflicting new misery, but in the eternal loss of what might have been eternally enjoyed. He first tells us that "separation from God is death," *i.e.*, involves death as its penalty, or, to use his own words, "consists in the loss of all the benefits which God has in store." He then adds: "Now *good things are eternal* and without end with God, and *therefore the loss of them is also eternal and*

* iv., xx. 6; iv., xxvi. 2; ii., xxix. 1; iv., xxxiii. 11; iv. 3; iv., xi. 4; ii., xxxiv. 3; v. xxx. 4; v., xxvii. 2.

never ending."[*] Here is Irenaeus' "everlasting punishment." It is an everlasting loss of blessing thrown away. Here is Irenaeus' "everlasting death." It is not, as Augustinian theorists describe it, a death which is always coming but never comes: it is a death which covers over its victim with a pall of everlasting darkness. An eternal loss is with Irenaeus an eternal punishment. All past punishments inflicted in this life upon sinners are for this reason infinitely less than the future punishment. The death which God inflicted upon sinners such as Dathan was a "temporal" and a "typical" death. It cut them from a life of a few years' duration: it cut them off from a life which was itself due to death. But the second death cuts off from an eternal life, and is therefore an eternal death.[†]

In forming our judgment of the real views on Irenaeus, we have gone upon the surest ground, not deriving it from one or two passages selected as most favorable, but from his own meaning put by himself upon his language, as seen by a careful perusal of his entire work. We will now in conclusion present our readers with one considerable extract from him, and ask them whether it does not entirely agree with our previous reasoning, and whether *any* second opinion as to its meaning can be *fairly* entertained.

Irenaeus is arguing with persons who held that there *could be no immortality or endless existence for any created souls.* His argument has nothing to do with the ill or well-being of souls, but simply with their continued existence. Those with whom he contended held that either souls must have been *uncreated* if they are to abide forever; or that, *if created,* they must come to nothing and perish like all other created things.[‡] The

---

[*] v., xxvii. 2.

[†] iv., xxviii. 1, 2.

[‡] ii., xxxiv. 2.

knowledge of the theory which Irenaeus reasons against will be our guide to the meaning of his reply, if, indeed, his words required any explanation.

In answer then to the above persons who held that "souls which only began a little while ago to exist cannot endure for any length of time," Irenaeus says:

> "As the heaven which is above us, the firmament, the sun, the moon, the rest of the stars, and all their grandeur, although they had no previous existence, were called into being and continue through a long course of time according to the will of God, *so also anyone who thinks thus respecting souls and spirits,* and, in fact, respecting all created things, *will not by any means go far astray,* inasmuch as all things that have been made had a beginning when they were formed, but *endure as long as God wills that they have an existence and continuance.* The prophetic Spirit bears testimony to these opinions, when He declares, 'For He spake, and they were made; He commanded and they were created: He hath established them forever; yea, for ever and ever.' And again, He thus speaks respecting *the salvation of man*: 'He asked life of Thee, and Thou gavest him *length of days for ever and ever,'* indicating that it is the Father of all *who imparts continuance for ever and ever on those who are saved. For life does not arise from us, nor from our own nature;* but it is bestowed according to the grace of God. And therefore, he who shall preserve the life bestowed upon him, and give thanks to Him who imparted it, shall receive also length of days for ever and ever. *But he who shall reject it, and prove himself ungrateful to his Maker,* inasmuch as he has been created, and has not recognized Him who bestowed the gift upon him, *deprives himself of continuance forever and ever.* And, for this reason, the Lord declared to those who showed themselves ungrateful towards Him: 'If ye have not been faithful in that which is little, who will give you that which is great?' indicating that those *who, in this brief temporal life, have showed themselves ungrateful to Him who bestowed it, shall justly not receive from Him length of days forever.*"[*]

[*] ii., xxxiv. 3.

For our part, we do not know how any man of honest mind and common understanding can put a second meaning upon this long extract from Irenaeus. There are, however, men who stand deservedly high in estimation who do put a second meaning upon these words. Dr. Roberts, the translator of Irenaeus, gives the following annotation upon them: "As Massuet observes, this statement is to be understood in harmony with the repeated assertion of Irenaeus that the wicked will exist in misery forever. *It refers not to annihilation,* but to *deprivation of happiness.*"

We will merely say that we have read Irenaeus and have *never* met with any assertion of his that "the wicked shall exist in misery forever." We will add that if such an assertion of his could be adduced it would only prove that Irenaeus contradicted himself as many men have done. We will lay down our indignant protest against a principle of interpretation which would make words of no use whatsoever to convey meaning. To tell us that "existence," and "continuance," spoken in the very same connection of the "enduring" of sun and moon and soul and spirit, mean "happiness"—whether learned editors tell us this to save their author's consistency, or to prop up any favorite theory of their own—is just to tell us that we may cease the use of words altogether, because they may have any meaning that any one may choose to put upon them. To say that "sweet" means "bitter," or that " light" means "darkness," is just as allowable a use of words as to say that the "enduring" and "continuing" of one of God's works, such as the sun in the sky or the human soul, means, "the happiness" of these works. We dismiss such interpretation as an insult to our common understanding. Irenaeus, notwithstanding his Benedictine editor and his Presbyterian translator, tells us that the wicked will not continue to exist forever, because God does not will them to exist. God did will his "happiness" and his "well-being," but he marred them. God does not will his continued existence, and therefore he will cease to exist. Such is the testimony of the learned, holy, and martyred Bishop of Lyons, in the second century of Christ. Such was the testimony of the primitive church, in agreement with apostolic teaching. Such is the doctrine which we uphold, and which, long obscured by philosophical dogma, human tradition, medieval subtleties, and modern prejudice, is again shining out before the minds of God's people in the churches of Christendom.

18

Rise of the Theory of Eternal Life in Hell

THE DOCTRINE OF LIFE and immortality through Christ, held by the Apostolical Fathers, and the best of their immediate successors, began at an early period to be altered and corrupted. *Philosophy* was the means which Satan used to introduce the error which first struggled with and finally succeeded in strangling the truth. The noblest system of philosophy that had ever emanated from the human mind, that of Socrates and Plato—the idea in that philosophy which seemed most akin to the grand truth of Christianity, the immortality of the human soul—was the weapon which Satan, transforming himself into an angel of light, used to fight, and to fight with terrible success, against the truth. He will confound the immortality taught by Plato, with the immortality taught by Christ: he will persuade men that there is not much difference between them: he will flatter the religion of the despised Nazarene by showing that in one main feature it is sustained by the noblest minds of Greece and Rome: he will introduce Plato as the precursor of Christ, of Paul, of John: he will show that Christ did but open out more fully and stamp His authority upon what Plato had been painfully striving after in the schools of Athens.

His point established, the astute mind of the fiend saw he could introduce into the church a doctrine which would blacken the character of

God, alienate the human mind from Him, send men for refuge from its excessive horrors to imaginary purgatories, keep the human mind in perpetual agitation, veering ever between a cruel dogma, a destructive leniency, or an indiscriminate infidelity. All this he saw with his penetrating intellect would be gained, could he but induce the church to believe that Plato taught the truth on the question of the immortality of the soul. He succeeded by means of philosophers who became Christians; but who brought with them into the church more or less of their philosophy. They forgot—or did not choose to follow—the example of Paul in philosophic Corinth: "I determined not to know anything among you, save Jesus Christ, and Him crucified" (1 Cor. 2:2). They would know something of Plato too. Had not his grand soaring mind all but anticipated Christ?

The reader of Scripture knows how earnestly and frequently Paul warned the church *against philosophy* (1 Cor. 1:22; Col. 2:8). He is the only one of the apostles who has distinctly done so. But he, well-acquainted with all the philosophical systems, has spoken out clearly and emphatically in their condemnation. Clement of Alexandria, on his words in Colossians 2:8, says, that Paul is "branding, not all philosophy, but the Epicurean and the Stoic."* He considered much of the Platonic philosophy as "a divinely-ordered preparation of the Greeks for faith in Christ." Paul himself, however, made no exception of this kind, nor did he consider that there was any real affinity between the Gospel of his Master and any system in credit with the Greeks (1 Cor. 1:23). He does not merely condemn the Stoic and Epicurean schools only and exempt that of Plato. Instead, he prohibits with all the weight of his authority the introduction of any philosophical system or dogma into the church. He warned that it would spoil and corrupt; not elevate, refine, or strengthen truth.

---

* *Misc.* i., xi.

It might be and was true that every system of philosophy had its *portion* of truth; but he knew that every system also was poisoned with error. Plato, as a guide for the church, stood no higher with him than Zeno, Pythagoras, or Epicurus. While he has quoted more than once from the poets, he has never quoted from the philosophers of heathenism.

Many of the early fathers forgot this warning of the apostle; and it is among these precisely that we find the origin of error in the Christian church upon the great doctrine of future punishment. Educated in Platonism, they did not like to renounce it, and they flattered themselves that they might, with great advantage to the cause of Christianity, bring a portion at least of their old learning into its service. Origen, in the third century, expresses this general bias, when he says that, "If any one were to come from the study of Grecian opinions and usages to the Gospel he would not only decide that its doctrines were true, but would, by practice, establish their truth, and supply whatever seemed wanting, from a Grecian point of view, to their demonstration, and thus confirm the truth of Christianity:" and he accordingly advised those who would understand Holy Scripture "to extract from the philosophy of the Greeks what may serve as a course of study as a preparation for Christianity."[*] Milner testifies to the injurious effects produced by Platonism upon Christianity in the second and third centuries.[†]

The influence of Plato appears even in the language of such men as Justin Martyr and Irenaeus. Both of them use expressions which we never find in the Apostolical Fathers. Some doubt may perhaps, not without reason, be thrown upon the genuineness of some of the phrases in Irenaeus, coming to us through a translation made at a period when the Augustinian error ruled in the church. Of the phrases in Justin, however,

---

[*] *Against Celsus*, b. i., c. ii., *Origen to Gregory*.

[†] *History of the Church*, Cent. ii., c. ix.

there is no reason to doubt. The true doctrine of punishment held by these fathers prevented the Platonic language from having its natural effect. Thus, if Justin in one place speaks of the immortality of the soul, and even supposes that philosophers derived their ideas of its immortality *from Moses and the prophets,* he in another shows how little he was influenced by this philosophic dogma, by his full and graphic description of *the manner in which* a soul may die and "cease to exist."* All that he meant by the immortality of the soul was that it did not die when the body died, but remained alive in the intermediate state between death and resurrection.† He used a philosophical and unscriptural phrase: but the general truth of his doctrinal views presented its injurious effects upon his own teaching. He helped however materially by such language to produce the effects which its use must eventually bring about. Had he protested against the *language* of the Platonists as he did most plainly against the *logical consequences* which the Platonists drew from their language, Justin might have done in the second century what we are doing in the nineteenth.‡ But Justin loved the language of philosophy while he rejected its spirit. In his very dress he wore the garb of the philosopher, while his heart was true to Christ. In this he did deadly injury to truth though he dreamed not of doing it. He helped to sow seed the nature of whose fruit he had no knowledge of.

But the seed of Platonism fell into different soil than the hearts of men like Justin, Irenaeus, and even Clement of Alexandria. It produced among the successors in time of Justin effects which it did not produce in him, and which were yet its natural and inevitable effects. Frequently reasoning against portions of the Platonic philosophy, often affecting to despise it,

* *First Apology*, c. xliv; *Dialogue with Trypho*, c. vi.

† *Dialogue with Trypho*, c. v.

‡ *Ibid.*

the Christian fathers as a general rule adopted the Platonic dogma, "*every soul is* immortal."[*] This became the motto upon the patristic banner. On this point Plato took rank, not among prophets, and apostles, but above all prophets and apostles. A doctrine which neither Old Testament nor New taught, directly or indirectly, nay, which was contrary to a great part of the teaching of both, these fathers brought in with them into the church, and thus gave to the old sage of the academy a greater authority and a wider influence than he had ever attained, or ever dreamed of attaining.

It was, in effect, Plato teaching in the church, under the supposed authority of Christ and His apostles, doctrines subversive of and contrary to what they had one and all maintained. *This dogma of Plato was made the rigid unbending rule for the interpretation of Scripture.* In this lay its deadly effect on truth. No Scripture, no matter what its language, no matter what the natural usual sense of its language, could be interpreted in a sense inconsistent with Plato's theory.

Under its influence, words assume new, unnatural, distorted, far-fetched meanings. Christ and Paul, and John and Peter, all are forced to Platonize. The deduction of reason, more than half doubted by the reason of Plato himself, scouted by the reason of the vast majority of mankind, was by these Platonizing fathers palmed off upon men's minds as the teaching of Revelation. What Socrates taught with faltering tongue, what Plato held in one place and rejected in another, what Cicero hoped might be true while he dreaded that it might not, Tertullian and Augustine taught as an indubitable truth.

We do not find the origin of the doctrine of eternal existence for the wicked among any of the names which we have for one reason or other learned to respect. We find it with men whose names are now scarcely known. The very first who can with truth be brought forward as holding it

---

[*] Tertullian, *Resurrection*, c. iii.

is Athenagoras. He lived from about A.D. 127 to 190. He was born at Athens, was educated there in the philosophy of Plato, became a Christian, and settled at Alexandria, where his great object seems to have been to show that Christianity and Platonism *were one and the same in substance.* His name commanded no respect in his own day, and his writings were suffered to sink into almost entire oblivion.[*] They deserved the neglect they met with. Beyond any question, he held the doctrine of eternal life for the reprobate as it was afterwards elaborated by Augustine. He rested it on the ground of the immortality of man, and *this immortality of man he based upon an argument of reason.* He laid it down that *God's object in making man was that man might live.*

Hence, he argues, as God's end cannot positively be defeated, man must continue to live forever, be he good or evil, miserable or happy. "Nothing," he tells us, "that is endowed with reason and judgment has been created, or is created, for the use of another, whether greater or less than itself, but *for the sake of the life and continuance of the being itself so created.*" Again he says: "According to the view which more nearly touches the beings created, God made man *for the sake of the life of those created, which, is not kindled for a little while and then extinguished*;" and he thereafter argues that "since among the works of God that which is useless can have no place," and "*since the cause of man's creation is seen to lie in perpetual existence, the being so created must be preserved forever.*" Hence, he concludes, that as the wicked must live forever they must meet with an eternal life of misery.[†]

The argument of Athenagoras is well deserving the attention of our modern Augustinian theorists. It shows them the source and origin of their

---

[*] Ante-Nicene Christian Library, Edinburgh; T. and T. Clark, Introductory Notice to Writings of Athanagoras.

[†] *Resurrection of the Dead*, c. xii., xiii., xviii., xix.

creed. It is based upon the reasoning of such men as Athenagoras. It is preeminently a rationalistic deduction. The wicked *must* be miserable forever, because they *must* live forever; and they *must* live forever because God made them for the purpose of living! This is the rationalism of Athenagoras adopted blindly by men who ought not to drink at such a fountain. It seems to us rationalism of a wretched kind.

One text of Scripture Athenagoras never dreams of advancing for his opinion: but then he has in place of it his master's sonorous phraseology for our nature. With him, as with Plato, the soul is immortal: it must continue to live: it was made immortal at its creation, and cannot be subjected to death; for it is, and was, and always will be incorruptible. Athenagoras, being a Christian as well as a Platonist, took the liberty to add to his master's theory. Plato dropped the body altogether at death, and was only too glad to do so, as being with him only an obstruction, a prison, a curse to the soul. Here Athenagoras was compelled by his Christian position to strike out a new line for himself, which diverged, we must say, as much from Scripture as from Plato. The body, which our Alexandrian philosopher very properly supposes to be an essential part of man, and not merely an old garment or an old house which the wearer or the tenant could quit at will, was originally created immortal, but became mortal by Adam's sin. With this part of his theory no fault can be found. It is perfectly scriptural. It is in what follows that he errs. He supposes that at the resurrection *the bodies of all men*, the wicked as well as the righteous, *will resume their original immortality.* The glorious chapter of St. Paul, in which he describes the resurrection of the just, and the change which passes upon their corrupt, dishonored, weak, and natural bodies, to fit them for an eternal life, is, without the smallest hesitation, applied by Athenagoras to describe the resurrection of the wicked.* Monstrous as the

* *Resurrection*, c. iii., x., xvi., xviii.

idea is, abstaining as most of our modern Augustinians do from this perversion of Paul's grand chapter, such an application is absolutely necessary to their theory; and Athenagoras was but reasonable here. The mortal body must put on immortality and incorruption if it is to endure an eternity of pain.

The truth is that if the reasoning of Athenagoras was correct, it would have led him to the theory of Origen *and not* to that of Augustine. That it did not do so is to us conclusive proof that at this period of church history the theory of a restoration from hell was one of those things of which so much as the remotest idea had not crossed the imagination of any one pretending to be a Christian. The time had not come for it, the time could not come, until the human mind was compelled to fly to it for refuge from a diabolical creed. For, most assuredly, the reasoning of Athenagoras correctly carried out would have led him to the conclusion of Origen.

One of his principles is that God's object in creating man could not be defeated: another of his principles is that "God made man for Himself," that "the final cause of an intelligent life and rational judgment, is to be uninterruptedly with those objects to which the natural reason is chiefly and primarily adapted, and to *delight unceasingly in the contemplation of Him who is, and of* His decrees."* No other conclusion could logically follow but that all men, however fallen, must be some time or other restored, so as to answer the end for which they were originally created. Their restoration to a holy delight in God was just as much a consequence of Athenagoras' principles as the restoration of their bodies to immortality, or the eternal existence of the entire man. But the meteoric light of Universalism was not visible in the sky of the second century. If it had even but faintly colored it, our Alexandrian philosopher would have anticipated Origen instead of Augustine.

* *Resurrection,* c. xii., xxv.

One word more, before we take our leave of Athenagoras. It bears reference to his use of a most important scriptural word. We beg the attention of our Augustinian friends to it, and to its bearing upon this controversy. Athenagoras was an excellent Greek scholar, and knew the meaning of that Greek word which is rendered by our English word "perish." He also tells us repeatedly the sense which ought to be put upon it. Thus, in one place he describes the Epicurean doctrine of the annihilation of body and soul by their saying that they "perish:" in another place he states that it has the very same meaning as that strong expression "to annihilate:" in another he opposes that which is perishable to that which *is eternal:* and in another he describes the old Stoic doctrine, that all things will one day *come to an end,* by saying that "they will perish."[*]

How then does Athenagoras use this word when he comes to speak of the future life both of just and of unjust? He denies that the term can be applied to *either class!* He tells us that if the unjust were said to perish it would be equivalent to saying that they would be annihilated! He accordingly boldly says, speaking of the unjust as much as of the just: "God has not made us that we should perish."[†]

Will our Augustinian friends save us the trouble of application? They know that God's Word has repeatedly said that the wicked will perish. Will they not then come over to our opinion that the wicked will, according to God's Word, be annihilated? It is an ugly long Latin word, but after all it only means, as we use it, "to be destroyed," "to come to nothing." Will they not allow so much as that Athenagoras knew the meaning of one of his own Greek words? This is all we ask them to allow; the rest will follow. If to "perish" means to be "annihilated"—and Athenagoras tells us that is its proper meaning—then, surely, the Bible teaches the annihilation of the

---

[*] *Plea for the Christians*, c. iv., xxi., xxxi., xxxvi.

[†] *Plea*, c. xxxi.

wicked. If we are to follow good old Moses Stuart's axiom, that, "We are to come to our conclusions by enquiring what the language means which the sacred writers have employed, and that the meaning of this is to be made out by philology, *i.e.*, by an investigation conducted agreeably to the principle of language," we cannot avoid this conclusion.* Surely Athenagoras knew the meaning of his own Greek language, and we only follow him to this extent. Where he goes beyond this, and contradicts the Bible, by saying that they, who, according to the Bible, will perish, shall not perish, here we take the liberty to leave Athenagoras for the Word of God.

While Athenagoras, the Platonist, is at Alexandria, maintaining the novel doctrine of eternal life in hell, he has a worthy fellow-laborer in Mesopotamia in the person of Tatian. Dr. Roberts has, with great liberality, placed him in his list of ante-Nicene Fathers. Mosheim has, with more propriety, placed him in his list of ante-Nicene *heretics*, as a founder of the sect known as Encratites, Hydroparastes, and Apotactites. It is curious and instructive to trace, where we can, the progress of error. Tatian had been in his earlier years a scholar of Justin Martyr, and after the death of the latter professed great reverence for his old master's opinions, and affected to consider them identical with his own. Justin, a great admirer of Plato, had, as we have seen, to a great extent adopted the phraseology of Plato concerning the soul, and called it *immortal* and *incorruptible*.

We have already explained that all which he meant by these phrases was that the soul was immortal *as compared with the body*, not dying with it, but existing in a separate state in *Hades*, while, after the judgment, he taught that it would die with the body in hell. Tatian, aware that Justin taught prominently the death of the soul, introduced a theory of its death which might seem to harmonize with that of Justin, while it was really contradictory to it. He supposed that when the body of the wicked died the

* Moses Stuart, *Exegetical Essays*, Philadelphia, p. 201.

soul also died with it, being forsaken by the higher spirit; but that at the resurrection it is raised to life again with the body. This early heretic held beyond a doubt the Augustinian theory of punishment. He speaks of the wicked as, at the resurrection, "receiving *the painful with immortality,*" and that their soul "rises again at last, at the end of the world, with the body, *receiving death by punishment in immortality.*"*

Tatian's description of eternal punishment is well worthy of notice. It will be remarked that in order to express his view he is obliged to introduce *a term of the utmost significance not found thus applied in Scripture.* That term is *immortality.* In all its various definitions of the eternal punishment of the lost Scripture never once speaks of their immortality. In his short address, Tatian introduces it at least twice. The introduction of a new phraseology is significant of the introduction of a new doctrine. On this, however, we will say more a little farther on.

The other matter we would note is the hopeless confusion of language, the perplexed jargon, which the introduction of this new doctrine necessitates. The expression, "receiving death by punishment in immortality," is in itself a contradiction in the terms. Ask a child or an unlettered person what it means, and you will see their bewilderment. The constant use of this kind of language blinds people to its lingual enormity.

What is there like it in Scripture? Scripture always contrasts death and life as exact opposites. Tatian makes death and immortal life to be one and the same! The notion of people receiving death by their receiving immortality in any condition is a barbarity of language worthy of the barbarous creed which has introduced into Christian literature a jargon which is mistaken for theology of a very exalted kind.

To a period perhaps somewhat later than the time of Athenagoras and Tatian belong "The Recognitions of Clement," and "The Clementine

---

* *Address to the Greeks,* c. xiii., xiv.

Homilies." These poor productions, in which heresy and error vastly predominate over truth, were attributed in ignorant ages to Clement of Rome. Indeed, even still, some men in high places in the Christian community are found to maintain that they are from his pen.* They are generally, however, esteemed spurious; and as such we treat them. Of these two works it is not known whether both are from the same hand, or which, if from different hands, was written first. We will first give a passing notice of "The Clementine Homilies."

It is difficult, if not impossible, to ascertain the exact sentiments of the writer of this work on our question of punishment. In different parts of it he appears to hold opposite opinions, in one place teaching our view of destruction, and in another the Augustinian heresy. Thus, in one passage, he says,

> "Those who do not repent shall be destroyed by the punishment of fire, even though in all other things they are most holy. But, as I said, at an appointed time a fifth part, being punished with eternal fire, shall be consumed. For they cannot endure forever who have been impious against the one God."

We could not more plainly describe our own view, except that we do not pretend to define the proportion of mankind to be punished, or suppose that the impious may be very holy persons. But in another place he is equally distinct for the Augustinian view. Here he makes Peter thus address the wicked:

> "Though by the dissolution of the body you should escape punishment, how shall you be able by corruption to flee from your soul which is

---

* *Future Punishment* by Joseph Angus, p. 2; Ante-Nicene Fathers, Recognitions of Clement, Introductory notice.

> incorruptible? For the soul even of the wicked is immortal; for whom it were better not to have it incorruptible. For, being punished with endless torture under unquenchable fire, and never dying, it can receive no end of its misery."[*]

Here we have a genuine Augustinian utterance. We beg our readers to mark the novel phrases, "incorruptible," "immortal," "never dying," which are never applied *in Scripture* to the wicked, but are judged essential by the spurious Clement to express his theory of punishment. Into the attempt to reconcile the passages we will not enter. Their contradiction may indicate interpolation, as some suppose to have been the case. If the entire work is from the same hand, he would seem to have lived at a period and a place where opinion was changing from the apostolic to the Augustinian point of view, and that he sometimes gives us one view and sometimes the other.

"The Recognitions of Clement" very strongly resembles "the Clementine Homilies." Various reasons have been given for the strong family likeness. In one respect, however, as it appears to us, they differ. In "The Recognitions" we see nothing of the inconsistency of statement which we have remarked in "The Homilies." "The Recognitions" are, so far as we know, thoroughly and consistently Augustinian. The immortality of every soul is laid down repeatedly in the most distinct terms. The argument on which its immortality is based is the justice of God. As God frequently leaves the wicked unpunished in this life, the writer supposes that they must suffer anguish for eternity in the next; and that, consequently, the soul must be immortal to endure it. The writer supposes that the wicked *might* have been sufficiently punished in this temporal life by temporal sufferings; but as these temporal sufferings have not here been inflicted they must be converted into eternal sufferings in the next life, which is very usurious interest to enforce for deferment of payment, seeing

[*] *Clementine Homilies*, Homily iii., c. vi; Homily xi., c. xi.

the deferment was not the act of the wicked but of God Himself. Having thus satisfactorily proved the immortality of the souls of the wicked, the rest follows as a matter of course. The eternity of pain follows from the eternity of existence.

To common logicians it might appear that the apostle Peter, through whom the writer utters his own sentiments, seems to reason in a circle. He first insists that the wicked ought to suffer eternally in the next life, and that therefore their souls must be immortal: and then he proceeds to demonstrate that, since their souls are immortal, they must suffer through eternity. But, whatever we may think of the quality of his reasoning, his theory of punishment is of the genuine Augustinian type. The heathen offenders and the ungodly among professing Christians suffer alike. "If," he says,

> "any persist in impiety till the end of life, then, as soon as the soul, *which is immortal,* departs, it shall pay the penalty of its persistence in impiety. For even the souls of the impious are immortal, though perhaps they themselves would wish them to end with their bodies. But it is not so; for they endure without end the torments of eternal fire, and to their destruction *have not the quality of mortality.*"*

It is indeed instructive thus to note the origin, among men of the lowest character, of views, which, subsequently adopted by men of a far higher reputation, have for long centuries depraved and corrupted the doctrine of the church. A brief sketch of the plan of "The Recognitions" may therefore not be without use. It is on the plan of "The Clementine Homilies." A century or more has passed since Clement, the fellow-laborer of Paul, has passed to his rest, and another man, of a different mould, seeks to impose his own views upon the church under a venerable and venerated

* B. iii., c. xxxix; xl; b. v., c. xxviii.

name. He accordingly supposes the genuine Clement to have been, while yet a philosopher, distracted with doubts as to the nature of the soul. He hears of Christ and His apostles, and meets Peter at Caesarea. His inquiries give rise to a long and strange argument between Simon Peter and Simon Magus on this intricate question, in which Peter discusses the famous "genitus" and "ingenitus," with all the glibness of Plato, and enters on the most mysterious questions in so sophistical and strange a way that, but for the name, one would be much more disposed to attribute the sentiments to the magician than to that "servant and apostle of Jesus Christ," who has left us two precious epistles.

Peter, in this most extraordinary controversy, affirms the soul to be immortal in its nature, and of a changeless substance which can know neither influx nor deflux, addition nor subtraction, mutilation nor conjunction, until we fancy, save for the different style, that we are listening to the Athenian philosopher enlightening his disciples, or to Augustine, gravely discussing the *quality of a soul.*

One cannot help feeling disposed at times to think the magician is much the best reasoner of the two. Indeed, Peter himself seems to have suspected the same; for at length, baffled apparently by Simon's pertinacity of opposition and the keenness of his arguments, the weary apostle takes refuge in a vision, which demonstrates what he had failed to prove to Simon Magus by his arguments—the immortality of the soul. In the writings of Athenagoras and Tatian, in the shameless forgeries and unhallowed vagaries of "The Recognitions" and "Homilies of Clement," lies the mean origin of a dogma which now overshadows the Christian church.

19

Tertullian

IN ATHENAGORAS, TATIAN, and the spurious works attributed to Clement of Rome, we have the earliest known advocates of the theory of eternal life in hell. From their writings we gather the marvelous power which the introduction of the Platonic dogma of the soul's immortality had upon the doctrine of punishment. But this theory required a more powerful advocacy than that of men of small or evil repute in their day. It found its required advocate in the person of Tertullian. A master of the Latin tongue, of reasoning ability, of a vehement nature and a vivid imagination, he was well suited to impress an idea on an age disposed to accept it; and, in spite of his heresies, despite his strange hallucinations, he left the lasting impress of his mind upon the church of succeeding times.

Accordingly, the theory of eternal torments culminated in the second century in this fierce African theologian. He did not hold it more plainly than Athenagoras and Tatian, but he impressed it with a power to which they were strangers, and be freed it from some of their statements which would expose it to animadversion. The weight of his personal character altogether exceeded anything to which they could lay claim. The grounds, therefore, on which such a man based his theory, the arguments by which he supported it, and the conclusions to which these led him, well deserve a separate chapter.

From the perusal of Tertullian's works we gather three great axioms or principles of his which influenced and molded his entire teaching on the question of future punishment. The first two were philosophical dogmas, for which he pretended little authority from Scripture; the third was his idea of the meaning of a common scriptural term, which meaning was, undoubtedly, imposed upon his mind as the true meaning from his previous reception of the philosophical dogmas referred to. His three principles were: first, the immortality of the soul; second, the distinction which he drew between what he called "divine fire," and "common fire;" thirdly, the sense which he placed upon the scriptural term "unquenchable." On each of these we will say a few words, required in order to exhibit the tone of mind ruling at this period, and subsequently among the fathers of the Church.

While Tertullian plainly and unequivocally rejected a portion of Plato's teaching on the nature of the soul, he held its inalienable immortality just as strongly as Plato did. He rejects the Platonic idea that souls are unborn and uncreated, and so exist from eternity. In opposition to this he taught that they were created substances, having a beginning in time.* But while he thus differed from Plato on the *past existence* of the soul he was at perfect accord with him as to its *future existence.* Once born and created it possesses a life of which it is never under any change of circumstance to be deprived. It subsequently possesses an existence like that of God. Plato's dogma is the watchword of Tertullian—"Every soul is immortal."

Beyond any question the theory as held by Plato was far more reasonable than as held by his Christian disciple; for that which can have

* *De Anima*, c. iv.

no end could scarcely have had a beginning. However, the unfortunate stand-point of Tertullian, at once a Christian and a Platonist, compelled him at whatever sacrifice of consistency and logic to deny a main feature of the Platonic theory. On the future eternity of the soul he was however firm. It could not, with him, die, or cease to exist. Fallen or unfallen, upright or wicked, redeemed or reprobate, it possessed an immortal life.

In his ignorance of the Hebrew language, Tertullian tries to gain authority for his opinion from the account of the creation of man given in Genesis 2:7. He considers that when man is there said to "become a *living soul*" his immortality is expressed. He ought to have known that the same expression was applied in Genesis 1:20-21 to the lower creatures. The account that "God *breathed*" into man the breath of life is strongly relied on by him. His labored and inconsistent deductions from this, trying to keep clear of Plato, and yet at the same time retain a part of Plato's view, shows us the utter fallacy of the ground he took. He thus in one place defines the soul:

> "The soul we define to be *sprung from the breath of God, immortal,* possessing body, having form, simple in its substance, intelligent in its own nature, developing its powers in various ways, free in its determination, *subject to the changes of accidents, in its faculties mutable,* rational, supreme, endued with an instinct of presentiment, evolved out of one (archetypal) soul."

Tertullian evidently considers the soul to have been made out of *some part of God—His breath.* From the quotation already given appears the difficulty of his so defining the soul as to be consistent at once with this divine origin and its condition as seen in fallen man. Hence he calls it at once sprung from the breath of God and immortal, and yet subject to changes of accident and to mutability! His difficulties still further appear a little after. He is speaking of Plato's opinion of the soul as "immortal, incorruptible, incorporeal, invisible, incapable of delineation, uniform, supreme, rational, and intellectual." Tertullian justly observes of this: "What more could Plato attribute to the soul, if he wanted to call it God?" Conscious however of his own dangerous proximity to Plato's view from his theory of the origin of the soul *from the breath of God,* he draws a distinction after the following fashion: "We," he says,

> "who allow no appendage to God (in the sense of equality) by this very fact reckon the soul as very far below God; for we suppose it to be *born, and hereby to possess something of a diluted Divinity and attenuated felicity, as the breath of God, though not His Spirit;* and although immortal, as this is an attribute of Divinity, yet, for all that, passable, since this is an incident of a born condition, and consequently from the first capable of deviation from perfection and right, and by consequence susceptible of a failure in memory."*

It is surely pitiable to hear a man of Tertullian's ability talking in this way. His efforts to combine human philosophy with divine truth only land him in hopeless perplexity. What is his distinction between God's breath and God's spirit, when both are evidently belonging to the being of God, it is difficult to see. He asserts a difference, but does not attempt to explain it. His view of the soul, as in its immortality Godlike and in its mutability but like any other creature of time, and as thus possessed of "*diluted Divinity and an attenuated felicity,*" is ridiculous in the extreme. We may well call what he considered philosophic theology but attenuated, diluted, emasculated Platonism. But such was his opinion of the nature of the soul. While he considered it in its intellectual and moral nature as mutable and capable of all evil, he considered it in its physical capacity as possessed of

* *De Anima*, c. xxii., xxiv.

an immortality equal to that of God, and to be itself a part of the divine substance.[*]

Tertullian, however, did not rely solely, or probably chiefly, either on the scriptural or the philosophical arguments supposed to establish his ideas of the soul. He knew that while a few Platonic philosophers held a theory in one respect like his, though in other respects wholly unlike, the great mass of philosophers and the vulgar multitude, regarded his and Plato's ideas as mere fanciful figments.[†] Indeed, he himself, while at one period he lauds the arguments of Socrates and Plato on the immortality of the soul, in other moods treats them with something very much approaching contempt. "All the wisdom of Socrates at that moment," he says, "proceeded from the affectation of an assumed composure, rather than the firm composure of ascertained truth. For by whom has truth ever been discovered without God?" While of the famous demon of Socrates he speaks in anything but flattering terms: "They say," he observes, "that a demon clave to him from his boyhood—*the very worst teacher certainly.*"[‡]

But Tertullian was not without supernatural aid of his own. Speaking modestly of himself, he says: "We too have merited the attainment of the prophetic gift." And he had also a valuable co-adjutor to supply any deficiency in his own gift, or to confirm his testimony by a second witness. "We have now amongst us," he tells his opponents, "a sister, whose lot it has been to be favored with sundry gifts of revelation." On the strength of his own and his spiritual sister's prophetic gifts, he expounds the mystery of the condition and qualities of the soul, and attributes to it form and limitation, length, breadth, and height, color and substance, eyes, ears, fingers, bosom, tongue, and other members, and maintains against Plato

[*] *Against Marcion*, b. ii., c. v.

[†] *De Spectaculis*, par. 30; *Resurrection of the Flesh*, c. iii.

[‡] *De Anima*, c. i.

that the possession of all these does not at all endanger the soul's immortality.[*]

Besides this great fundamental axiom of the immortality of the human soul, which led him into an hundred absurdities, and which he supported by philosophy, Scripture, and personal revelation, Tertullian had another idea which guided him to his view of future punishment. It was that strange *philosophical* opinion which in our chapter on Justin Martyr we have noted as commonly held at that period, of an *essential difference* between two supposed kinds of fire. "The philosophers," he says,

> "are familiar as we with the *distinction between a common and a secret fire.* Thus that which is in common use is far different from that which we see in Divine judgments, whether striking as thunderbolts from heaven, or bursting up out of the earth through mountain tops; *for it does not consume what it scorches, but while it burns it repairs.* So the mountains continue ever burning; and a person struck by lightning is even now kept safe from any destroying flame. *A notable proof this of the fire eternal! A notable example of the endless judgment which still supplies punishment with fuel!* The mountains burn and last. How will it be with the enemies of God?"

It is most instructive to mark the grounds on which the theory of eternal anguish found admission to the Church. Christian divines now accept the conclusion which such men as Tertullian arrived at, while they are sadly ignorant of the steps by which those conclusions were reached. We just look at a certain dogma as very ancient, and commonly received in remote times, while we do not study the current ideas and mode of thought of those remote times which brought about the general acceptance of the dogma. Thus the two axioms or principles which we have just

[*] *De Anima*, c. ix.

considered led Tertullian easily and irresistibly to his theory of punishment. The wicked are in hell! They cannot die there!

Why?

Oh, the soul is immortal.

But what of the body? Must it not consume under the action of the fire as here it would when exposed to such an influence?

No. We have even here fire which does not consume, because in the very act of consuming it *reproduces* what it consumes. Such is the lightning from the skies; such are the flames of Etna and Vesuvius. All philosophy accepts this, and it cannot be denied. *Such is the fire of hell!* Consequently, the body of the wicked cannot be consumed in it. It will scorch, and pain, and agonize, through all eternity, because through all eternity it nourishes and supplies that bodily substance which it scorches, and pains, and agonizes, but never consumes? "From its very nature it directly ministers to them incorruptibility." The devouring flame supplies its inexhaustible fuel! Roaring, crackling, raging, scorching, paining, in the lurid vaults of hell, it supplies the bones, and marrow, and blood, and flesh, round which it roars, and crackles, and rages, with a noise as loud as the shrieks and wailings of the damned. Such was the philosophical theory which forced Tertullian to his view of future punishment.* Men now laugh at the philosophical dogma. They accept the diabolical conclusion which was based upon it! Tertullian was infinitely more reasonable than they.

There is a feeling, natural even to fallen men, tenderly cherished and nurtured by the Gospel of Christ, which might have interposed and forbid the conclusion of Tertullian, even though it had no logic or no dogma to present. It is the feeling *of pity and of mercy* which is implanted in us by our Maker.

* *Apology*, para. 48.

> "Wilt thou draw near the nature of the gods?
> Draw near them then in being merciful."

In our comparatively humane age, this feeling is ever rebelling against the dogma of endless misery. Supposed to be the doctrine of God's Word—taught to us at our mother's knee and preached to us by men whom we look upon as ministering in God's stead—loudly proclaimed as the church's faith always, in every place, and by all the faithful accepted, save by a few miserable heretics—spite of all, mercy is ever raising her powerful protest in our midst. From the depths of the heart of such men as Tillotson, and Watts, and Butler, and Taylor, and Barnes, come ever welling up the irrepressible feelings of anguish, dismay, and almost madness, at the thought of that which they feel themselves compelled to believe. Grand old Luther looked at Dante's and Tertullian's hell, and groaned out, "It is the highest act of faith to believe that God is merciful."

But such a feeling was faint and low in Tertullian's bosom, and probably in Tertullian's age. It was an age of cruelty—it was the age of the heathen games, when women and children feasted their eyes at the sight of the blood flowing from the gladiator's wounds. It was the age of heathen persecution, when Christians were exposed to wild beasts and burned in fires, for refusing to deny then Lord. The cruelty of the age was reflected in such minds as that of Tertullian. For the present sufferings of the church he consoled himself, not as Paul did by the thought of the "far more exceeding and eternal weight of glory" which should succeed the "light affliction which was but for a moment," but by the grim reflection that he should behold his persecutors suffering what they had inflicted, yea, incalculably more. Says the stern African,

> "How shall I admire, how laugh, how rejoice, how exult, when I behold so many proud monarchs and fancied gods groaning in the lowest abyss of darkness; so many magistrates who persecuted the name of the Lord,

> liquefying in fiercer fires than they ever kindled against the Christians; so many sage philosophers blushing in the red-hot flames, with their deluded scholars!"

Such was the spirit engendered in Tertullian. And so the conclusion which the strictest logic led him to from what he supposed to be indisputable facts was not counterbalanced by any pleading of mercy. Eternal misery was his intellectual creed, and his heart rejoiced at the prospect of it.*

We have seen the grounds which led the ablest of the earlier teachers of endless misery to his conclusion. They were the philosophical figments of the immortality of the soul and of the nature of what was called *divine* or *secret fire*. These two dogmas, operating on a callous heart, led him to the creed for which he contended so strenuously. When we lay aside the philosophical figments we lay aside also the horrible conclusion against which all our heaven-born sentiments of pity revolt.

It only remains for us to show the alteration and perversion of scriptural language to which this conclusion led Tertullian and his contemporaries, as it has led every one of their followers from that day to this. It led him, and all his school, to these two things: first, in their descriptions of future punishment, to introduce a language not merely strange to, but contradictory of that of Scripture; secondly, to pervert the sense and meaning of those words which the Spirit of God has used in Scripture to set forth the doom of the lost.

And, first, Tertullian introduces into his descriptions of future punishment a nomenclature not only novel to, but contradictory of, the nomenclature of Scripture. Thus he speaks perpetually of the "incorruptibility" of the wicked, body and soul, in hell: of the wicked, as much as of the righteous, he affirms "immortality:" he speaks of man as made *out of* "the substance" of God: of the soul as a "divine nature," and

* Salmon, *Eternity of Punishment*, Sermon ii.

"an eternal substance!" Of the soul of the wicked he tells us that it stands in no need of "salvation," being already "safe" by its essential immortality: and of the bodies of the wicked he affirms that they will in the day of resurrection obtain "salvation" through Christ! "Eternal life," he tells us, will be their lot. "Destruction," he says, cannot happen to the soul, while the bodies of the wicked will be rescued from "destruction" in the resurrection![*] It is quite plain to any reader of Scripture that this language is never applied to the wicked in Scripture but that it contradicts the scriptural language which is used of them.

We will show from a single example the serious nature of this use of language by Tertullian. Every reader of Scripture knows that there is no more usual description of the punishment of the wicked than that they will be "destroyed," or suffer "destruction" in hell. Tertullian had a very clear and very decided meaning for this word "destruction" to which we would request the particular attention of his modem followers. He knew that "destruction" meant what we affirm it to mean, that is, *the annihilation of organized being*. Thus, in one place he tells us that it was by this phrase that Epicurus conveyed the idea of the utter cessation of existence at death. In another place he tells us that destruction differs altogether from *change*, that whereas to be changed "is to exist in another condition," to be destroyed "is altogether to cease to be what a thing once was," to cease to have "existence," to be identical with "the annihilation of any substance." In another place he tells us that the condition of the body in the grave, when it has seen corruption, is "destruction; and that if God were to leave the body forever in this condition it would be His *abandoning it to everlasting destruction*."[†] With Tertullian's clear view of the meaning of destruction, it only remained for him, in consistency with his view of

[*] *Apology*, par. 48; *Resurrection*, c. iii.; xxiv; *Against Marcion*, b. ii., c. v.

[†] *De Anima*, c. xlii; *Resurrection*, lv., ix.

future punishment, to deny that the wicked will be destroyed; he has accordingly plainly done so. Of the soul of the wicked he tells us that we are "to believe it 'lost,' *not in the sense of destruction, but of punishment,* that is, *in hell.*"* We would draw the attention of the Augustinian theorists to this. Tertullian, who knew the meaning of the word, is compelled, in order to carry out his views, to contradict the Scripture. In what does he differ from his modern followers? In this, that while he contradicts the language of Scripture, they, when they do not, as they are constantly doing, exactly imitate him in his contradiction, do what is just as bad, pervert the language of Scripture from its natural and proper sense.

We will now give an example which shows that the theory of Tertullian compelled him, *knowingly and confessedly*, to alter the proper sense of some of the most common terms of Scripture to a non-natural and improper sense. What we mean is simply that Tertullian knows and acknowledges that certain words used in Scripture to express future punishment have properly a certain meaning: that the theory of punishment which he holds and believes to be scriptural does not permit these words to be understood in their proper meaning: and that consequently they are to be understood in some improper and unnatural sense. The proper inference, we contend, would have been "that the theory which required such violence to be done to the language of Scripture was unscriptural; but the veil of philosophy was on Tertullian's heart, and he could not see this.

Tertullian is commenting on our Lord's words in Matthew 10:28, "Fear not them which kill the body, but are not able to kill the soul; but rather fear Him who is able to destroy both body and soul in hell." Tertullian very properly makes "kill" in the first clause of this verse to correspond with "destroy" in the second. He also very properly says that

* *Resurrection of the Flesh*, c. xxxiv.

what God is here declared to be able to do He will do to the wicked in hell. He also knew the true and proper sense of the words "kill" and "destroy." His meaning for the latter we have already shown. We will now show what he means by "dying," or "death," a word so warped from its proper sense by the modern imitators of Tertullian.

These say that "death" means "some condition or change of life," generally supposed to be a change for the worse. But how does Tertullian define it? "The word *dead*," he says, "expresses simply what has *lost the vital principle* by means of which it used to live. Now *the body is that which loses life, and as the result of losing it becomes dead. To the body therefore the term* dead *is only suitable.*"* We thus see that Tertullian held that the terms "to die," "to be destroyed," and "death"—all of them with him synonymous—were not at all suitable for the soul, and could only with propriety be affirmed *of the body* after death and until resurrection.

Here then came Tertullian's perplexity. He was in a strait between his correct knowledge of the meaning of words and a theory of punishment which he was persuaded was true. These troublesome words, which he knew could not *suitably* be applied to the soul at any time, or to the risen bodies of the wicked after resurrection, he must needs confess were applied in Scripture to both body and soul of the wicked! What was he to do? He could not blot them out of Scripture. He could not deny that both body and soul would be killed and destroyed by God in hell. He could not deny that the only *suitable* sense of these words was that body and soul would be annihilated and cease to exist. What was he to do? Give up his theory?! No. What then? *Put a forced, improper, unsuitable sense on the words of Scripture, and then justify this by saying that the theory of Scripture demanded that its words should not be understood in their suitable sense, but in an improper, forced, unnatural, and unsuitable sense!* This is what

* *Against Marcion*, b. v., c. ix.

he has done. He is still keeping Matthew 10:28 in view, and supposing an opponent to argue from it that the wicked would cease to exist in hell. He says,

> "If, therefore, anyone shall violently suppose that the destruction of the soul and the flesh in hell *amounts to a final annihilation of the two substances,* and not to their penal treatment (as if it were to be consumed not punished) *let him recollect that the fire of hell is eternal,* expressly announced as an everlasting penalty; and let him then admit that it is *from this circumstance* that this never-ending killing is more formidable than a merely human murder, which is only temporal."*

This reasoning of Tertullian is well worthy of consideration. You will remark that he does not attempt to deny that the proper meaning of the "destruction of the soul and flesh in hell" is "the final annihilation of the two substances." He could not do this; for he knew well that that was the proper meaning of the words, as he had himself taught in a hundred places. But his theory of hell, which he thought that of Scripture, forbid him to allow to the words their proper sense. Up came to his mind his theory of the immortality of the soul and its endless sufferings, and *therefore he must deprive the language of Scripture of its proper force. "The fire of hell is eternal"* he says, putting on the eternity of the fire the sense which his theory of the soul required and therefore the words of Scripture must needs be taken in a non-natural sense!

And mark also what underlay the whole of his reasoning upon this subject. *He supposes the loss of existence by one who might have had it forever as no punishment!* In one place he distinguishes "destruction" from "punishment," as if destruction were not punishment. He here distinguishes "being killed," "being destroyed," and "being consumed,"

---

* *Resurrection of the Flesh,* c. xxxv.

from punishment, as though they were no punishment! Mark his words "as *if they were to be consumed, not punished!*" Consuming, depriving of existence, and that an eternal existence, was *no punishment* in Tertullian's eyes! Unless the flesh was scorching, the blood bubbling, the marrow boiling, in the consciousness of the wretched sufferer, the African theologian thought that there was no punishment! But our main point here is that Tertullian confesses that his theory of future punishment forces him to pervert the language of Scripture.

To our minds this is the plainest condemnation of a theory which requires a sacrifice of the most vital kind. Abandon the true interpretation of the words of Scripture on one great question, and where can you uphold it? Tertullian's treatment of its language is the condemnation of his system. In order to uphold the dogma of eternal misery and evil, we will not consent to the introduction of a principle of interpretation which would involve our Bible in a maze of inextricable confusion and obscurity.

Tertullian's admirable reasoning upon another great question should have prevented his fearful abuse of language when discussing that of future punishment. As strongly as we condemn his argument on the latter, we praise his truly noble argument "On the Resurrection of the Flesh." To our minds it is far the best thing that has been written on the subject. Here, indeed, his master-mind shows itself, for he is putting forth its great powers upon the side of truth. But here he takes the precisely opposite ground to that which he takes in his argument on future punishment. The specious artifice of the heretics in attributing to the phrases of Scripture a "figurative and allegorical" meaning he exposes with a master's power. He will have none of it.* And yet Tertullian should have remembered that they were only reasoning on the resurrection as he was accustomed to reason on the punishment of the wicked, *i.e.*, altering the meaning of words from

* *Resurrection of the Flesh*, c. xviii.

the ordinary and proper sense to one which was unnatural, or, at best, secondary and figurative. He should have remembered that the heretical meaning of "death," as "ignorance of God"—of "resurrection," as being "reanimated by access to the truth," as "bursting forth from the sepulcher of the old man," as "escaping out of this world, which is the habitation of the dead," had at least as much scriptural warrant as his interpretation of "death" as "misery," and "destruction" and "consuming," as "pain and anguish."

One word more on the language of Tertullian and his fellows, ancient and modern. They, one and all, in their descriptions of future punishment, introduce a language which, to say the least of it, is absent from Scripture. When they mean to set forth beyond mistake what they hold, they tell us that the soul is immortal and cannot die; that the bodies of the wicked will be raised incorruptible and immortal; that the wicked will never die, never perish, never be consumed, never be destroyed, and so on. *To appearance,* this language *contradicts* that of Scripture: at all events this language is *never* applied in Scripture to the wicked. What does it arise from? Surely the language of Scripture is sufficient to express the doctrine of Scripture. God meant us to understand His mode of punishment. Surely He has explained it sufficiently and beyond ambiguity in His Word. Whence then the necessity for that *Augustinian language* which is never found in Scripture? Whence the necessity to introduce language which so far at least as sound goes gives the lie to the language of the Bible? *Is not the source of this new language to be found in a new doctrine?* The terms of the Scripture are not able to express the theory of Augustine.

Well indeed it is for us that the Bible does not speak as these men speak. If it did, it would afford ground for the denial of its inspiration, which all the dissenters from its authority have never been able to discover. If it were to say that the wicked "shall die," and " shall *not* die,"—"shall live forever," and "shall *not* live forever,"—"shall be consumed" and "shall *not* be consumed,"—"shall be destroyed," and "shall *not* be destroyed,"—"shall perish," and "shall *not* perish,"—"shall come to an end," and "shall *not* come to an end,"—vain would be our most strenuous efforts to maintain its authority. Then, indeed, the ungodly would laugh at its threats. But this is what all our Augustinian theorists are doing in every pamphlet and work they put forward. Mr. Grant does so over and over, and vindicates the practice.

Having seen the grounds on which Tertullian arrived at his view of future punishment, it only remains for us to notice his use of this dogma. As in his arguments for his theory he is more forcible than his predecessors; so in his description of the endless agony of the lost he throws them completely into the shade. He does not draw any discreet veil over his scene of punishment. Without asserting that he took a positive delight in the contemplation of it, though his own words could justify our saying so, he at least depicts its fancied circumstances with a minuteness and a force that have only been surpassed by the imagination of Dante, or the agonizing details of a Roman Catholic Friar or a Protestant Revivalist.[*] Nor is put into a dungeon: deprived of all but the necessaries of existence: tortured by day and by night: guarded, lest his own hand should rid him of a miserable life: and all this to go on till nature thrusts within the prison bars an irresistible hand, and frees the wretched from his existence.

Now what would be the effect upon the community of such a course? The joy at the criminal's overthrow, once universal, would rapidly change into pity, into indignation, into horror, into the wild uprising of an outraged nation to rescue the miserable man from a tyrant worse than himself, and to hurl the infamous abuser of law and power from his seat. And this is but the faintest image of what a cruel theology would have us

---

[*] *History of European Morals,* W. E. H. Lecky, ii., 237; Salmon, *Eternity of Punishment,* appendix, note i.

believe of our Father which is in Heaven! Nature steps in, in the one case, and says there shall be an end. Omnipotence in the other puts forth its might to stay all such escape. *Forever and forever!* Millions of years of agony gone, and yet the agony no nearer to its close! Not one, but myriads to suffer thus! Their endless cries! Their ceaseless groans! Their interminable despair! Why heaven and earth and stars in their infinite number—all worlds which roll through the great Creator's space—would raise one universal shout of horror at such a course. Love for God would give way to hatred. Apostasy would no longer be partial but universal. All would stand aloof in irrepressible loathing from the tyrant on the throne, for a worse thing than Manichaeism pictured would be seated there—*the one eternal principle would be the principle of evil.*

20

Rise of the Theory of Universal Restoration

NOT SURELY WITHOUT REASON did Paul warn against philosophy, when the admission of one philosophical dogma led good men, under the specious pretext of exhibiting the Divine justice and holiness as infinite, to paint God as a monster of unutterable cruelty. We will now see the wisdom of the apostle's warning in the result from this same source of another school of theology, which, while seeking to free God's character from the charge of injustice or cruelty, would probably, if generally accepted, be in its immediate consequences in this world far more injurious to truth and godliness. No language can express too strongly our conviction of the danger as well as the error of this latter view. It gilds with seductive light the ways of sin. It would, we firmly believe, if commonly accepted, in a single generation reduce the morals of the world to a level with those of Sodom. Its ablest advocates confess this. Bengel tells us that it is "a doctrine *not to be preached*." Dr. Thomas Burnet advocated it in Latin, and charges ministers on no account to proclaim it to their hearers.*

---

* Saphir, *The Lord's Prayer*, 378; Blain, *Death, Not Life*, 114.

The fearful picture of God, exhibited by Tertullian, could not be laid in its bare horrors before the mind without drawing forth some protest. The doctrine of the age upon the soul gave the shape to the protest, and Origen came forward to make it under the title of "universal restoration." Tertullian had consigned reprobate men and devils to endless pain in hell. Origen converts hell into a vast purgatory, and sends men and devils forth from it, purified and humbled, to the feet of the Great Father, and to the joys which are at His right hand for evermore. It is the old story of human thought from one extreme to its opposite. The truth always lies between the two.

Origen had seized hold of a scriptural truth, the final extinction of evil, which was just as much a part of our Father's revelation as Tertullian's eternity of punishment.* Each had his undoubted share of truth; and if the question lay between their two systems alone it could never be set at rest. If Tertullian could appeal to Scripture for the overthrow of the wicked, whether men or angels, as being of an endless nature, Origen could point from the same source to a blissful coming time when all that had breath should praise the Lord.

What was there which prevented Origen from going back to the old scriptural doctrine of *death* as the end of sinners, which places the two scriptural truths just mentioned in harmony and not in opposition? It was the very same dogma of the immortality of the soul which had led Athenagoras and Tertullian to their endless life in hell.† This dogma first taught by Satan to Eve, and handed down through Egyptian priests and heathen philosophers to fathers of the Christian church, made the revolt from Tertullian to be only the exchange of one human system for another, instead of being a return from man's heresy to God's truth.

* *De Principiis*, b. i., c. vi.; b. ii., c. i.

† *De Principiis*, b. i., c. ii., para. 4.

Origen had exceeded the views of the earlier fathers on the soul. Jerome's charge against the school of Origen, that he and his followers held the souls of men and the angelic natures to be a part of the Divine substance and nature of God Himself, though it appears inconsistent with some of the statements of Origen, yet shows the tendency of his teaching, and the manner in which it was regarded in his time.[*] He certainly held the most exalted notions of the dignity and nature of the soul. It had with him an existence long anterior to that of the body, even though he may not have held it to have been created from eternity: it was wholly incapable of death or destruction: it possessed an immortality of which nothing could deprive it. Here was Origen's axiom, a first truth with him. It was in connection with this that he held the scriptural truth to which his opponents had shut their eyes—the abolition of evil: it was with this, as a main part of his system, that he looked on hopefully to the times of which the Scriptures are full, when all things should again be very good.[†]

How were they to be brought about? Not by the casting away of the barren branches, leaving only the fruitful branches on the tree (John 15:6). Not by the disappearance out of the realms of life of the wicked, leaving in the land of life only the lovers of God and of Christ. Not by the destruction of a single unit from the multitudinous creation which occupied in God's world a rank higher than the brutes. This could not be with Origen. With him, if it was not "life from eternity to eternity," it was at least "once living, always to live." Death might come and close the eye of the bright-plumaged bird; death might come and still the roar of the young lion that shook the earth; death might lay its unresisted hand upon that leviathan, so fierce that none "dare stir him up;" death might even for a space paralyze the strength of man's body, and corrupt the beauty of his

[*] Hieronymus, *Epistle*, 59; *Ad Avit*, c. iv; Origen, *De Principüs*, i., iii. 3; ii., ix., 1, 2.

[†] *De Principüs*, i., vii. 4; iii., i. 13; iii., vi. 5.

countenance, and mingle dust with dust—but to the Divine soul of man death and destruction could not come.

It was stronger than death: mightier than destruction: pain could not weaken it: fire consume it: it was indestructible. How then could the glorious picture of prophecy prove more than a fond conceit? Only by converting hell into a universal-purgatory, where evil was destroyed and the evil-doer purged, where sin was blotted out while the sinner was preserved.[*]

Heathen philosophy had uttered Origen's theory long before Origen was born, just as it had sketched out that of Augustine. Plato may be said to stand sponsor for both views. We have already seen that in his Tartarus he has given the exact prototype of Augustine's hell. But endless misery for the wicked was what Plato could endure only for *a very few*, whom he called "incurable." The vast majority of the wicked were, in Plato's conception, "curable". For all these, the scene of punishment after death was *the place of their purgation.* He had an Acherusian lake to which the majority of wicked souls went, and from which, after a longer or a shorter period of suffering, they were released. He had his lake of Acheron where souls of a moderate amount of crime went, and from which, after due suffering, they were released. Even into his Tartarus, into which incurable souls were sent for unending torment, some very wicked yet curable souls were also sent, and after suffering there came forth to pass through the places of lighter suffering to a complete purgation.[†]

We thus see that Plato suggested his idea to Origen as he did to Augustine. Very little need be added to Plato's teaching in order to make it one of *universal* restoration. It was but to suppose that his *few incurables*

[*] *De Principiis*, i., vi. 1, 2, 3.

[†] Plato, *Phædo*, para. 61, 62.

were not absolutely incurable, but might be ranked among the curable, and the full idea of Origen was displayed.

Heathen philosophy had given his idea to Origen; but he had, as a Christian teacher, to apply it to the language of Scripture. It took its place easily and naturally in the speculations of Plato; because he taught of those souls which he brought forth from his penal and purgative fires, that in those fires they did not die, did not perish, and were not destroyed. It might seem rather a stumbling-block to Origen that the souls which he brought forth from the fire of hell were said in Scripture to die, and perish, and be destroyed there. For Origen knew very well the meaning of those Greek words which are thus translated in our English version. He knew that the terms of the Greek language applied to the future punishment of sinners were the very strongest terms that could be chosen from that copious language to express the utter destruction of organization, the utter loss of life, and being, and existence. What was to be done with these? Were they to be explained away?

That is what the holders of Augustine's theory have done. They have ransacked the language of poetry and passion, of exaggeration and hyperbole, to find out remote secondary senses to impose on the plain terms of the Divine law, and, where these have failed, they have put senses on those terms which neither poetry nor passion, exaggeration nor hyperbole, justify. With them *death* means *life*, and *life* means *happiness*, and *being destroyed* means *being made miserable*, and so on.

Having put these convenient meanings on the phraseology of Scripture, and interpreted it as not one of them would dare to interpret the code of a human legislator, they look placidly upon a thousand texts which contradict the lie they teach from platform, and pulpit, and press, and instill into children's minds almost with their mother's milk.

Origen could not, or would not, do this. He gives, as any Greek scholar not possessed with the spirit of Augustine would do, their proper force to the terms of the New Testament, the same meaning which Plato, or Demosthenes, or Cicero, would attach to them.

We will give an example of this. Every one is familiar with the solemn warning of our Lord: "Fear not them which *kill* the body, but are not able to kill the soul: but rather fear Him who is able to *destroy* both body and soul in hell." We remark in the English version the change from "kill," in the first clause, to "destroy," in the second, a change exactly answering to the Greek original, which lives *apokteino* (αποκτεινω) in the first clause, and *apollumi* (απολλυμι) in the second. The maintainers of Augustine's theory attempt to take advantage of a change which is in reality only a heavier blow to their system. They generally explain "destroy" as a term of *inferior* force to "kill."

Now anyone who came unprejudiced to this passage of our Lord would acknowledge that every law of right reason would lead us to conclude that the force of the term in the second clause must *at least equal* that in the first, else the warning is diminished in its intensity. Let us hear the Greek scholar, Origen, on the proper force of this word "destroy." He is commenting on 1 Corinthians 3:9, in connection with Jeremiah 1:10:

> "See what is said to the people of God, 'Ye are God's husbandry, ye are God's building:' therefore the words of God over nations and kingdoms are, 'to root out, and to throw down, *and to destroy.*'"

If it be rooted out, and that which is rooted out *be not destroyed, that which is thrown down still exists.* It is therefore the result of God's goodness, after the rooting out, *to destroy what is rooted out;* after the throwing down, *to destroy what is thrown down.*"* Such is the mighty power which Origen, a Greek scholar, gives to this word "destroy." With him it means *blotting out*

* *Commentaries,* Matthew 10:28.

of all existence, obliterating the very form and appearance. It is thus a stronger word in sense than "kill." Death, for a time at least, leaves the shape and parts unaltered: destruction removes the organization and resemblance altogether.

But, it will be asked, if such be the true force of the words applied in Scripture to future punishment, how did Origen defend his theory of universal restoration with these meeting him in the face? Very easily. Origen never found any difficulty in Scripture. If it was apparently for him, well and good; if it was apparently against him, he made it without any ceremony speak as he wished. Scripture has, with him, not only a "historical, but a spiritual method of interpretation:" it has "a meaning, not such only as is apparent at first sight, *but also another, which escapes the notice of most.*"*

Origen, it must be confessed, very frequently takes the latter meaning; for his explanations of Scripture constantly merit the praise of excessive singularity. But it will be evident to all that in laying down the above rule of interpretation, Origen gives himself full scope for assigning any meaning that he pleases to Scripture, and fully merits Mosheim's description of him as one who "neglects and despises, for the most part, the outward letter; and in this devious path displays the most ingenious strokes of fancy, though always at the expense of truth, whose Divine simplicity is scarcely discernible through the cobweb-veil of allegory."†

Every reader of Scripture knows that its solemn warnings are addressed *to the sinner in person*: "O wicked man, thou shalt surely die." Death, destruction, perdition, loss of life—all the multiplied phrases and illustrations of the Bible, are in it directed against *the persons* of the wicked. With regard to those redeemed ones in whom while sin is destroyed they

---

* *De Principiis*, i., iii. 3; Preface, para. 8.

† Mosheim, *Eccl. History*, Cent. iii., c. iii. part ii.

are themselves saved, we constantly find such expressions as "the old man crucified," "the body of sin destroyed," "the flesh crucified," "the old leaven purged out," and "the deeds of the body mortified."* But expressions of this kind are never used in Scripture of the wicked. It is *they themselves* who are threatened with destruction. Origen's simple mode of neutralizing their force is by directing them against *their sin.*

True, that few readers of Scripture perceive this application of Scripture; but Origen perceives it and that is enough. It is one of those meanings which "escape the notice of most," but lie open to his gaze. And so his point is gained. Their force cannot be too strong for him; for with his spiritual direction it makes for him and not against him. So he does not attempt to diminish it.

The Augustinian, directing them correctly against the sinner, puts upon them a false meaning: Origen, directing them with his spiritual vision against his sin, leaves them their proper sense. Both pervert Scripture, and it is difficult, perhaps impossible, to say against which the charge lies heaviest.

We meet with Origen's free and easy method of interpreting Scripture everywhere throughout his writings. The object of the fire of hell with him is thoroughly to root out and destroy *wickedness* of every kind. Iniquity, and evil thoughts, and false dogmas, and the scandals which offend, are the fuel for the unquenchable fire of hell.† On these it preys with ruthless force. Till these are thoroughly extinct, completely eradicated, blotted out of all being, the unquenchable fire of hell burns on. But this process, which is destructive of evil, is a purgation to the evil doer. While the sin that had hindered his entrance into his Father's Kingdom at an earlier period is being diminished to its extinction, the sinner is growing into the likeness

* See Romans 6:6; 8:13; 1 Corinthians 5:7; Galatians 5:24.

† *De Principüs*, ii., x. 4, 5, 6.

of God which has been defaced. The process complete, they who had suffered and been purged in hell take a place, a lower one, it is true, but still a place, in glory.

Origen's view required the admission of two things which no genuine person who reveres and follows the Scripture will allow to him. He required first, as the very foundation of his system, that the Platonic dogma of the *inalienable immortality of all souls* should be admitted. He found no difficulty on this point in his day. We now ask for a better proof of this than heathen philosophers give us, and which did not satisfy even themselves. Finding Scripture not merely silent but putting its decisive negative on the Platonic dogma of immortality and the modified one of the Christian fathers, we reject it as a tradition of men.

We know that Platonism here had its element of truth. It was the longing of the heart for what man once had and lost through sin. We know that Platonism finds its glorious response in Christianity—in that Gospel of Christ which brings, as its inestimable gift, eternal life to those who believe in the Son of God. But the system of philosophy which controverted the school of Plato had also its element of truth. While our sympathies are with Plato in the mighty argument of life and death, we must needs admit that Lucretius *reasoned* better than the greater sage of Athens. If human reason and speculation alone were to decide the question, reason would decide in favor of Epicurus and Lucretius.

The longings and aspirations of the soul would indeed always enlist some on the side of its immortality; but it would not be on reason they could rest, but on some undefined, indistinct, shadowy, yet dearly cherished hope, coming they could not tell whence, shining they could not be certain whether with true or fatuous light, but which they would and must follow, for everywhere else there were only the shadows of death. To this unbroken darkness, the philosophy of Lucretius led. It had its miserable element of reality. It spoke with truth of an eternal death for souls that would not seek the life.

The other requirement of Origen was liberty to alter the application of Scripture to suit his views. Neither can we admit this. While against the followers of Augustine we bring the heavy, sore, awful charge of altering the meaning of the plainest language of Scripture, in order to force life on those for whom God had decreed death, against Origen we must bring the equally grave charge of so dealing with Scripture as to make it absolutely worthless as an authoritative teacher of truth. What it says of *the sinner* we have no right to apply to *his sin.* If hell has within its terrible womb the elements of utter death and destruction, it is *for the wicked* they are being stored up there. *It is they themselves that die, and* perish, and come to a fearful end.

But Origen had one grand truth in his system—the glorious scriptural truth of the extinction of all evil. There is a time to come, to which prophecy points onward, when the evil which has, for wise and wondrous and merciful purposes, been permitted to obscure the bright face of heaven to our poor contracted view, shall have passed away. The idea of Augustinian theorists, that evil for a time and evil for eternity are essentially one and the same thing, is as opposed to Scripture and God's mind as it is ridiculous in the eye of common sense.*

It is making no difference between time and eternity; whereas to him who embraces eternity time is as nothing. God expressly tells us that the question of *duration* is with Him of the utmost consequence. Why does He permit the triumphing of the wicked? *Because it is short.* If anyone were to say that God might just as well permit the wicked to triumph forever as He has permitted him to triumph for a time, God would answer him even through uninspired Zophar precisely on this point of duration: "Though

* Rev. W. Ker, *Popular Ideas of Immortality*, 2nd ed., 64.

his excellency mount up to the heavens, and his head reach unto the clouds; *yet he shall perish forever.*" And so with other things of a painful kind. With God, "*heaviness may endure for a night*;" but it shall not endure forever.

The transitory and the temporary are not with Him the same as the enduring and the eternal: with Him, the heaviness which endures for a night is borne for the eternal "joy which cometh in the morning" (Job 20:5; Ps. 30:5; 1 Pet. 1:6). It is not the same thing to God that evil and its sufferings should be allowed for some few thousand years, a speck indistinguishable between the two eternities of the past and the future, evil too, of which good will be the final goal; and that evil, black, foul, and unmitigated, should through all eternity exist in the center of God's world of righteousness. With this truth, the final extinction of evil, in his possession, and the dogma of the inalienable immortality of the soul admitted, the theory of Origen is fully able to stand its ground against the rival view of Augustine. It possesses *at least as much* truth, and presents a more pleasing view of God.

But it is after all a human system, and as such is to be condemned. God's Word contradicts it in a thousand places. It holds out *no hope* to those who stand condemned in the judgment. This world and its peoples will again be all-righteous, all-rejoicing; but the reprobate will have passed away out of being, their names blotted from the book of life.

Whatever be our opinion of Origen personally, of his learning, his brilliancy, even of the truth of much of his teaching, his teaching *here* places him among those prophets condemned by Ezekiel for "strengthening the hands of the wicked, that he should not return from his wicked way, *by promising him life.*"

In that future age which has no end, the reprobate have no abiding name or place. Their image has vanished out of the city. Life for them, whether a thing to be desired or shunned, whether with Origen in heaven or with Augustine in hell, is the devil's lie, repeated now from a thousand high places, as it was once whispered in Eve's credulous ear in the garden, when the tempter said: "Thou art immortal;" "Thou, certainly, shalt not die."

Only second to the condemnation of Scripture is the fact that of the theory of universal restoration Origen is *the earliest known advocate.* The modern advocates of Universalism are compelled to admit that it found no advocate in the primitive church.[*] Among the *followers* of Capocrates, a heretic of the second century, it is said that a theory resembling that of Origen prevailed,[†] just as the Augustinian theory was held by men of heretical tenets before it was adopted by men of a sounder faith: but we cannot find, either among heretical or orthodox teachers, the *name* of a single writer who advocated the theory before Origen. It finds no countenance whatever in the writings of the apostolic men who walked with Peter, and John, and Paul. Eternal punishment is their uniform teaching.

Just as little countenance does it find in any existing writings of the second century. It required the rise in this century, and the prevalence towards its close, of a theology more black and cruel than heathenism had ever taught, to enable even Origen, with all his vast learning and daring genius, to put forward in the first half of the third century after Christ his theory of restoration. Pleasing as it was to human sin, supported as it was by the man of the greatest genius among the fathers, having in it a most important element of truth, it made no progress in the church. The men of the first centuries knew that Origen was not connected with Christ—could not stretch back his hand and grasp that of an apostle. They knew that his doctrine had no foundation on the rock; but was a vision floating

[*] Andrew Jukes, *The Second Death*, 2nd ed., 92.

[†] Hippolytus, *Refutation of Heresies*, b. vii., c. xx.

in the air, a fancy dreamed on a summer night: and so it soon came to be treated as a heresy; and Augustine rose up and crushed it out of the church for twelve hundred years and more.

For the benefit of our readers we subjoin a table which will enable them at a glance to see the relative antiquity in the primitive church of the three great theories of future punishment which are at this day maintained in the Christian church. The dates given for the death of each father are, of course, only guaranteed for as a probable approximation to truth.

Theory of Scripture: ***Eternal Death***	**Died (A.D.)**	**Theory of Augustine:** ***Eternal Life of Misery***	**Died (A.D.)**	**Theory of Origen:** ***Universal Restoration***	**Died (A.D.)**
Barnabas	90				
Clement of Rome	100				
Hermas	104				
Ignatius, Martyr	107				
Polycarp, Martyr	147				
Justin Martyr	164				
Theolphilus (of Antioch)	183				
		Athenagoras	190		
		Tatian	200		
Irenaeus Martyr	202				
Clement Alexandrinus	212				
		Tertullian	235		
		Hippolytus	240		
				Origen	253
Arnobius	303				
		Athanasius	373		
				Gregory, Nyssa	394
		Augustine	430		

From the above table we see how comparatively late the theory of Augustine appears in the list of patristic writings, while that of Origen's is later still. That blank space between them and primitive truth is fatal to both. Of Origen, we now take our leave. In one grand feature he commands our entire sympathy. He looked forward to the extinction of evil. His yearning for it was true—was but following out the judgment and reason as well as the longing of every right heart. We cannot look at evil—its hatefulness, its misery, its pollution—and think that with such a God as ours this evil will be permitted to extend or to exist forever. So thought Origen, and Scripture bears him out.

But he erred most fatally as to the means. He left the plain words of Scripture to carry out a human tradition. The inalienable immortality of the soul was the *ignis fatuus* which led this brilliant thinker through depths and over heights which weary the imagination of common minds to follow him. It compelled him to promise life where God had threatened death. His theory is, no doubt, very captivating, very seductive; but it is false. It is destructive of the true nobility of that nature a false idea of whose nobility led Origin into his error.

To suppose that a responsible being, capable of good and evil, may deliberately choose the latter, and deliberately continue in it, and yet that God is bound in every instance to win or to force back that responsible agent to the path of life which he had forsaken, is destructive of the quality which distinguishes the higher from the lower order of creation, namely, *the freedom of their will.* God says to those whom, in making capable of knowing Him, He has made capable of sharing in his own immortality: "You may and can choose evil, and with it death." Origen says to them, "You cannot, and you shall not: the evil you would choose shall be severed from you, do what you will; the good you would not shall be forced upon you, struggle against it as you may." He reduces the creature, made to walk in the field of freedom, to the creation regulated by the iron law of necessity.

21

Conclusion

AND NOW WE BRING OUR work to its close. Its argument has led us to the most glorious hope and expectation which a being loving God can possibly entertain—the termination of moral evil. As it is a part of our Father's revelation that evil had an origin, so we rejoice to find it another part of that revelation that it will have an end. It is not from eternity, and it will not be to eternity. The condemned heresy of Manichaeism is not the doctrine of the Bible. Evil is a thing of time, and is not an essential part of the constitution of God's universe. The ages to come will roll on ignorant of evil, as were those former ages before the archangel fell. Evil will be blotted out. All God's attributes—His mercy, His holiness, His justice, His power—are pledged to extirpate it.

To do so is a necessity of that nature of His which has its own binding eternal laws within itself. Hell is not the eternal abode of evil, concentrated in intensity, deepening and darkening throughout eternity, ever mingling its deep wails and its loud blasphemies with the hosannas of earth and heaven. It is not the everlasting exhibition of a scene with whose moral horrors all the sensuality, and devilry, and hate, and despair, that have been exhibited in earth's foulest dens, could not compare. The frenzies of Bedlam, were earth one Bedlam: the despair of suicide, were each one of earth's sons and daughters to resolve on rushing from a hated life: the hatred of the heart, were each heart to hate as Cain when he stood by Abel in the old field of murder: all these could not exhibit even a feeble resemblance to that which hell would present—if Augustine's view were true.

Thank God it is not true.

We have shaken off a hideous nightmare. We have renounced Satan's lie of the immortality of sinners. The hell which God has prepared is not for Augustine's purpose. He will, indeed, gather into it all things which offend—all the foul rakings of hate, and pride, and falsehood, and selfishness, and lust. But it is with the ominous purpose of Jehu, when he said, "Gather all the prophets of Baal, and all his priests; let none be wanting: and the house of Baal was full from one end to another." So will hell enlarge her borders; and the evil of the universe shall descend into it, and fill its wide domain, to be extirpated and blotted out forever.

Such is the hell of Scripture, the very counter-part to that fearful scene which Augustine has depicted. The very thought of it is too horrible to think. We reject it as a black lie, a foul slander on the character of our God. However ancient this worn-out lie, it is no part of the faith once delivered to the saints. We renounce it as a fable; a monstrosity worthy of the Koran, where it takes its fitting place; unworthy of the Gospel, where it finds no place.

We leave it to the disciple of Mohammed, lying on his couch of sensuality, to look down with cruel delight upon a scene of unutterable and endless misery.* This is not the consummation which the disciples of Christ, or the worshippers of the Father of mercies, are called on to rejoice in. They could not look on it and rejoice. They could not regard pain as

* Koran, c. lxxxiii.

endless without feeling that unalloyed joy could never be their own.* They will contemplate the destruction when it comes with satisfaction because in it they see evil and misery forever banished from God's world, and God reigning supreme in the affection and loyalty of all that breathe.

From all this stand-point we view the final scene of retribution. There is heaven, and there is hell. The redeemed enjoy the one: the lost are subjects of the other. The book of Revelation describes the latter: "Death and Hades were cast into the lake of-fire. This is the second death" (Rev. 20:14). All that has been and continued to be evil: the fallen angels who now move in earth and air; the spirits who are kept in chains of darkness; the multitudes whom the last day will find impenitent and unholy; have all been consigned to one common scene of punishment.

According to their deserving is their suffering. The time for each one's suffering over, he is wrapped in the slumber of eternal death. Gradually life dies out in that fearful prison until unbroken silence reigns throughout it. They who would not find life have found death. But the scene remains forever.

As Sodom and Gomorrah have exhibited to every succeeding generation of men the Divine vengeance upon full-blown iniquity, so will the charred and burnt-out furnace of hell afford its eternal lesson to the intelligences of the future. As angels wing their way from world to world, as the redeemed touch with fresh delight their harps of gold, as new orders of life are called into being, so the nature and the end of evil are always remembered in that scene where so many of the inhabitants of heaven and earth have bid an eternal farewell to that life of God which is so full of joy.

That lesson of awe is read and pondered on by all. But it will be a lesson read without the shudder of anguish. The dead have drunk the waters of Lethe, "the silent stream," and forgotten long ago their misery.

---

* Psalm 58:10; T. R. Birks, *Victory of Divine Goodness*, 179.

There is no eternal antagonism of good and evil, no eternal jarring of the notes of praise and wailing. Evil has died out, and with it sorrow: throughout God's world of life, all is joy, and peace, and love.

SCRIPTURES COMMENTED ON

12810026R00161

Printed in Great Britain
by Amazon.co.uk, Ltd.,
Marston Gate.